WOMEN AS NAZIS: FEMALE PERPETRATORS OF THE HOLOCAUST

WENDY ADELE-MARIE

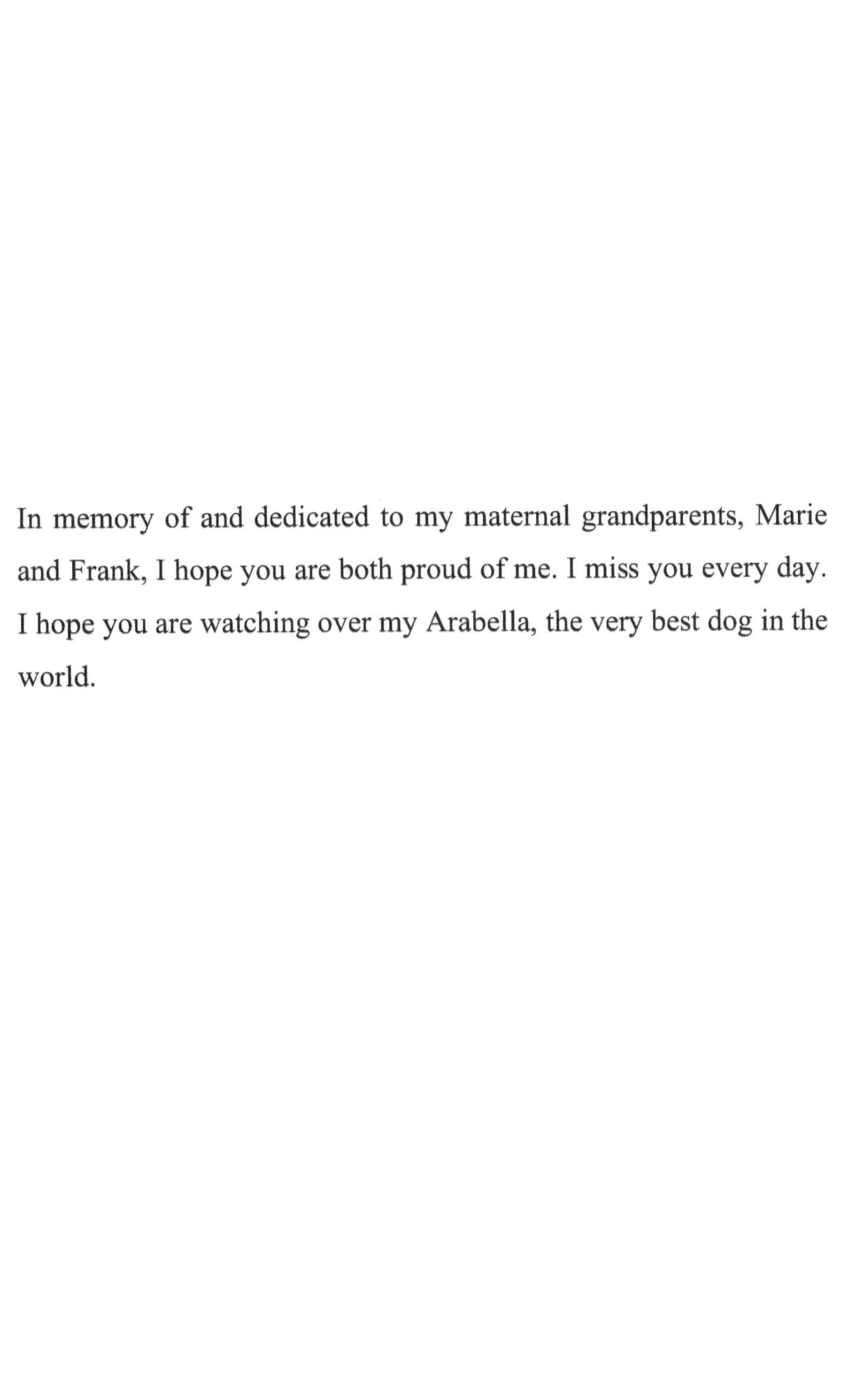

In memory of and dedicated to my maternal grandparents, Marie and Frank, I hope you are both proud of me. I miss you every day. I hope you are watching over my Arabella, the very best dog in the world.

TABLE OF CONTENTS

FOREWORD

Wendy Adele-Marie's new study of Nazi women as guards, overseers, and others who worked in the concentration and death camps during the genocide and Holocaust of the Second World War is an invaluable addition to a growing body   of scholarship on women as victims and—in this case—perpetrators of genocide and Holocaust.

This book is based on years of wide-ranging research in archives, personal accounts, biographies, scholarly works, and trial records. It is, in my judgment,   one of the most comprehensive and perceptive analyses of why Nazism appealed   to so many German women and why hundreds of these women turned into "killing machines" in the concentration and death camps during the Second World War. Her analysis of the motives of these perpetrators is superb. She offers compelling conclusions that many German women joined the killing enterprise willingly out of greed, opportunism, fanaticism, resentment, and a need to exert   an "agency" of power that they lacked at home. The great irony is that they supported to the end a regime that at heart had an abiding contempt for the female gender. Wendy Adele-Marie explains this seeming contradiction with great clarity and much detail with conclusions not only from the historical record, but also from the insights of social psychology.

It has been said that the Holocaust negates all comfortable categories of thought and belief. How could a "cultured "and "educated" nation in the heart of Western Christian Civilization carry out the first intended *complete* genocide in human history? What prompted a flawed individual like Oskar Schindler who was an adulterer, a gambler, and an alcoholic to save hundreds of Jewish lives, while Commandant of Auschwitz Rudolf Höss, a devoted middle-class family man, hard-working and kind to animals, become one of the greatest mass-murderers in history? Here, accordingly, Wendy Adele-Marie poses the question of how the stereotypically "gentler", nurturing, compassionate female gender can turn sadistic, violent, and lethal both individually and   collectively.

Wendy Adele-Marie's in-depth case studies of female guards, overseers, *Kapos,* and medical personnel in the camps are chilling reminders that women can be as cruel as men and can sometimes try in this area to outdo their male counterparts. Her case studies are both riveting and revealing. She explains clearly and cogently the common threads of motives and behaviors shared by these perpetrators. She also illuminates most usefully the sequels to the careers of these murderesses with detailed analysis of their war-crimes trials and in the case of   such figures as Hermine Braunsteiner, the struggle to bring these perpetrators to justice long after the end of the war.

This study merits a prominent place in the recent scholarship of Nazi Germany, the Holocaust, women's history, and not least in the never-ending search for our understanding of human behavior. It will be useful to both the general reader and specialists in the field, for it stands as a warning against the dangers of fanaticism, prejudicial hatred, temptation, and the total corruption of absolute power.

Leon Stein, Ph.D.,
Professor Emeritus of History at Roosevelt University and Education Director
Emeritus at the Illinois Holocaust Museum and Education Center

PREFACE

So shalt thou feed on Death,
That feeds on men,
And, Death once dead,
There's no more dying then

Shakespeare, *Sonnet* 146, 13.

The motivation for this book came about well over a decade ago when Dr. Leon Stein and I had a conversation about women and genocide. He suggested   that I look into nurses who worked in the camp setting during the Holocaust. He and I then coordinated a conference for Roosevelt University that dealt with the topic of women and the Holocaust, and included female survivors and resisters as speakers. All of this led me to examine more on women and the Holocaust, and at that point I started to focus on perpetrators after reviewing the Bergen-Belsen trial transcripts, then later the Ravensbrück as well as the Nuremberg trial transcripts.   I was shocked (because, I am sure like many people, I had not thought about women as genocidal perpetrators in the Holocaust) to learn how many women   were involved not only with Nazism, but with day-to-day management of the concentration and extermination camps. I was even more surprised to see how   little information and scholarship was available about these women. Choosing only the few that this book focused on was very   difficult.

Women took an active part in mass genocide, and scholarship for decades overlooked these women. Interestingly, I found that at the Belsen trial in 1945, out of forty-five defendants, nineteen women were charged with war crimes. These women, guards, nurses, and *Kapos* (block commanders), included Juana

Bormann, Herta Ehlert, Herta Bothe, Gertrude Fiest, Ilse Forster, Ida Forster, Klara Opitz, Ilse Lothe, Hilde Lohbauer, Charlotte Klein, Gertrude Sauer, Hilde Lisiewitz, Anna Hempel, Irene Haschke, Helena Kopper, Hildegard Hahnel, Frieda Walter, Elisabeth Volkenrath, and the angel of death, Irma Grese. In another instance, I located copies of post-war judgments from both the East and West German trials, and discovered twenty-nine women, in addition to the ones listed above, received sentences varying from three years in prison to death. I then decided to look into why Nazism appealed to German women. Throughout my research, I was constantly astonished at the number of women who took part in genocide and other crimes of the Holocaust, but was also equally saddened at how few women were brought to justice.

Several sources suggested that more than three thousand women were trained as camp guards at Ravensbrück, the main women's concentration camp. However, research also suggested that there were over three hundred camps for women, out of over ten thousand camps, which implied that the actual number of female camp guards and other workers may have been higher than we can currently estimate.[i]

Many records were destroyed, but existing documents, and also the testimonies of survivors, have proved invaluable. Somewhat worrisome was that when I began my research, what details I did find about these women were never presented in a comprehensive manner until very recently. Excluding accounts by survivors themselves, little was published on female perpetrators. Renate Wiggerhaus, Gudrun Schwarz, Irmtraud Heike (who has written on this subject since 1994); and Daniel Patrick Brown were leaders in this field (especially Brown with his groundbreaking biography of Irma Grese and then with his comprehensive *The Camp Women*, an important resource); most recently Sarah Helm has continued to shed light on this understudied arena of Holocaust and Nazi historical research. Hence, in writing this book, which has taken over a decade, I felt that case studies of a select few

---

[i] My thanks to Dr. Leon Stein for his assistance with this analysis.

women closely involved with the atrocities of the Nazi régime would be of benefit to future scholars of the Holocaust, Nazi Germany, and women's   history.

It remains important to remember that German (and indeed, other) women during World War II played an important role in all levels of the war, from maintaining farms while the men were away to conducting business for the Nazi régime. Millions more were not perpetrators, and it is unfair to portray all German women as such. Women's contributions, whether to the benefit of society or not, have been largely ignored, especially in the context of war, although recent scholarship seeks to balance that redress. I was also motivated to try to discover why women involved with the misogynistic Nazis did what they   did.

It remains difficult to understand why women could commit so many atrocities against children and members of their own sex; hence, answering why was also exceedingly difficult. I have realized, however, that in war and with regard to crimes against humanity, there was no separation of the sexes. War atrocities cannot be segregated by gender. While for decades little information existed about most of the women who were involved with or worked for the Nazi régime, studies such as those presented here are an important contribution to understanding the intersections between gender, the Holocaust, and Nazi Germany.

In conducting my research, I used survivor interviews, trial transcripts, and other primary information. Often, the words of the female perpetrators themselves provided me with the necessary and sometimes subjective framework to create a biographical portrait of these women.

ACKNOWLEDGEMENTS

I have many, many people to thank who supported this project. I owe an enormous debt of gratitude to Dr. Leon Stein. Since 1999, when he first suggested the topic of female culpability in genocide and the Holocaust, his help, guidance, encouragement, mentorship, and friendship have proved invaluable in the development of my work as a scholar of the Holocaust. It was because of his influence that I became a professor and specialized in the Holocaust. A special thank you to my mother Francine for everything. I especially thank Wini and Philip Drell for the discussions on Phil's images taken when he filmed and photographed from D-Day to liberation of the camps as part of the "Stevens Irregulars." I am also indebted to them for the gift of books from Philip's library as these books have been invaluable in my research. For her friendship and assistance with various projects, continued advice, reading the final draft, copy-editing, and for providing comments, Felice Clark. I thank the United States Holocaust Memorial Museum for research assistance.

Finally, this book is for the victims of the Nazis. Their voices cannot be forgotten, but, perhaps, to understand why, we must understand whom. The involvement of female perpetrators guilty of genocide and other crimes during the Holocaust cannot and must not be overlooked. The millions who died in the Holocaust are the reason for this book.

PART I: FROM NAZISM TO GENOCIDE

CHAPTER I

INTRODUCTION

Anyone in this day and age who believes that the "gentler sex" encompasses all that is sweet, soft and sighing, luscious and loving, kind to men and to animals, content to be the loyal and understanding helpmate of her chosen hero, is in for a shock in these pages.[1]

The insistence of the Nazis on the separation of the sexes allowed, for example, the creation of Nazi organizations for women which perhaps had little real power, but whose actual operation was in the hands of the women themselves.[2]

Women who worked for the Nazis were responsible for some of the most horrific crimes of the Holocaust. What led women to take a job with a government that advocated torture and death? While not all women who were involved with the Nazis were murderers, many women who worked for the Nazis in the concentration and extermination camp setting used whatever means necessary to mistreat, subjugate, torture, and murder. Female perpetrators were not forced to subject prisoners in their charge to abuse. Numerous women who worked as camp guards were volunteers. Even more had to be conscripted. Other women became involved in different ways. Were the women who were involved with or who worked for the Nazis aberrations or merely pawns in Adolf Hitler's government? Why were some women more prone to sadism than others?

With its party's advent to power in Germany in 1933, National Socialists sought to return women to subordinate positions in German society, which meant that women were to disregard any prior economic, political, or societal quest for emancipation. Women were to return to their domestic spheres, and, preferably, proudly have babies for the Fatherland. The Nazis wanted to eliminate, "within a hundred years, the dark German type by mating them with blond women" in order to create a master race of 'racially' pure, blond haired, blue eyed people.[3] To succeed in this goal, which the Nazis believed was necessary so that pure Germanic blood would survive, the régime established a hundred-year plan, conceived in part by Heinrich Himmler, Hitler's *Reichsführer*, *SS*. Himmler established "*Lebensborn* (Spring of Life), an SS maternity organization whose main function was to adopt racially suitable children for childless SS families and to assist racially sound unwed mothers and their children."[4] Children who matched racial Aryan tenets, with the hopes of creating the blond master race, were stolen and given to SS families to raise; over 12,000 children were kidnapped and given to SS families.[5] *Lebensborn* was described as "stud farms where SS men and suitable young women were mated to breed a master race."[6] A government that encouraged fertility this way, and used women to achieve racial goals, certainly did not view women in an egalitarian fashion, nor were full civil and political rights promoted; the Nazis held most women in complete contempt.

However, while many women were marginalized during this régime in order to assert Hitler's political ideology, they could also alter their status within their private spheres should they wish it and have the ability to do so.[7] This was not easy. Moreover, the societal marginalization espoused by Nazism helped to authenticate the hyper-aggressive Nazi masculine ideal. If women returned to the domestic sphere, and if the enemy of the German man was destroyed, the Nazi ideal of masculinity would reign supreme, and Germany would be better for it. The enemy of the German man and woman was defined as Jews and others classified as "unworthy" of life.[8] Thus, Nazism appealed to many women, partially because the party offered a restoration to feminine honor and proffered a new status for women, even though it centered on domesticity. Despite the masculine-oriented ideology of the Nazi party, during the 1930s and 1940s, many women in proudly paid allegiance to the Third Reich.

This was in spite of Nazi beliefs, which mandated that women not interfere with the principles of the party.   Although women could be Nazi party members, they could not join elite sectors of the Nazi party. However, they could marry a Nazi official to gain authority or influence. Outside of marriage, female allegiance further manifested itself via employment as *Aufseherinnen* or in other positions found throughout different sectors of the   camps.

Conceivably, women working in the camps did so because this type of employment provided them with a sense of purpose and a feeling of unity against   a common enemy. Countless women volunteered or applied for a position in the camps. These positions varied from secretaries to switchboard operators. However, many women were conscripted for work; conscripts had no choice else they were imprisoned.[9] The camp structure allowed some women to be   promoted to better positions (only within the constraints of the female hierarchy) and potentially, although this was not always the case, make more money than they could at other jobs. Women could also work in the camps as an *Aufseherin* (female overseer). Some were later promoted to *Oberaufseherin* (female head overseer) or assigned other ranks. Estimates on the number of *Aufseherinnen* vary; recent figures suggest that Ravensbrück trained up to four thousand women. Nazi records indicated that by January of 1945, over three thousand *Aufseherinnen* worked at numerous camps. There were dozens of sub-camps just for female prisoners, who were then guarded by women.[10] Women worked in many other positions in the camp system.

Other women worked for the Nazis as doctors; were married to Nazi officials and then were employed in the camp structure; or were forced to work as *Kapos*. Despite any preconceived notions that existed about the soft, nurturing feminine sphere, and regardless of gender segregation within the Nazi hierarchy   of power, female doctors, camp guards, *Kapos*, and, at least in one case, a Nazi wife, were all responsible for many of the atrocities committed within the camps. Moreover, many women employed by the *Schutzstaffel* (Protective Squadron, known as the SS) guards were as vicious as men, if not more so. Average women from all areas of Austria and Germany, and from different socioeconomic backgrounds, had the ability to transform themselves into Nazi death machines.

These women, some easily, went from an idealized domestic sphere into a world that was horrific and unimaginable. Countless women who worked for the SS blurred gender roles in the camp structures by imitating male SS and taking part   in the abuse and murder of millions.[11] Indoctrinated with hate, *Aufseherinnen* and other women who worked in the camps were taught to be ruthless, if not indirect killing machines, and enjoyed a certain level of independence. It remains difficult   to interpret how a world of torture and death could offer women a viable change   in their socioeconomic status, and whether this alteration was fully realized (at   least by the women themselves), partially because of the lack of available material on female perpetrators.[12] Women's roles were tightly conscripted by the Nazis,   and ironically, the horrendous camp structure provided some minimal   fluidity.

Laws were passed that were designed to limit women's public roles. Specifically, the July 1933 decree that stated "up to their 35th year women were candidates for matrimony and therefore not to be granted permanent salaried status as State or municipal employees or in semi-public institutions."[13] Although rare, some women found "no obstacles were placed in the way of women of exceptional talent and energy ... two such examples were Leni Riefenstahl, the film producer, and Hanna Reitsch the woman test pilot and aviator, both of whom were highly regarded by Hitler."[14] Although these women were extremely atypical, other women could become involved with the Nazis. While the Nazi avocation of traditional roles appealed to many women, not all wanted to be confined to the private sphere. Nazism attracted some women who looked at the party as one that restored feminine honor and ideals, but most women found it difficult to achieve any real status in the party or in government. Nazism certainly sought to halt any precedent of female emancipation. For some women, employment in the camp structure was just that, a job, but for others, work became a way to circumvent Nazi limitations.

With the rise of Nazism, women were no longer allowed to attach themselves to social organizations that favored emancipation and equal rights. Once Hitler came to power in 1933, women were encouraged to join   state-sanctioned organizations, and return to their homes to fight for the new domesticity that was sweeping Germany.[15] In addition to encouraging and promoting the role of women within the home, *Kinder* (Children), *Küche* (Kitchen), *und Kirche* (and Church), Hitler promised an end to Jewish control and domination of German commerce, assuring a return of businesses and any subsequent profits back to the Germans.[16] Consequently, while Hitler's ideology promised a return to morality and economic prosperity, his *Weltanschauung* (ideological world outlook) warned that much of Germany's success, however, would have to come from women who would "rescue the German   family."[17]

Rescuing the German family meant having as many children as possible for the *Führer*. In some cases, women were awarded medals, which were known   as the *Mutterkreuz* (Mother's Cross). These medals came in three versions, bronze (four children), silver (six children), and gold (eight children), all for having large families. One Nazi document asserted, "German women wish in the main to be wives and mothers … they have no longing for the factory, no longing for Parliament, no longer for the office."[18] This document went on to state that what all German women wanted above anything else was "a cosy home, a loved husband, and a multitude of happy children" which the Nazis argued was for women, "closer to their hearts."[19] However, not all women wanted to be consigned to the domestic sphere and sought ways to become involved with the Nazis. One such way was via employment in the camp structure, and then later   via war work. The Nazis made great use of women before and during the war; whether these women worked as secretaries, radio operators, laborers in munitions factories, or other war-related activities, the Nazi régime allowed, and then required, that some women work to help provide service to the Fatherland, thus allowing men to concentrate on the warfront.[20] Propaganda had encouraged such work. Propaganda also presented women with conflicting ideas as to what their exact role should be for the state. Should they stay in domestic roles or work for the government in some capacity? Some women resolved the conflict by working because they wanted to, or they sought to alter their status. Others were conscripted, while still countless more worked due to economic necessity. Propaganda blurred women's roles in several ways by presenting messages that advocated domesticity and also state service, albeit in differing capacities. Women were often left to resolve any communicational conflict on their own. Use of propaganda was not new. The Nazis had used propaganda since the party first began, and it also became an integral part of the Nazi war against the   Jews.

Hitler's ideology that impregnated German society was marked with a series of successful vile propaganda campaigns led by Joseph Goebbels, Reich Minister of National Propaganda, which demonstrated the virulent Nazi hatred of Jews. Hitler had some ambivalence about making a formal decision with regard to who was actually a Jew. However, although he had ordered Hermann Göring, *Reichsmarshall*, and Reinhard Heydrich, *SS Obergruppenführer*, second in command of the SS, to come up with a solution to the Jewish question, he remained ambivalent for "political rather than moral" reasons. Nevertheless, as   one of their major goals, the Nazis planned to ensure that all areas they conquered
in Europe, as well as globally, would also be   Jewish-free.[21]

Part of this ideology arose from the fact that the Nazis had constructed a need for racial cleansing, which was accompanied by a drive for *Lebensraum*, or living space. Consequently, their agrarian-oriented ideology dictated a bizarre and horrendous need to purify the German race by killing all of the Jews and others deemed undesirable by Nazi ideology, whom the Nazis perceived as standing in the way of their goal.[22] Goebbels, considered the "alpha and omega of his propaganda system," was responsible for developing Nazi propaganda.[23] Anti- Semitic newspapers were published detailing contempt and hatred for the Jews, warning women especially about 'dangers' that Jews presented. Jewish men were presented as threats to German women. Despicable slogans and campaigns also appeared warning all Germans of parasitical Jews, which further escalated   hate.

As the furor against the Jews grew, propaganda increased to reassert German nationalism and also promote women's roles. Following Hitler's new domestic ideology, and recognizing the need to inform German women of their new roles, on 18 March 1933, Goebbels gave a speech, entitled "German Women," at the opening of an exhibition. In this call-to-domestic-arms speech, Goebbels revealed the new role that German women should expect to play within the new Nazi administration. In addition to speeches, film was another way the Nazis could spread propaganda. Goebbels instituted an extremely regimented bureaucracy devoted entirely to film, and one of his goals was to create films glorifying Nazi ideology. His various offices were responsible for overseeing and commissioning state-controlled films, all designed to meet stringent regulations. Implied anti-Semitic messages in film helped the Nazis find support for their measures against the Jews. Anti-Semitism, wrapped up in propaganda, was used to forewarn Germans of what could happen should the Jews be allowed to take   over their country.[24] Propaganda created for women was conveyed in such a way that women felt the government thought them important. Goebbels also used propaganda to warn Germany that the more women allowed themselves to become part of the public sphere, the greater the likelihood that Germany would

continue to decline.[25] The family was presented as one of the most important parts of the Nazi state because it had a "specific duty to fulfill. It was seen as the germ cell of the nation and as the source of *völkisch* renewal, through reproduction. As such, it became the most important eugenic tool."[26]

However, many German women did not want to simply put aside previous achievements they had made in the public sphere and begin having babies for the Fatherland. Instead, some German women chose careers in the Nazi party, hoping to regain, perhaps, some measure of equality. Not all women who worked for the Nazis were German, but those women who became involved had to prove they had the proper racial background expected of them; consequently, most had an Austrian or German background. Even if imprisoned, women could alter their status against that of other prisoners if appointed as a *Kapo*. Many of the female camp *Kapos* were not necessarily Austrian or German, and they were not employees of the Nazi régime either. Like conscripts, these women did not have a choice, but once ensconced as a *Kapo*, she could enjoy a distinct status from the other female prisoners, engaging in smoking, smuggling, or even, as one survivor related, she witnessed "a *Kapo* and her girlfriend play 'wedding' all night." [27]

Again, the Nazis themselves, in a perfect example of the many contradictions that surrounded Nazi ideology, realized that despite a philosophy that relegated women to a traditional domestic sphere, working women were necessary during the war: "Thus they found that during the World War II they   had to try to persuade married women and even mothers to go out to work, and   not devote themselves entirely to home and family, the role deemed most suitable
for women in Nazi theory."[28] Moreover, National Socialism represented a way out of traditional domesticity and may have seemed exciting to women who wanted out of the day-to-day drudgery of an ordinary existence. Certainly to the younger people of Germany, National Socialism was appealing in many ways,   and not only for reasons of social promotion or status. As one German woman   put it, "National Socialism … had a resonance that was simply undeniable. It   made young people enthusiastic. There's no question at   all."[29]

Enthusiasm may have had its roots in perceived societal gains, or even in one's sense of duty for one's country, appealing perhaps for women. Working for the SS offered women not just a way to make money, but to achieve status.[30]
Moreover, in the camps, women were often able to assert authority, something they could not always publicly do. Employment in the SS office also offered a way to connect to what was going on in their government. Women could become part of the Nazi government in a variety of ways. They could join the SS Women's Corps, volunteer, enlist as air ward maidens, work as nurses, or, once   the camp system was established, work in the concentration or extermination camps. However, an idealized, extraordinary existence working in the camp structure did not exist.

What existed for women involved with the camps was a life full of abuse, hatred, mental as well as physical horror, dual sexual dominance, masochism, and murder, although many did not see it that way.[31]   Countless camp women were incredibly indoctrinated with hate and felt that their work served a purpose. They were also equally determined not to admit to accountability; at their trials, these women denied most charges brought up against them. Undoubtedly, many female guards were "cruel women, no doubt at all. And there are hard women. The concentration camp guards must have had the devil in their bodies."[32]

For many of the new Nazi female recruits, all inborn nature and nurture traits were displaced in order so that they could control what they were indoctrinated to believe as their enemy, the Jew, and other members of society deemed imperfect by Nazi propaganda and ideology. As the war went on, and as the camp structure grew, more and more women were needed for work as the men were increasingly sent to the front lines. Women guards were to be viewed as   equal to the males, and some women saw this as a total truth, executing an agency of power in a way that either mimicked the male SS guards or went one step further. Shockingly, many SS female contractors strongly believed in all aspects   of the *Weltanschauung* of the Nazi party, accepted their propaganda, and viewed working for the SS in the camps as an appealing career choice. National Socialism and its structures appealed to women for several reasons, perhaps because in part it provided an ideology in which they could   participate.

---

[1] Andrew Ewart, *World's Wickedest Women: Intriguing Studies of Eve and Evil Through the Ages* (New York: Taplinger Pub. Co. 1964), 7.

[2] Jill Stephenson, *Women in Nazi Society* (New York: Barnes & Noble Books, 1975), 32.

[3] John Toland, *Adolf Hitler* (New York: Doubleday & Co., Inc., 1976), p. 764.

[4] Ibid.

[5] Andrew Malone. "Stolen by the Nazis: The tragic tale of 12,000 blue-eyed blond children taken by the SS to create an Aryan super-race." *The Daily Mail Online.* www.dailymail.co.uk/news/article-1111170/Stolen-Nazis-The-tragic-tale-12-000-blue-eyed- blond-children-taken-SS-create-Aryan-super-race.html (23 April 2010).

[6] See Toland, p. 764 and refer to "Stolen by the Nazis" for more on what happened to the women who had babies with SS men, and also for what happened to the children.

[7] See Claudia Koonz, "A Tributary and a Mainstream: Gender, Public Memory, and Historiography of Nazi Germany" in *Gendering Modern Germany History: Rewriting Historiography,* edited by Karen Hagemann and Jean H. Quataert (New York: Bergbahn Books, 2007), especially pp. 151-152, where Koonz stated that it was true of oppressive regimes when private spheres were mandated as the norm for women, it can then be seen how these actors "simultaneously allowed the women who operated within those spheres to exert agency, in fact, that is precisely how oppression functions. Ordinary women could be the victims of misogyny as well as beneficiaries (and sometimes facilitators) of racial persecution."

[8] Enemies that were non-Jews were defined as, but not limited to: Communists, the mentally and physically disabled, political dissenters, Roma, and people belonging to various religious sects such as the Seventh-Day Adventists.

[9] See Brown, *The Camp Women*, pp. 15-20, especially for why conscription was needed.

[10] Children and homosexual men were also imprisoned at these camps. See http://www.jewishvirtuallibrary.org/jsource/Holocaust/cclist.html. Gudrun Schwarz stated in 1994 that "Die genie Zahl der Aufseherinnen ist nicht bekannt." (The exact number of women guards is not known). See "SS Aufseherinnen in N-S Konzentrationslagern (1933-1945)" *Dachauer Hefte* 10 (1994): 32 and 35. It is believed now, in 2010, that ten percent of the total camp guards were women. See Isabel Kershner, "Women's Role in Holocaust May Exceed Old Notions" *New York Times*, 17 July 2010. http://www.nytimes.com/2010/07/18/world/europe/18holocaust.html (6 September 2010). Daniel Patrick Brown's groundbreaking *The Camp Women: The Female Auxiliaries Who Assisted the SS in Running the Nazi Concentration Camp System* has the most definitive list of women auxiliary guards; he suggested that based on his exhausting research,   3,508 female guards worked for the SS in the camp structure out of 51,000 SS men who also worked in the camps. Brown's conclusion supports Schwartz's, in that compiling a complete record of the female guards was difficult because of the lack of extant records. See Daniel Patrick Brown, *The Camp Women: The Female Auxiliaries Who Assisted the SS in Running the Nazi Concentration Camp System* (Atglen, PA: Schiffer Military History, 2002), p. 9.

[11] Although they were able to enjoy a certain measure of autonomy within the camp hierarchy, women were usually not promoted to the rank of officer, and they were less likely to be convicted of war crimes and crimes against humanity.

[12] Recent scholarship on women and the SS has been included as much as possible throughout this study.

[13] George Bruce, *The Nazis* (London: The Hamlyn Publishing Group, 1974), p. 99.

[14] Ibid. These women were not the norm, certainly. Bruce asserted further "speaking generally, however, Hitler wanted more children for the Hitler Youth and young men for the expanded *Reichswehr*" an assertion that challenges his theory that "no obstacles" existed for women even if they were of "exceptional" ability. See Ibid.

[15] It was interesting to note that in times of revolution or war, women were often relegated back to their domestic spheres. In France in the years preceding the French Revolution, women made gains towards emancipation. However, from 1787 on, the roles of women declined and eventually their conduct was legalized with the Napoleonic Code, which saw the "deterioration in the legal status of women, who were allowed no control over the family property, and could not acquire, sell, or give property without their husband's consent." See Alfred Cobban, *A History of Modern France: Volume Two: 1799-1871* (Baltimore, MD: Penguin Books, 1969),   pp. 27-28. In addition, although during World War II American women played an essential role in war operations, at the end of the war and well into the mid-1960s, women were sent – or, essentially encouraged to go – back to their domestic sphere. See Elaine Tyler May, *Homeward Bound: American Families in the Cold War Era*, 2nd ed. (Basic Books, 1999).

[16] Joseph Goebbels, the Reich Minister for National Propaganda, demonstrated   the virulent Nazi hatred of Jews. Goebbels was responsible for the development and administration of German propaganda during the 1930s and 1940s. Goebbels rose to power along with Adolf Hitler, and was responsible for creating, directing, and instituting Nazi propaganda with a "Machiavellian sense of political reality." Moreover, the acceptance of mass, total genocide was facilitated by the Nazi use of propaganda. Nazi propaganda was used in a variety of mediums, including film, radio, posters, cartoons, and newspapers. For the quotations on Goebbels, see Ernest K. Bramsted, *Goebbels and National Socialist Propaganda, 1925-1945* (Michigan: Michigan State University Press, 1965), pp. 9 and 455. The Nazis also used songs, some especially designed to appeal to women, to spread propaganda. See Eberhard Fromann, *Die Lieder der NS-Zeit: Untersuchungen   zur Nationalsozialistischen Liedpropanganda von den Anfängen bis zum Zweiten Weltkrieg* (Köln: Papy Rossa, 1999).

[17] Jack G. Morrison, *Ravensbrück: Everyday Life in a Women's Concentration Camp, 1939-1945* (Princeton: Markus Wiener Publishers, 2000), pp. 4-5.

[18] Bruce, p. 119.

[19] Ibid. In deconstructing the idea behind the Nazi view of women's roles post January 1933, Bruce provided a quote from one of Hitler's speeches where he addressed a group of German women. In this speech, Hitler stated, "In my new army I have given you the finest fathers of the world." Bruce correctly identified that "sinister motives lay behind this sentimental wording: the harsh fact of woman's total subordination to Adolf Hitler's militaristic and expansionist foreign policies." See Ibid for the quote; Bruce further related Albert Speer's role in trying to get more women to work for the war effort, and initial resistance efforts against the same. [20] See Alison Owings, *Frauen: German Women Recall the Third Reich* (New Brunswick, NJ: Rutgers University Press, 1994), 24, and refer back to p.10. See also Daniel Patrick Brown, *The Beautiful Beast: The Life and Crimes of SS-Aufseherin Irma Grese* (Ventura, CA: Golden West Historical Publications, 1996), 2. Brown also explained the application process for the *Aufseherinnen*. Note that when the war broke out the women were then under the supervision of the *Waffen* SS.

[21] See Christian Gerlach, "The Wannsee Conference, the Fate of the German Jews, and Hitler's Decision in Principle to Exterminate All European Jews" *Journal of Modern History* 70, no. 4 (December 1998), p.781.

[22] See Ibid.

[23] Bramsted, 455.

[24] See David Welch, *Propaganda and the German Cinema, 1933-1945* (Oxford: Oxford University Press, 1983), 18. Welch discussed the various types of film propaganda that Goebbels oversaw, which included educational, national, and cultural films. Posters, radio, and public actions against the Jews also helped to indoctrinate the masses against Jewish people. In addition, children were taught in elementary school the difference between an Aryan and a Jew, and with compulsory membership in youth organizations that glorified the Nazi state, children were forced to take in propaganda about enemies of the German state.

[25] See Joseph Goebbels, *German* Women, in "Deutsches Frauentum" *Signale der Neuen Zeit. 25Ausgewählte Reden von Dr. Joseph Goebbels.* Munich: Zentralverlag der NSDAP, 1934. http://www.calvin.edu/academic/cas/gpa/goeb55.htm (12 April 2001).

[26] Lisa Pine, *Nazi Family Policy: 1939-1945* (Oxford: Berg, 1997), 10. *Völkisch* in this context meant nationalistic.

[27] See Elizabeth Baer and Myrna Goldenberg. *Experience and Expression: Women, the Nazis, and the Holocaust* (Detroit: Wayne State University Press, 2003), p. 278. Many women who were involved with the Nazi party did not commit war crimes or crimes against humanity. For a good overview of German women in Nazi Germany, see Clifford Kirkpatrick, *Nazi Germany: Its Women and Family Life* (New York: Bobbs-Merrill, 1938).

[28] Stephenson, pp. 6-7. See also pp. 98-99, for more on Hitler's realization, circa 1935- 36, that for the war effort to succeed, women would be needed in the labor force. Conscription was later enacted, leaving many women no choice but to work in the camps. For the volunteers, they signed up willingly and had a different status than the conscripts. Many signed up for economic reasons. Several women, when brought to trial, stated money was a major motivating factor behind working as an *Aufseherin*. See Sir David Maxwell Fyfe, *War Crimes Trials: Volume II – The Belsen Trial* (London: William Hodge and Company, Ltd., 1949). Appendix III.

[29] See Owings, "Frau Regina Frankenfeld," 391.

[30] Irmtraud Heike revealed that women camp guards were paid on the same scale as public employees; following this, monetary factors were not always behind the decision to work in the camp setting. Moreover, Heike stated that in some factories women stood a chance to make more than working as guards. See Irmtraud Heike, "Female Concentration Camp Guards as Perpetrators: Three Case Studies" in *Ordinary People as Mass Murderers: Perpetrators in Comparative Perspectives* (New York: Palgrave Macmillan, 2008), pp. 124-125.

[31] For example, Elisabeth Volkenrath blamed Heinrich Himmler for her guilt. See my chapter on Volkenrath.

[32] Owings, 11. What about the hundreds who escaped justice?

CHAPTER II

WHY NATIONAL SOCIALISM APPEALED TO WOMEN

Wedded to the State

But the most brilliant propagandist technique will yield no success unless one fundamental principle is borne in mind constantly and with unflagging attention. It must confine itself to a few points and repeat them over and over. Here, as so often in this world, persistence is the first and most important requirement for success. [1]

Your body does not belong to you, but to your blood brethren and your…Volk. [2]

Why did National Socialism attract women despite the fact that the ideology was misogynist and riddled with contradictions? What could it offer them that previous ideologies could not or would not? Perhaps the answer lies not within the doctrine itself, but with the women who interpreted Nazism for their own gains. National Socialism did not allow for an equal role for women in German society, and fired women from "civil service and teaching positions, although oftentimes for political reasons" whereas "in some professions, the percentage of women actually increased. For example, women doctors increased

from 5.6 percent in 1930 to 7.6 percent."[3] Despite some marginal gains in a few

professions, women were discouraged from taking on formal careers.[4] With the

rise of Nazism in the early 1930s, women were discouraged from attaching themselves to social organizations that favored emancipation and instead were encouraged to join groups coordinated by the government. The Nazis saw this as necessary to rebuild Germany from the destruction that they believed was wrought upon the German people by the Weimar government that preceded them. The Nazis saw the preceding Weimar Republic as a period of not only decadence, but a time in German history where "the Jew, as the 'peoples' vampire', leeched the gold of masculinity from his 'host' by infecting all with his erotic effeminacy."[5] In the view of Hitler and Nazi party members, the Jew was to blame for the downward spiral that German society endured after World War I. Moreover, Nazi ideology blamed Jews for the rise of feminism, female promiscuity, prostitution, and the lack of morality in Germany. The Jewish man was depicted as a parasite that sought to corrupt good German women. In addition, the Jewish man was often portrayed as someone who wanted German women to have promiscuous sex outside of their (Nazi-designated) racial sphere, and live a life full of depravity and decadence. Thus, the extermination of the Jew coincided with the Nazi desire to protect women and idealize, on terms outlined by the Nazis, femininity: "In seeking to eradicate the Jew, Hitler also sought to eradicate the sexual woman. The Führer's conception of a good woman was simple ... the goal of female education has to invariably to be the future mother."[6] A Hitlerian theory was this: domesticity and childbearing for state survival. After Hitler came to power in 1933, women were encouraged to return

to their homes to fight for the new domesticity that was sweeping Germany. The preferred role for women in the Third Reich was to have babies, and to be the prolific mother of the new German state. While National Socialism espoused romanticized domesticity and female subservience, the incongruous Hitler critically "relied on the devotion and support of women, even though he banished them to periphery of political life and often treated them with indifference in private. His narrow, cramped views on women's role determined the destiny of millions."[7]

Despite contradictions, part of Nazi ideology promoted by Hitler included his argument for the concept that true femininity was rooted in domesticity, and a "constant yearning for motherhood."[8] Following Hitler's new gender segregated objectives, women were indoctrinated at an early age as members in such compulsory organizations as the BDM *(Bund Deutscher Mädchen*, the League of German Girls or the girl version of the Hitler Youth). These organizations impressed on young German women racial ideals and also the idea that having babies for the state was the greatest honor that a woman could hope to   achieve.

The second honor accorded to these young women was the chance to serve their state as possible "defenders of the homeland," which suggested that women could play a role in serving the state.[9] The Nazi hyper-masculine ideological belief in private, fertile spheres for women clouded rationale from people such as Albert Speer who argued that women could be used for labor purposes for the   state. However, very early promotion of labor was seen as unnecessary; it would   be after the war was under way that labor demands made it necessary for most women to go to work.[10] Nevertheless, fertility for the state remained a   constant.

It was also emphasized by the Nazi state that women should have as many babies as physically possible. Women such as Magda Goebbels, wife of propaganda minister Joseph Goebbels, especially personified the ideal Aryan German mother. In an interview with the *Vossische Zeitung*, a German newspaper, Magda Goebbels strongly asserted that "When the German woman is confronted with the choice between marriage and career then she always will be encouraged to choose marriage since that is undoubtedly best for a woman.   I am
attempting to make the German woman more beautiful."[11]

Magda Goebbels, who was very attractive in the Nazi ideal construct, attempted to make the Nazi ideal of the German (and later Austrian) woman appear more beautiful by publicly emulating an idealized domestic role   for   women; following in her example and within the framework of this new role, women were to have as many babies as possible to ensure the continuation of the German *Volk* (nation, people). This ultimate construction of femininity by the Nazis, based in fertility, became a way for women to take part in the construction   of the new state. Indeed, at a very early age, girls were "encouraged to prepare for motherhood and given practice in tasks befitting the woman's role in the *Volksgemeinschaft*"{People's Community}.[12]

Young girls were led to believe that they too mattered to Hitler and that he took a personal interest in them. The intended outcome was for young girls to feel as if they had a crucial role to play in the construction of the Nazi state, although privately. Their ultimate duty for Hitler was to "bring healthy children into the world, to bring them up for the nation, and in his way to do their part in the preservation of the life of their Volk."[13] The allure of *Volksgemeinschaft* for women meant that their predetermined historical roles would be advocated, highly valued, and encouraged. Perhaps some women truly believed that by buying into the Nazi national agenda, they could enter the public sphere on any level because the state made it seem possible, even the ultimate avocation of personal sacrifice for Hitler.[14]

For women, as sanctioned by government propaganda, and encouraged by government economic incentives, having a fertile womb became an ideal achievement and a way to take part in nationalistic pride. This pride manifested itself in a fevered attempt by some women to become pregnant for Hitler, as doing so enabled the woman to feel a deep connection to him. Magda Goebbels was one of a select group of women specifically used to define the Nazi construction of a feminine mother ideal. She had seven children, two boys and five girls, and publicly emulated the new role for German women Hitler sought to project in various media.[15] But why was the role of the new *Deutsche Mutter* (German mother) so incredibly important? Hitler had promised women who bore children "glory as wives and mothers, who would bear the children of the Thousand Year Reich."[16]

In order to ensure that Germany would continue as a viable state, and, at least in the eyes of the Nazis, an emergent world power, it was necessary for the population to increase. At the same time, with the needed and expected rise in the German birthrate, Hitler cried for the need for *Lebensraum* (living space) for the German people. He espoused his theories that the Germans had suffered horribly, especially since the close of World War I, and he blamed the Jews for the economic and social hardships many Germans faced, including the loss of nationalism. Many Germans lost their homes, businesses, and farms after World War I, and things got worse when hyperinflation emerged. Then, when conditions worsened with the advent of the worldwide Great Depression, the promises of Hitler and the Nazi party resonated with many.

Hitler also promised that Germany would soon recover and once again enjoy economic prosperity. Consequently, while Hitler's ideology promised a return to morality and economic prosperity, much of Germany's success would have to come from women who would "rescue the German family."[17]   The Germanic Aryan race had to increase and multiply in order to ensure that Hitler's ideal state would rise and continue. Therefore, National Socialism sought to establish a subservient role for women, where the woman would act, in most cases, as a breeder for the Nazi war machine.[18]

In addition to establishing a subservient role for women, Hitler also blamed the Jews for those German women who demanded equal rights and who   did not embrace his domestic-oriented policies.   Hitler saw himself as the father   of the nation, and as a surrogate husband of sorts for women. German women were to be wedded to the state by devoting their bodies for the reproductive purposes of Nazi Germany.   In yet another Nazi contradiction, Hitler advocated not only domestic femininity, but sought to downplay the sexuality of women, while promoting fertility. He did this by portraying himself as the protector of German womanhood against the "incursions of the vampire master," the   Jew.

Hitler saw the Jew as responsible for the degradation of German society, and sought to "eliminate the snake of primal eroticism, the Jew who is trying to possess her [the German woman]."[19] Furthermore, Hitler also saw the male Jew as someone who "fed on femininity," a monster who sought to destroy, both morally and racially, the German woman.[20] Nazi ideology emphasized domesticity as a way to protect women from corrupting elements as the Jews,   who were surmised as potentially seeking to suck the virtue from the souls of German women. Thus, one of the only ways a woman could protect herself, the same woman who "was the conduit to degeneration, the weak link in the evolutionary process", was to become a mother.   Impregnation by a pure Aryan man was the only way a woman could "break the teeth of the vagina."[21] Therefore, Hitler would protect all German women from any enemy in exchange for domestic and reproductive devotion to his nationalistic cause. Incredibly, Nazism, an ideology that did not allow women to rise to positions of actual authority, nor be ever fully accepted as equal party members, and of which its male members looked down upon women working outside of the home, still appealed to millions of   women.

At first, women did not realize what exactly Hitler's policies were concerning public roles for them, since he initially hesitated on "making a clear programmatic statement concerning the role of women."[22] Many feminists,   when Hitler came to power, saw a chance to elevate their societal and political role and argued for emancipation. German women looked for a new role in the Third Reich, and sought to take full advantage of whatever roles would be prescribed   for them outside of the typical domestic element. In one such 1933 example, a book entitled *Deutsche Frauen an Adolf Hitler* (German Women to Adolf Hitler), appeared in which several German female authors/feminists argued directly to Hitler that in the history of Germany, women often held positions equal to men.[23] These female authors cited four areas as their proof, including "matriarchal prehistory, a criticism of patriarchy, women's proven ability in the political arena, and the genesis of a new human being who combines female and male characteristics."[24] Many women who opposed discriminatory policies and sexism, whether covert or overt, faced tremendous backlash from Nazi party men who felt that women had no place in the public sphere (unless, of course, as warranted for party propaganda purposes and later war work) and sought to uphold gender segregated political participation. Contradictions in Nazi policy and actions did not go unnoticed. Nazism, at its core, held women in contempt. Still, many women did not give up and wanted access to the public sphere. They continued to protest their separation from party activism and government   roles.

Women who were against discrimination and sexism as espoused by the Nazis, made it clear what they opposed and why. Many argued that the majority   of the male members of the Nazi party were chauvinistic, and cited that, as far back as 1924, women left the party because of the overt sexist elements of the male Nazis. Many German women did not view the female Jew as equal, as many women understood the tenets of Nazism, which decreed that any woman who was not of full German origin, much less a Jew, could not hope to attain a position resembling egalitarianism in the Third Reich.[25] Ironically, the Nazis held women in contempt, falsely promising egalitarian status. Nazi policy was racist, but also inherently sexist.[26] Nevertheless, many Nazi men and, indeed, some women, still believed that the German woman's ultimate role was to have a baby to ensure that the German race would grow. By creating an ideal domestic sphere for her family, the German woman could construct a fertile agency that suggested race   and state servitude, even within the context of the   home.[27]

Thus, reproduction meant having babies not only for the family, but also for the state. Women were also assured that a baby and a sound home life was the ultimate goal that women could strive for, which would bring harmony to both home and country. Not all women agreed with this domestic construction of female roles. Some members of the *Frauenwerk* (Women's Bureau) contested the removal of women from positions of authority in the régime, as well as the treatment of married women who worked. Other women, arguably feminist in approach, felt that the Nazi party was in danger of collapse lest women not return
to the public sphere.[28]

Feminists argued that for the Nazi party to succeed, such sexist elements had to be suppressed and that women needed to be not only taken seriously, but   also given a role that would put them on the same economic, political, and societal rank as men. During the Weimar Republic, these feminists noted, over thirty women were members of the Reichstag, and it was these same women involved with the politics of the Weimar Republic who had continually fought for equal rights in terms of economic, political, and societal standing. Factions arose because members of the Nazis seized on problems that had already existed within the feminist movement, and capitalized on the difficulties the women had with   each other. The Nazis also sought to demonstrate, especially to young women   and non-feminists, that the members of the old-guard Weimar feminists could not understand what women really needed and wanted from political and social organizations as well as their government. [29]

Nazi-era feminists argued that the decadence of the Weimar Republic was something that women spoke out against. These feminists also asserted that they were for a new Germany, provided, of course, that Nazi Germany recognized an equal role for them. Hitler, despite some women's arguments to the contrary, did not agree that women were on the same level as men. In an address to the Nazi Women's Association, he contemptuously asserted:

> Women's liberation is only a word invented by the Jewish intellect, and its content is stamped with the same spirit. The German woman never needs to emancipate herself during the really good times of German life. The world of the woman is…her husband, her family, her children and her house. For years National Socialists have resisted the admission of the woman to political life, which has been, in our eyes,   disreputable. [30]

Other women's movements and organizations responded to the rise of Nazism by also fighting for rights, but their goals and ideology were in total opposition to the pre- and post-Weimar feminists. [31] Instead of emancipation, these women wanted official recognition and national respect for domesticity. They widely espoused *Kinder, Küche, and Kirche* as their domestic call-to-arms. Having large families and supporting domesticity was a selfless way for Nazi women to support their men and their state, and was the antithesis of   what German feminists stood for. [32] In addition, their ideology matched that of Hitler, who saw the role of women as singular, and devoted to the state. There was little room for interpretation for any other role for a woman other than "the production of offspring … their object was the earliest possible mating of vigorous males   with healthy females, their ultimate aim the maximal propagation of the species." [33]

Again, even very young girls were reminded that the most important role they could have in the future was to be a mother. German girls who joined the BDM *(Bund Deutscher Mädchen,* the German Girls League or the girl version of the   Hitler Youth) were sent to training camps to learn camaraderie and sportsmanship; in actuality, membership was compulsory and they were indoctrinated with National Socialist policies.[34] Young women would receive a dual education. Involved with organizations run by National Socialists, they were also encouraged to exercise and take care of their bodies, so that later in life they could bear as many children as possible for the state, not just for themselves.

The Nazis also sought to discourage women from seeking higher education, as women who wanted to go to college were considered infected by the forces of the bourgeois Jewish intellect.[35] Young girls were continuously molded so that they would personify the ultimate Nazi woman. This feminine ideal was personified by being identified as Aryan, physically fit, subordinate to men, and one who was willing to have babies for the state.[36] The SS also had special requirements, including schools, for women who wanted to marry SS men. The requirements included passing background checks, physical examinations, and a willingness to have children. SS officer Joseph Altrogge said of the German woman that

> We must choose her for her physical, racial, and genetic characteristics and not consider at all her name, status or money...we want strong women, ready to take upon themselves the mission the German nation assigns them. German women recognize their responsibility. Those   who avoid it are not worthy of being called German women.[37]

Aryan women were encouraged not to smoke, wear makeup or unattractive clothing, but were instead continually expected to act feminine, albeit as defined by the Nazi construct, being reminded that their main duty in life, besides total allegiance to the state, was to seek male companionship in the hopes of getting married and having as many children as possible.[38] Women were provided with several female Aryan role models, including author Gertrud Scholtz-Klink, a handsome blond widow with four children. Scholtz-Klink, who had established herself as a political leader as early as 1928 within National Socialist organizations, was appointed *Reichsfrauenführerin* (leader of the women of the Reich) on 24 February 1934.   She was an example that German women of all ages emulated.[39] Women were also not expected to work, and were encouraged to stay home to fight for the new domesticity that would save the German state. Women who went against these ideals confronted numerous   problems.

Women who did work often faced discrimination. On the other hand, some single women were "required by the Labor Service to work for a year in agriculture or domestic service."[40] Hitler failed to see that women deserved equal rights or any consideration at all other than respect for their domestic contributions to the state. Hitler's ideology sought to demonstrate that women who remained celibate, failed to have children because of personal choice, or who joined a convent, were lacking in one thing, ideal male companionship, and were thus dangerous to the survival of the state. Hitler, who commented that "the female has recourse to all kinds of methods to dispossess her rivals…Must one regard this innate savagery as a fault? Is it not rather a virtue?" would also say "women have the talent, which is unknownst to us males, for giving a kiss to a woman-friend and at the same time piercing her heart with a well-sharpened stiletto."[41]

Arguably, Hitler felt that in order for Germany to prosper as a viable state, nature would have to assist women in leading them to their true, innate, and assigned roles: *Kinder, Küche, Kirche.*[42] In reality, and in another example of the contradictions that surrounded National Socialism as an ideology, the economics of Germany were not such that all women could stay home and be *Hausfrauen* (housewives). Especially after 1939, Hitler and the government needed women to work outside of the home in order to ensure that the economy would   prosper.[43]

With the German economy recovering from the depression, combined with Hitler's desire to build up his armed forces, women were needed for jobs in farms, factories, dairies, and shops. Some single women had to work because they had no other means of support, whereas others would be required to work. Married women were often discriminated against in the workplace even if they worked because of economic necessity; thus, a conclusion can be drawn that for the state, the ultimate role for women was to marry, stay home, and have multiple babies. This contradictory and unrealistic familial ideal was not always possible, and became improbable, especially after Nazi Germany began to suffer   defeats.

Domesticity, despite the Nazi objectives that glorified it as the true and legitimate sphere for women, was no longer a viable option for all German women if the German state wanted to continue to prosper. Consequently, women were needed to work as men were being sent off to war; as losses loomed after 1943, women's participation was desperately needed, even though Hitler at first   did not agree wholeheartedly that women were needed in the factories in the same way American women were being put to work.[44]

Thus, women were encouraged, although on a smaller scale than that of   the United States during the 1940s, to join the workforce to support the state.[45] There were still more women whose husbands did not make enough money to support them as well as any children, which necessitated that the woman find a   job to ensure that her family would survive.[46] Working in menial positions, such   as working in factories, was not enough. Many women also felt that when SS men recruited for positions in the camps, it was hard to refuse such offers even though working in the camp structure did not necessarily mean more   money.

For some women, any entry into the Nazi power structure could be co- opted by them as a way to achieve any gains possible. Some sought to use this access to change their life positions, and held onto whatever alteration they were able to achieve. Women could meet a male Nazi higher-up and marry them, achieving a position of authority (however constructed by the male Nazi hierarchy and as seen with Ilse Koch), or work for the SS. Although women could not join   the SS, they could work for them as an *Aufseherin*. Few of these women enjoyed earning more money than some of them had made before, or believed that they could make elsewhere. If nothing else, the job for some women had the added panache in that they wore government-issued, clean, crisp, (and in their minds) impressive uniforms.[47]

Some women also had the chance to work their way up within the hierarchy of the camp structure, which was an opportunity denied to women at many other places of employment.[48] Such raises in positions included appointments as *Erstaufseherinnen* (head guard), *Lagerführerin* (camp leader), *Oberaufseherin* (Senior Overseer) and *Rapportführerin* (Report Leader). Was the SS, with promises of promotion in these positions, despite obvious sexist elements, an alternative for those women who did not want to serve the *Führer* by having babies? Many women sought other options to domesticity, and working   for the SS was one of them. Advertisements were run that sought women to fill positions such as air raid wardens, camp guards, secretaries, nurses, and factory workers. Later, the Nazis had to resort to conscription of women. Interestingly, some of the SS female contractors, when brought to trial, stated that money was   the major motivating factor behind their joining the Nazi party and working for   the SS.[49]

Many Austrian and German women responded to advertisements, were recruited by friends, their SS boyfriends, or by SS men who told them that, if they came to work for the *Führer*, they could make more money and possibly rise within the Nazi party, which was not necessarily the truth. Working for the government, even in a concentration or extermination camp setting, seemed a viable solution for some women who could or did not want to get married and/or have children. Some married women (with or without children) worked in the camps and did so for economic reasons. For some women, positions in the camp meant that they could possibly make more money than they could in other jobs,   and could retain a semi-autonomous status. Although, if a woman chose to get married and/or have children, her life would then possibly revolve around having as many children as possible for the state as part of her "expected duty." Even   with children, many women stayed in the workforce just to support a new or an existing family.

The Nazi emphasis on fertility at the cost of personal sacrifice was ambiguous. A number of women had as much sex as possible out of wedlock in order to get pregnant. This lack, for the time, of sexual morals, was viewed as necessary even though women sacrificed their reputations in order to serve their country. This precept of "wombs for Hitler" appeared to be a way for some women to identify with the state. Notably, several women who worked in the camps had as many babies as possible with different men. Survivor accounts especially recount reckless sexual behaviors, contradicting Nazi marital constructs. One Ravensbrück survivor described her feelings about these women:

> It is true that moral standards of German women have always been a matter of surprise. It sometimes happened, when we were asked to work with a small squad, that a garrulous and ill-disciplined guard would relate her personal adventures.   It appeared absolutely normal in her eyes that she, though unmarried, should already have given birth to several children of different fathers.[50]

Perhaps for some women, sexual liberation under the guise of serving the national interest was really a way to emancipate themselves from expected social and moral norms of the early twentieth century. Could these women be considered feminists? To live a life centered on domesticity for many women would be to give up the advances that their predecessors had made towards emancipation; this possibility demands a closer look at the importance of feminism and feminist struggles during the Nazi era.

Feminism rose in Germany in the period that followed World War I.[51] Feminists were clamoring for equal positions in German society, but, with the rise of Nazism, they were quickly silenced. When the Nazi party was established, women were categorically denied any position of power within the party. As a result, many women who identified with the Nazis and who were involved with the burgeoning women's rights movement in Germany found themselves struggling for an identity.[52]

Hitler seemed to provide an answer for many women who were looking for an egalitarian role in society. Several organizations developed under the Nazi umbrella that attempted to meet what the Nazis saw as the needs of the feminists. However, such organizations were not truly equal in that they were only designed by the Nazis to fulfill what they viewed as a supposed feminine need to have a role in society outside the home. These state-run organizations served to remind women that their true role was to be "companions to warrior husbands in forging the Thousand Year Reich." Other statements by the Nazis also asserted their masculine ideology: "we [the Nazis] believe that every genuine woman will, in her deepest feelings, pay homage to the masculine principle."[53]

When Hitler rose to power, many female politicians were ousted from their positions. If anyone resisted, including women, they would be arrested and thrown into prison.[54] As many of the German women's organizations were forced to either join the *Frauenfront* (national women's movement) or dissolve their clubs altogether, the nationalistic camaraderie offered by the *Frauenfront* was appealing. Women had no other choice but to fall in with Nazi politics, as there was often no other answer for them. Moreover, there was no other public sphere for them to move into other than the one endorsed by the Nazis: "The women who embraced the cause, and those who voted for Hitler, were prepared to barter political power in return for the privileges offered by the Nazis to women exclusively in their roles as wives and mothers."[55]

Feminism stood for the antithesis of Nazi ideology that glorified a return to the domestic sphere for women, but women from all levels of society were able to find employment if they sought it — from factory work to administrative positions — no matter how contradictory Nazi-defined statuses for women remained. Could it be argued then that women wanted any position, whether as employment as a guard, or as a spokeswoman noted for her fertility, as a way to simply be recognized in some twisted form of "egalitarianism?"

Within a few years of Hitler coming to power, hundreds of thousands of women found camaraderie, and even some measure of autonomy, within the now concentrated Nazi women's movement.[56] Even after difficulties with National Socialism surfaced, which included denial of equal public, social, and economic rights, women still supported Hitler and his régime for several reasons. The Nazis sought out female support for their causes. Propaganda suggests that the Nazis targeted women because as guardians of the home and private sphere, women were viewed (although on a small scale) as potential influencers towards their spouses or other male relatives. If the women supported the Nazis, why would   they not promote their policies within the home   structure?

At first, women supported Hitler and National Socialism because both represented and offered a new way of life, in terms of promises of fiscal growth and prosperity, as well as assurance for a return to family values after periods of devastating post-war economies, hyperinflation, then depression.[57] Later, when problems emerged with the party, women still supported National Socialism, partly because of indoctrination and even perhaps an innate belief that the German people simply had no better choice than the Nazi party.[58] Although promises were made for the betterment of society again, Nazism also sought to cement the fact that women had one legitimate public and private sphere: motherhood.[59] Domesticity was idealized and women were rewarded for it. Motherhood was not much of a gain for some women if they could not afford a family, and it was especially difficult for countless women after the war opened on 1 September 1939.[60] Despite ideology that did not offer women much beyond accolades and

assistance in exchange for staying in their domestic sphere, many women still wanted, and struggled for, a new role for themselves under   Nazism.

Even with the advent of state-run women's organizations, some women attempted to go beyond what the government offered. They wanted to maintain some measure of social autonomy, despite Nazi ideology that was against women taking part in groups outside of state-sanctioned organizations. Consequently, although they supported Hitler, and agreed in principle with some core Nazi tenets, countless women were frustrated by limitations. Some women spoke out:

> Leonore Kühn, long a leader in the middle-class women's movement, decided to support Hitler. Arguing logically from separatist premises, she declared that since women and men inhabited different worlds, it followed that women needed vastly improved education opportunities so that they could staff and direct their own activities. "We applaud *Kinder, Küche, Kirche,* but we demand two more, *Krankenhaus* and *Kultur.*"[61]

However, the *Weltanschauung* (ideological world outlook) put forth by Hitler and especially the propagandist Goebbels, did not intend, at least on the surface, for women to work outside of the home. Nazi ideology demanded that the German woman be devoted to the state and to have as many children as her body would allow.

Moreover, Goebbels argued that unless women returned to their traditional domestic spheres, the roles of the sexes would be completely reversed, since "the feminization of men always leads to the masculinization of women."[62]   Goebbels acknowledged that while women were an important part of German life, he stressed that their most important role was to maintain family and home. In a veiled warning to German women with regard to the low German birthrate, Goebbels emphasized the need to bring as many Aryan children into the world as possible in order to secure the future of the Third Reich.

Goebbels also recognized that while German women played a brave role in World War I, he suggested that it was now up to the women to ensure that Germany could rise again as a great world power via their uteruses. Goebbels reinforced and continually reiterated, using a variety of methods, fertility- emphatic propaganda that the Nazi state wanted German women to realize that unless they did their part to raise the birthrate, Germany would again perish at the hands of their enemies. Propaganda correlated babies with state-recognized reverence as well as the ideal form of domestic harmony: "The concept of the
German woman will again earn the honor and respect of the entire world."[63]

The ideologues of National Socialism, such as Goebbels, attempted to restore the valiant and courageous idea of domesticity, and again placed great honor on motherhood. Conversely, in an example of the many contradictions that surrounded Nazism, the same philosophy also gave a number of German women, vis-à-vis working for the régime, a chance to obtain position and power, something some women felt had been historically denied to them. Thus, Hitler was seen as a pseudo-emancipator, when quite the opposite was true. Emancipation had indeed risen in the preceding Weimar Republic, but any gains that the women's movement had made were almost obliterated by Nazism.

What makes this analysis seemingly contradictory was that since the Nazis had technically forbidden emancipation for women, women still felt that they could self-emancipate by joining up with the governing party of Germany. Consequently, as the need for labor increased during World War II, some German women were encouraged or conscripted to work outside of their traditional sphere. Therefore, if they chose to do so, women could work in different areas of the Nazi administration, sometimes, but not always, for better money than they could earn in factories and elsewhere.[64] Again, discrimination against women existed in the workplace, whether in a factory or office, but for many women, the attraction of working for the state was too much to   resist.

In addition, working for the Fatherland gave the women a chance to channel their resentments on a society that had consigned them to a domestic sphere, even with the understanding that the woman's main role was to bring as many babies into the world as she could for Hitler. A Nazi woman could occasionally interpret Hitler's policies as she wanted, and bring that nationalistic, racist ideology into her own private domestic realm. She could control how much indoctrination to bring into her familial sphere, and she remained in charge of her own interpretation of the Nazi ideology sweeping Germany. Within their own private domestic sphere, women could find different ways to support Nazism, for example, women could name their children after Nazi leaders as another way to

show their devotion to the state.[65]

If the state needed her, then a woman could serve; whether it was private   or public was not often of the woman's choosing. Scores of women would willingly do what was asked of them, and for whatever purpose promoted by Hitler and the Nazis. It remains difficult to understand the conflicting nature of   the aspirations of German women under Hitler, "for women, belonging to the 'master race' opened the option of collaboration in the very Nazi state that had exploited them," and employment in even the camp structure was attractive to women because it "represented upward mobility for the young women."[66] Could   it be that the more women were involved in Nazi ideological goals, the more that

Hitler would be able to cover up his actions? For example, with women at the forefront of the camps as guards, their gender could hide truths. The Nazi régime did allow for women to step out of the domestic sphere in order to help provide service to the Fatherland, even if the service was to work as a SS contracted guard in a horrific setting.[67]

In addition, the Nazis may have rationalized that the world could not and/or would not be able to comprehend women committing crimes against humanity by taking part in the atrocities of the camps. Furthermore, the Nazi concept of the nature/nurture issue, which idealized a woman's role in society, categorically seemed to deny that a woman could or would take an active part in genocide. It remains a fact that despite any misconceptions about women, transforming seemingly naive women into killing machines was not as complex as it would seem, since "the incredibly insensitive attitude that the Nazis promoted" allowed women "to view the inmates as the absolute dregs of humanity."[68] Employment as a guard offered an alternate status or simply just a paycheck. Women were not informed of their exact duties or working conditions when first going through the process of applying for work as a camp guard, but instead were told to expect light work. Horrors were to come for the new hires; much of it was later constructed and promoted by the women themselves once they went to work as guards. Few women could have conceived what was ahead in the camps. For some, a job was a job, and, just maybe, a chance at a better life.

For women who had no spouse, or who just wanted to work outside of a factory or dairy, Nazism offered women of the lower social classes mobility. National Socialism was especially successful with women since it rose as an ideology "during a black period in Germany's economic history in which the disintegrating influence of the Industrial Revolution was accentuated by the depression."[69] Many women were exposed to National Socialism via any involvement with the BDM. So, for some young women, working for the SS may have been a logical transition, especially since the BDM made the connections for them. Instead of total domesticity, SS connectivity allowed some women to reconstruct their lives. Many women took this connectivity and expressed severe anti-Semitism just as their male counterparts did. In addition to providing a way out of a traditional domestic sphere, could some women simply have been more pre-disposed to anti-Semitism than men? Would this presupposition then have just possibly facilitated women's decision to first take jobs in the camps, and, for some, act out in horrific ways?

Whether any predisposition to anti-Semitism made it easier for women to join in the torture and killing of Jews, there was a possibility that "females were slightly more likely than males to be anti-Semites in the early Nazi party…the accumulated and corroborated evidence indicates the females were indeed more anti-Semitic than males."[70] It remains critical to remember that the women who worked in the camps were by no means isolated, or unique in comparison to their male counterparts. Men committed acts of unfathomable cruelty just as the women did. Does gender matter then when studying women in the camp   system?

Yes, in the sense that in a time when women were not conceived as equals, in a society where equalitarianism was a relatively unheard of concept, women went to work in a system that allowed for them to express, whether voluntarily or forced, their angers, frustrations, resentments and expressions of new-found power in a way that only men could previously. These women mimicked SS men in such a way as to gain totality and control their own agency. They also acted out against women who they felt were too soft or showed compassion to prisoners.[71] Thus, an organization such as the SS had an appeal for women who were looking to become involved with Nazism in a way not associated with   domesticity.

---

[1] Adolf Hitler made this statement in his book *Mein Kampf.* This particular quotation was taken from Hilmar Hoffmann, *The Triumph of Propaganda: Film and National Socialism, 1933-1945*, 2nd ed. (Oxford: Berghahn Books, 1996), 140.

[2] Cate Haste, *Nazi Women: Hitler's Seduction of a Nation* (London: Channel 4 Books, 2001), 87.

[3] Jackson Spielvogel and David Redles. *Hitler and Nazi Germany*: A History, 6th ed. (Boston: Prentice Hall, 2010), p. 171.

[4] Spielvogel pointed out that the war changed everything since female labor was absolutely necessary to win the war. He further argued "The Nazis would almost certainly have insisted on returning women to their 'natural' occupations if they had won the war." See Ibid., p. 171.

[5] Bram Dijkstra, *Evil Sisters: The Threat of Female Sexuality and the Cult of Manhood* (New York: Alfred A. Knopf, 1996), 407.

[6] Ibid., pp. 406-407.

[7] Haste, pp. 7-8.

[8] Dijkstra, p. 403.

[9] Brown, *The Camp Women*, p. 15.

[10] Ibid. Brown also pointed out that Albert Speer wanted women in the workforce because necessity mandated it so. See Ibid., pp. 15-16. Interestingly, Adolf Hitler personally employed a female air pilot, Hannah Reitsch, one of Germany's greatest pilots, and the only woman to receive a Luftwaffe flying medal. He also employed a female chef. See Wendy Adele- Marie, "Axis Women." *Women and Work* (Chicago: Roosevelt University, 2004).

[11] Kirkpatrick, pp. 117 and 319.

[12] Donald D. Wall, *Nazi Germany and World War II*, 2nd ed. (Belmont, CA: Wadsworth, 2003), 105. Note also that Dr. Leon Stein pointed out that the concept of a "people's community" was attractive to many Germans but that this idea was a hoax.

[13] Ibid., 106.

[14] See Peter Fritzsche's *Germans into Nazis* (Cambridge, MA: Harvard University Press, 1998), p. 199. See also Brown, *The Camp Women*, p. 9. The idea of self-sacrifice and even martyrdom for Hitler and the party was not new. This concept was presented in propaganda, most effectively in film, notably with *Hitlerjunge Quex* (Hitler Youth Quex, Han Steinhoff, 1933). See Wendy Adele-Marie, "Hitler and the National Socialist Party" in Encyclopedia of Documentary Film, edited by Ian Aitken (New York: Routledge, 2006), pp. 569-560.

[15] Magda Goebbels had a son from a previous marriage and had six children (five girls and one boy) with Joseph Goebbels.   For her service in promoting domesticity, she received the *Mutterkreuz* (Mother's Cross). However, during the last days of the Third Reich, the Goebbels and their six children joined Hitler and Eva Braun, Hitler's longtime companion in Hitler's bunker in Berlin. The Goebbels gave orders that their children should be administered a shot of morphine, and that a poison capsule be given to them. All six children died. The Goebbels then committed suicide. Goebbels' son from her previous marriage had fought for the German armed forces. By the time of his mother's suicide, the Russians had captured him. See Hans Peter Bleul, *Sex and Society in Nazi Germany* (Philadelphia and New York: J.B. Lippincott Company, 1973), pp. 62, 96-97. See also Haste, pp. 232-234, and for the death of the Goebbels and their children, see especially p. 235. Gertrud Scholtz-Klink, a widow and mother of four children, was the head   of the Nazi's Women's League (NS-*Frauenschaft*). The League recruited thousands of women to help construct the proper imaging of a Nazi woman in the *Volksgemeinschaft*. This woman was subservient to men, understood her role in the private sphere, and placed emphasis on profound fertility. See Wall, pp. 106-107.

[16] See Haste, p. 237. Note that even if a woman was a lesbian, her duty was still to reproduce and become a mother for the state. Female homosexuality had its stigmas, but was not deemed as offensive as male homosexuality, although many Nazis had a problem with women guards and their expressions of lesbianism in the camps. See Ibid., 293. In the Nazi male mindset, there were problems with lesbianism as far as the Hitlerian worldview was concerned. Some of the perceived difficulties included the fear that lesbians would attempt to recruit good, heterosexual German women for their "unnatural" sex practices. Homosexuality among women raised so much concern that there was even discussion about forcing lesbians to mate with men in order to cure them. Note however, that lesbians were never persecuted on the same level as male homosexuals. See Claudia Schoppmann, *Days of Masquerade: Life Stories of Lesbians During the Third Reich* (New York: Columbia University Press, 1993), passim.

[17] Morrison, pp. 4-5

[18] Leila J. Rupp, *Mobilizing Women for War: German and American Propaganda, 1939-1945* (Princeton: Princeton University Press, 1978), see pp. 11-16. For Rupp's interpretation on the status of literature on women and Nazi ideology, reference n. 6, pp. 13-14.

[19] Dijkstra, 438.

[20] Ibid.

[21] Ibid.

[22] Richard L. Johnson, "Nazi Feminists: A Contradiction in Terms," *Frontiers* vol. 1, no.3 (1975):56

[23] For some of these role models, reference Katherine R. Goodman, *Amazons and Apprentices: Women and the German Parnassus in the Early Enlightenment* (Rochester, NY: Camden House, 1999), passim.

[24] Ibid.

[25] Johnson, 58. In this article, Johnson outlined exactly what German feminists wanted, and, more or less, demanded from their Führer: equal opportunities under the Third Reich. Johnson also argued that the basic tenets of Nazism, elitism and racism, would in no way allow women to attain equality. See also pp. 59-60. Perhaps women who became involved with the SS decided that whatever role was afforded to them was the best possible under the circumstances. Many women cited that economic opportunities played a big role in their decision to work at the camps. For more on this argument, see my chapter on Irma Grese. The reader must note that in 1921, the Nationalsozialistische Deutsche Arbeiterpartei, the NSDAP, voted that "a woman can never be admitted into the leadership of the party and into the executive committee." See Karl Dietrich Bracher, *The German Dictatorship: The Origins, Structure, and Effects of National Socialism* (New York and Washington, DC: Praeger Publishers, 1970), 87.

[26] See Cornelie Usborne's entry on Gisela Bock, in Kelly Boyd, ed. *Encyclopedia of Historians & Historical Writing, Volume One* (London: Fitzroy Dearborn Publishers, 1999), p. 99.

[27] Kirkpatrick, 203.

[28] Walls, pp. 106-107.

[29] Ibid., 53. Kirkpatrick suggested that the struggle between feminists and women not involved with the feminist cause escalated before Hitler came to power. See Ibid., pp.54-57.

[30] Bracher, 60. See also pp. 58-59 for more on the feminist movement under the Weimar Republic.

[31] See Rupp, pp. 29-31.

[32] Ibid., 29. See also Wall, pp. 109-110.

[33] Bleuel, 148.

[34] Ibid., 83-84.

[35] Pine, 51. See also Haste p. 83.

[36] Aryan was defined by Nazi eugenic policy as someone non-Jewish, non-colored, and having Nordic lineage. For more on the definition, see *"Arier, arish* Aryan" in Heinz Paechter, *Nazi Deutsch: A Glossary of Contemporary German Usage* (New York: Frederick Ungar Publishing, Co., 1944). 18. Note also that birth control and abortions were declared illegal for Aryan women. See Bleuel, 318.

[37] Tom Segev, *Soldiers of Evil: The Commandants of the Nazi Concentration Camps* (New York: McGraw-Hill, 1988), 75. What it meant to be an Aryan was formally defined on 10 September 1935, with the passage of the Nuremburg laws. See James M. Glass, *Life Unworthy of Life: Racial Phobia and Mass Murder in Hitler's Germany* (New York: Basic Books, 1997), 129, and Walter Laqueur, Ed. *The Holocaust Encyclopedia* (New Haven and London: Yale University Press, 2001), pp. 451-455.

[38] One of Hitler's rules for women guests at Berchtesgaden was "Women guests are forbidden to use excessive cosmetics and must on no account use colouring material on their fingernails." See Jon E. Lewis, Ed. *The Mammoth Book of Eyewitness History: Firsthand Accounts of History in the Making from the Ancient to the Modern World* (New York: Carroll & Graf Publishers, Inc., 1998), 396.

[39] See Gertrud Scholtz-Klink, *Die Frau in Dritten Reich* (Tübingen: Grabert, 1978), and Haste, p. 93. For a short biography of Scholtz-Klink, see Shaaron Cosner, *Women under the Third Reich* (Westport: Greenwood Press, 1998), 140. Besides Magda Goebbels and Scholtz-Klink,

other women emulated the ultimate construction of the Nazi *"Frau,"* such as Winifred Wagner, Viktoria von Dirksen, Helen Bechstein, and Baroness Karin von Kantzow, Hermann Göring's first wife. See Ian Sayer and Douglas Botting, *The Women Who Knew Hitler: The Private Life of Adolf Hitler* (New York: Carroll and Graft, 2004), passim.

[40] Wall, pp. 107-108.

[41] Adolf Hitler, *Hitler's Secret Conversations: 1941-1944* (New York: Signet, 1953), 338. See p. 339 for Hitler's view on women who did not have children or who failed to find a suitable male mate. The stiletto theory would hold true when examining some of the *Aufseherinnen*.

[42] Ibid., 339.

[43] Yehuda Bauer, *Rethinking the Holocaust* (Yale University Press: New Haven and London: 2001), 170. Bauer discussed that women were a necessary part of not only ensuring the growth of the economy, but were a much needed part of ensuring that Hitler's war machine would continue.

[44] See Adele-Marie, *Women and Work*, passim.

[45] See D'Ann Campbell, "Women in Combat: The World War II Experience in the United States, Great Britain, Germany, and the Soviet Union," *Journal of Military History* 57,   no.2 (1993): 301-323.

[46] By 1939, the year Germany invaded Poland, close to thirty-five percent of women returned to the work force. See Haste, p. 85.

[47] See Heike, "Female Concentration Camp Guards as Perpetrators," pp. 124-125.

[48] Such as was the case with Irma Grese. She was making either the same or slightly more money that she had at a dairy, so money, although she was to state the contrary at her trial, was not the motivating factor to work at Ravensbrück. See Brown, *The Beautiful Beast*, passim. Not all women found that their families accepted them working for the SS in the camp structure. For the trial transcripts of Grese's sister, Helene Grese, revealed that her father was supposedly against   his daughters becoming involved in Nazi activities, see Fyfe, 248. Irma Grese was believed to have said that her father beat her severely when she came home on leave from her work in the camps wearing her uniform. See Fyfe, p. 711. Morrison reminded the reader that the Nazis did not allow women, technically, into the SS service. Instead, he offered, women were relegated – despite their position within the camp infrastructure – to the SS Women's Auxiliary. See Morrison, p. 24.

[49] Stephenson, pp. 6-7. See also pp. 98-99, for more on Hitler's realization, circa 1935- 36, that for the mounting war effort to succeed, women needed to be in the labor force.

[50] Denise Dufournier, *Ravensbrück: The Women's Camp of Death* (London: George Allen and Unwin, Ltd., 1948), 67. The Nazi government gave women who had babies, married or not, several forms of assistance, which included extra money and childcare. See Bleuel, pp. 202- 207.

[51] For more on the role of women during the Weimar Republic and their ideology, see Elke P. Fredericksen, and Martha Kaarsberg Wallach, Eds. *Facing Fascism and Confronting the Past: German Women Writers from Weimar to the Present* (New York: State University of New York Press, 2000), pp. 37-39, 40, 46, and 194.

[52] Haste, pp. 74-75.

[53] Ibid., 74. Women definitely did pay homage to Adolf Hitler. Haste stated that when Hitler ran for office and won in 1933, over half of the people who voted for him were women.

[54] Ibid., 79.

[55] Ibid.

[56] Frederickson, 30.

[57] See Haste, p. 78; Haste stated that the majority of the early female supporters of Hitler were politically conservative, and would not have necessarily aligned themselves with feminists.

[58] Pine, pp. 86-87.

[59] Haste, p. 78.

[60] Adele-Marie's grandmother Martha Reinke revealed to her in conversation that when pregnant in 1943, Allied bomb raids rained fire on German cities. These terror raids prevented her, and many women, from access to proper medical care. She revealed that during the war, motherhood became a burden.

[61] Claudia Koonz, *Mothers in the Fatherland: Women, the Family, and Nazi Politics* (New York: St. Martin's Press, 1987), 141-143.

[62] See reference for Goebbels's speech cited in n. 8.

[63] Ibid.

[64] Stephenson, pp. 6-7. See also pp. 98-99, for more on Hitler's realization, circa 1935- 36, that for the mounting war effort to succeed, women would be needed in the labor force.   Women who joined the Nazi party as auxiliaries or as volunteers were single, married, or often   had a husband or other family member already involved in the Nazi party. Several of the Nazi women, when brought to trial, stated that money was the major motivating factor behind their joining the party. See Fyfe, Appendix III.

[65] Adele-Marie's paternal grandmother named her only son after Joachim von Ribbentrop, Hitler's Reich Foreign Minister. See also Robert S. Wistrich, *Who's Who in Nazi Germany* (New York: Routledge, 1995), pp. 201-202.

[66] Sarah Gordon, *Hitler, Germans, and the 'Jewish Question'* (Princeton, NJ: Princeton University Press, 1984), 303.

[67] See Koonz, 6; refer also to Brown, *The Beautiful Beast*, p. 55, and Morrison, pp. 24-25. Morrison suggested that not all women would be confined to the domestic sphere. See Morrison, pp. 4-5.

[68] Brown, *The Beautiful Beast*, 57.

[69] Kirkpatrick, 206.

[70] Gordon, 303. Jews were not the only targets of the SS and the female SS contractors. See also Ellen Switzer, "Tomorrow Belongs to Me" in *How Democracy Failed* (New York: Athenaeum, 1975), 52-53. Why were females supposed to have been more anti-Semitic than the men? Gordon took her information from Peter Merkl's *Political Violence under the Swastika: 581 Early Nazis* (Princeton, NJ: Princeton University Press, 1975). Merkl's research suggested, "Females were not great aiders of Jews." Gordon also reminded the reader "accumulated and corroborative evidence indicates that females were indeed more anti-Semitic than were males. See Gordon, p. 303. However, Gordon also noted that Merck's tables, which used numbers from   1933, showed women were slightly over characterized than men as anti-Semites, thus, the data   may have been skewed to represent German women as more anti-Semitic than German men. See Gordon, pp. 58-60.

[71] Brown illustrated such an example with Klara Kunig, *Aufseherin* at NL Dresden-Universelle and Ravensbrück. She was "dismissed from service for being too shy and polite to the prisoners (delinquent in training)." See Brown, *The Camp Women*, p. 162.

CHAPTER III

DER SCHUTZSTAFFEL (THE SS – PROTECTIVE SQUADRON)

Ich schwöre Dir, Adolf Hitler
Ich schwöre Dir, Adolf Hitler, als Führer und Kanzler des deutschen Reiches,
Treue und Tapferkeit.   Ich gelobe Dir und den von Dir
bestimmten Vorgesetzen Gehorsam bis in den Tod, so wahr mir Gott helfe.[1]

Although the prewar image of women assumed readiness to take up 'unwomanly' work for the good of Germany, women were not subjected   to the kind of steady practical propaganda urging them to take war jobs, which the American government utilized.[2]

In 1925, the SS was formed to act as Hitler's personal protection unit, or his protective squadron. Later, the SS developed into Germany's primary distinctive security force. The forerunner of the SS was first established during World War I, when a special, sharply honed unit was required for varied, secret, and elite assignments. The men of the SS, seen as a special sort of paramilitary unit, wore sharp, crisp, uniforms, and received special treatment including incentives such as extra time off. By the mid-1920s, Hitler sought to reorganize the SS, also known by this time as *Schwarzes Korps* (black shirts), and used them to help assert his power within the National Socialist party. The SS quickly established themselves as an elite racial and political guard under the command of

Hitler, and later "were determined to be the masters of Germany and Europe."[3]

Nevertheless, despite its designation as an elite unit, the SS "remained rather insignificant," until Heinrich Himmler took control.[4] Himmler, who had been a member of the Nazi party since 1925, was first given a role in the SS as *Deputy Reichsführer-SS* in 1927. By 1929, Himmler was promoted to full *Reichsführer-SS*, and for the next several years, worked hard to establish the SS   as the premier force in Germany, and quickly moved to take over all rival factions, especially those later run by his competitor, Hermann Göring, Hitler's second in command.

In Berlin, in April of 1933, out of the roots of the Prussian political police, Göring founded the *Gestapo* (secret police), intended to destroy all opposition, political and social, to Nazism.[5] The *Gestapo* was a terrorist-like unit with little regulatory control, but by 1934, Göring lost complete jurisdiction to Himmler. The *Sturmabteilungen* (SA, Storm Troopers, or brown shirts), led by Ernest Röhm, an early Nazi supporter, initially comprised of Hitler's main power force until 1933. However, for Hitler, many problems existed with Röhm's control of the SA, including rumors of his alleged homosexuality and supposed rivalry with Hitler. Although Röhm controlled a unit that was comprised of many, many men, his position within the Nazi party and Third Reich hierarchy placed him squarely at odds with Hitler. Röhm was now a threat.

Rumors abounded that Röhm was going to attempt to overthrow Hitler. However, Röhm was murdered in 1934, and control of the SA fell apart. With Röhm's death, the German people saw the SS, and its leader, Heinrich Himmler, as the "guardians of national morals."[6] By 1936, Himmler was in charge of all police operations within the Third Reich.[7] He became the chief architect of the complex SS hierarchy, and it was under Himmler's direction that the SS grew into several different police units, including the unit that would be in charge of the concentration camps.[8]

As the Nazi party grew in strength, Himmler appointed Theodor Eicke to a position within the Nazi party, and within a few years, Eicke proved himself to be an invaluable part of the burgeoning SS administration. Dachau, Himmler's 1933 invention, was the first concentration camp designed to contain prisoners, including Jews, political prisoners, and others. It was at Dachau that Eicke proved himself to Himmler, and by 1934, Himmler had promoted Eicke to "*SS Gruppenführer*, the second highest position in the SS."[9] As anti-Semitic actions increased in Germany, there arose a need to establish more camps for   the prisoners. Eicke was the man responsible, under Himmler, to administer SS policies and create a tight, centralized, SS bureaucracy. Eicke was also put in charge of reorganization of the emerging camp structure. Himmler had wanted the SS to be extremely structured as well as efficient, and he selected Eicke to ensure that this was done. The SS was then to administer and control all of the camps and Eicke was responsible for ensuring that Himmler's orders would be followed. It would be Himmler who also felt that a women's SS bureau would be effective for many reasons, including referencing the Nazi tenet of self-sacrifice for the   state. It was then within this construct that Himmler bore the first responsibility   for bringing women into the SS-hierarchy.[10]

Eicke successfully created a select, orderly system of SS bureaucracy, which later employed women. He also centralized the camps, demolishing old ones as well as designing new ones. Eicke continually worked on the camp infrastructure from 1934 until 1936. Consequently, Eicke supervised building of new camps and brought all of the established camps under the complete jurisdiction of the SS.[11] After 1936, the Nazis opened many camps.   First, concentration camps were built, and then extermination camps soon followed.[12]

With the administration of the SS under a centralized command, Eicke was able to then establish, albeit always under Himmler's directive, a special section of the SS known as the *SS Totenkopfdivision* (SS Death's Head Division).[13] Within this division, Eicke established the *Totenkopfverbände* (SS Death Head Special Units). The individuals who were part of this particular SS division were indoctrinated with anti-Semitic ideology. They were also encouraged to use violent and torturous psychological, physiological, and physical measures to subdue, control, or subjugate the prisoners. As this unit would be in charge of the camps, they had to be extremely efficient, loyal, and tremendously controlled, both mentally and emotionally. Within a few years, Eicke had thoroughly eliminated all of the individuals who he felt could not be a part of this elite unit. He then began a process to select men for assignment to the camps (one such selection was Karl Otto Koch, whose wife Ilse would be known

as the "Bitch of Buchenwald"), and both Himmler and Eicke went to extreme lengths
to ensure they were among the SS elite:

> The original guard units at Dachau consisted generally of sadists and bullies
> left over from the Nazi party's political struggle. Eicke weeded these men
> out soon after he became commandant, and replaced them with reliable,
> disciplined SS officers, NCOs, and enlisted men. As he expanded the camp
> system, Eicke's Dachau SS cadre, especially his most trusted subordinates,
> served as the nucleus of the additional SS guard units for the new
> concentration camps.[14]

This meant neither the applicant nor his spouse could be Jewish, nor could
they claim any Jews as ancestors. Moreover, "an Aryan pedigree had to be produced
which demonstrated that for ordinary applications blood had been pure since 1800
and for officer candidates since 1750."[15] SS applicants also had to   pass through the
SS Racial Commission, which had a series of three tests all candidates had to pass.
These tests included physical and racial examinations. After these initial tests, further
assessment of all applicants took place, and even more tests were administered.[16]
Finally, if the candidate passed all tests, he   would
swear an oath of allegiance to Hitler, and go through a series of ceremonies,
culminating in a special one on the anniversary of Hitler's birth, where the successful
new SS member would be given all the remaining   accoutrements
necessary for SS membership.[17]

These soldiers underwent intensive training under Eicke's supervision, and
were responsible for guarding and implementing the procedures of the camps, under
the directives of Himmler and then Eicke.[18] These men also recruited and then hired
women to work as camp guards and as guard supervisors. However, it remains nearly
impossible to determine how many of these SS special guards were women, but
the number is believed to be upwards of 3,000, and possibly up   to 5,000. The Nazis
later made great use of German women during the war; whether these women worked
as SS guards, laborers in munitions factories, or other war-related activities, the Nazi
régime did allow for women to step out of   the domestic sphere, however
constricted, to serve the   Fatherland.[19]

Although women were able to enjoy a certain measure of autonomy within the SS camp hierarchy, they were usually not promoted to the rank of officer, and were less likely to be convicted after the war of crimes against humanity and war crimes. Interestingly, some members of the *Totenkopfverbände* (SS Death Head Special Unit), who were in charge of the camps, allowed the women guards some measure of autonomy, but "there was never any question about where ultimate authority and real decision-making power lay. Such power was in the hands of the SS."[20] Although such power was highly controlled and dispersed, women could, although rarely, break out of constructed roles by using their gender for government work, especially for undercover work.

The SS did use women as spies, as did the Gestapo. One case involved a female Gestapo agent who assisted two male agents in rooting out an Italian diplomat for blackmail purposes. The agents found a young girl who was able to infiltrate the home of the diplomat, and ensnare him in a compromising position. The three then were able to get the diplomat to share secrets and the girl was sent away. This instance remained rare, but important to note that women's work for either the SS or Gestapo did not always involve working directly in the camp structure.[21]

If a woman decided to work for the SS as a camp guard, she would have been fully aware of what was going on in both the concentration and extermination camps once there. Like the men involved with the SS, many women also believed that the camp structure was a necessary part of National Socialist policy, which dictated that in order for Germany to survive, all perceived enemies of the state, especially the Jews, had to be destroyed. These women were simply doing a job that they were paid to do; a job, in most instances, that was cruel, inhumane, and murderous in actualization.[22]

What cannot be forgotten, however, was that whether these women applied, were conscripted, or volunteered for the position, numerous women made a conscious decision to use this position of authority over the "other" in cruel ways. By acting out under the guise of helping the state by "controlling" the prisoners in their charge in whatever way they saw fit, these women gained temporary societal (although within the camp structure) authority and in some cases, career mobility by being recognized by male superiors for their brutality. However, not all female guards needed to engage in brutality, as Gerda Weissmann Klein, a survivor reminds us in her documentary *One Survivor Remembers.* An *Aufseherin* saved her life, something Weissmann Klein noted, which conveyed to her that not all Germans were cruel.[23]

More importantly, although their work was outside of the preferred Nazi domestic sphere, perhaps *Aufseherinnen* and other women who worked for the Nazis truly thought they would help Hitler control his enemies, as well as do their part to ensure Germany would continue to prosper. Certainly, as Daniel Patrick Brown has concluded (based on his assessment of Konnilyn Feig's analysis): "the Nazi system so debased the German woman that she could not exert any natural leadership without being considered anti-Nazi, except in her limited role as a concentration camp matron." [24] Taking a certain sense of nationalistic pride in

their duty to Hitler, no matter what that duty was, was also seen in the way many of these women conducted themselves, whether as a wife or as a worker, perhaps even believing that "Nazi women … created a sense of racial order behind the front."[25] How did women who wanted to work (and were not required to by the Labor Service) then find work in the camps?

When Ravensbrück, the first women's camp opened in May 1939, ads were posted and recruitment drives for guards began immediately. The recruitment drives promised "physically effortless work" along with uniforms, good wages, and a sense of work permanence, all better conditions then, the SS argued, they could find in a factory or elsewhere.[26] At first, the SS had problems filling the vacant positions, perhaps because of prior propaganda that meant the camp system was something to be avoided, as well as usual negative connotations typically associated with any penal system. Conscription and forced compulsion also took place to fill the vacancies. Brown suggested that some women might have been even abducted and forced to work as guards, under the threat that unless they cooperated they would be interred as a prisoner themselves.[27]

To work as an *Aufseherin*, women could not have any prior criminal record, and had to be in good health. The majority of *Aufseherinnen* were screened, interviewed, and trained at Ravensbrück.[28] If hired, the women were promised that they would receive full training, a uniform, a somewhat decent salary, and a place to live. The women would then undergo a period of instruction that differed in length and scope, at least initially.[29]   After being taught the basics of Nazi tenets, some women were chosen for yet another interview. The instructor was tasked with finding out just how much the trainee knew about the régime, and also what her own attitudes and personal value systems were.[30]

If the women made it through this process, they were set to begin training. Training for *Aufseherinnen* entailed learning how to spot potential problems in the camp, prevent escapes, and how to control prisoners. The *Aufseherinnen* also received guidelines that described the proper and acceptable way to punish prisoners. The *Aufseherinnen* were then assigned to work with an *Oberaufseherin* for further training. Once the training was complete, women could be assigned to Ravensbrück or would be sent to other camps to work.[31] Women who wanted to work in the concentration camp system would have to join the Nazi Labor Front, and pay a portion of their salary to a variety of mandatory funds. Once hired at the camp, the women were given uniforms and assigned to sleeping quarters. Many ate and slept at the camp, as it had become a *de facto* home for many of these women.[32]

A typical day for an *Aufseherin* would be this: rise, commence with her daily absolutions, put on her uniform, eat, and report for duty. Daily duties varied from calling *Appell* (roll call), to processing the prisoners, to disposing of the bodies.[33] When female prisoners arrived at a women's camp, several *Aufseherinnen* would greet them. The female guards would sometimes be carrying pistols, whips, and/or have large, trained attack dogs at their sides.[34] Prisoners would then be processed by the *Aufseherinnen*, which sometimes meant interrogation. Prisoners under close *Aufseherin* supervision would have to strip naked and have their heads shaved, would shower, and would be given a uniform, which all prisoners wore.[35] The prisoners would also be given identification badges, which were colored triangles.[36]

The *Aufseherinnen* always supervised the women prisoners. The prisoners would then go through another series of questionings, and were then assigned to their duties. Violence against prisoners was encouraged, and, if the *Oberaufseherin* did not perceive the guard as being cruel enough, they too could face punishment.[37] In terms of salary, the wages were not excessive, and many did not make more than what they would have outside of the camps unless they worked towards a goal of promotion and even then, "the possibilities for making a career as a guard were more limited for females than for their male colleagues in the SS."[38] An *Aufseherin* would be paid anywhere from 30 to 185 marks a month, depending on her marital status and if she had any dependents.[39] Where did these women work?

Although there were dozens of camps for women, some *Aufseherinnen* worked at camps that held men.[40] There were well over three thousand female camp guards working in numerous camps between 1938 and 1945, and again, that number may be even as high as five thousand. Four important camps that employed many of these women were Auschwitz, Bergen-Belsen, Buchenwald, and Ravensbrück.[41] Hundreds of thousands of children, men, and women were imprisoned, enslaved, tortured, and murdered at these and other locations.

---

[1] See G.S. Graber, *History of the SS* (New York: D. McKay, 1978), 82.

[2] Rupp, 167.

[3] Ian Kershaw, *Hitler: 1936-1945, Nemesis* (New York: W.W. Norton and Company, 2000), 129.

[4] Bracher, p. 138.

[5] Ibid., pp. 351-352.

[6] Graber, 47. Also see pp. 48-60.

[7] Ibid., pp. 38-41.

[8] See Christopher Browning, *Ordinary Men: Reserve Police Battalion 101 and the Final Solution in Poland* (New York: Harper Collins, 1992), pp. 4-5.

[9] Charles W. Sydnor, *Soldiers of Destruction: The SS Death's Head Division, 1933-1945* (Princeton, NJ: Princeton University Press, 1977), 17.

[10] Brown, *The Camp Women*, pp. 14-15. See also Adele-Marie, *Encyclopedia of Documentary Film*, passim.

[11] Ibid., see pp. 5-9, 18, 20-25.

[12] Roselle Chartock and Jack Spencer, Eds. *Can it Happen Again?: Chronicles of the Holocaust.* (Black Dog & Leventhal: New York, 1995), pp. 46-47.

[13] Ibid., xv.

[14] Ibid., 24.

[15] Graber, 81.

[16] Ibid., 82.

[17] Ibid., 83. Women could not join the SS, but could work for them in various agencies established by the SS bureaucracy. In addition to the guards, women also worked as administrative assistants, receptionists, and as nurses.

[18] See Segev, pp. 94-123, for more on Theodor Eicke.

[19] Although recent scholarship does suggest that fully ten percent of the guards were women. See Heike, "Female Concentration Camp Guards as Perpetrators," pp. 124-125. Did the women really understand what they were getting into once they went to work in the camp structure? Heike did an excellent job outlining perceptions and realities of the guards; further, she stated on p. 124, in reference to Lichtenburg and Ravensbrück that "the command staff, and thus the running of the camp, was entirely in the hands of the men, women were supposed to guard the inside of the camp. As a result, women essentially determined the day-to-day existence of the inmates of the camp." Heike illustrated, on p. 125, that once advertisements for *Aufseherin* were responded to, upon application "a woman would receive an information sheet in which the duties were extolled as 'light physical work'." Conclusions can be drawn that the majority of women, despite disclosures on the sheet that applicants did "not need any professional knowledge, since it is merely a matter of guarding the prisoners," could not have known the full and true horrors of the camps. In Brown, *The Beautiful Beast*, p. 57, he stated that "despite her limited education, it would be difficult to believe that Irma Grese did not comprehend just how involved she had become in creating the loathsome environment" that was the camp environment; further, Brown illustrated on p. 58 that Grese (we can deduct that this held true for other *Aufseherin* as well) that if the "others" as designated by the Nazis needed to be punished, that Grese felt that "she had the right, indeed the obligation (!), to mete out such punishment." Indoctrinated since youth to believe in the superiority of their status, women such as Grese truly felt that she was justified in her actions.

[20] Morrison, 14.

[21] Edmund L. Blandford, *SS Intelligence: The Nazi Secret Service.* (Edison, NJ: Castle Books, 2001), pp. 41-42. Blandford, on pp. 127-128, reveals how Reinhard Heydrich attempted to destroy some of the top generals that he and other Gestapo had issues with. One such way centered on marriages to women who Heydrich was able to distort their familial backgrounds as a way to discredit or get rid of the husbands. See also pp. 129-133.

[22] Segev, 216. As the camp structure grew, there also arose a greater need for personnel, and women were sought to fill the many positions offered by the concentration and extermination camps. Advertisements were run, and word of mouth also became a way for women to find out about jobs in the camps. See Appendix I for a sample of the *Aufseherinnen* application, taken from Brown, *The Beautiful Beast*, 26.

[23] *One Survivor Remembers*. DVD. Directed by Kary Antholis, 1995. The United States Holocaust Memorial Museum and Home Box Office, 1995.

[24] See Brown, *The Camp Women*, p. 9.

[25] For her analysis of Elizabeth Harvey's discussion on how women perceived themselves see Koonz, "A Tributary" p. 167.

[26] See Heike, "Female Concentration Camp Guards as Perpetrators," pp. 124-126.

[27] See Brown, *The Camp Women*, pp. 16-18. Brown also pointed out that "the overwhelming majority of female guards were drafted." He also argued that the SS made a distinction between women who volunteered and who were conscripted in that women who worked voluntarily were "considered more worthy". See p. 17.

[28] Morrison, p. 25. Morrison also suggested that with the increase in prisoners, not enough women were applying for jobs as camp guards. By 1943, Morrison stated, the Reich Labor Ministry resorted to conscription to fill all of the *Aufseherinnen* posts that they had available.

[29] See Brown, *The Camp Women*, pp. 17-18.

[30] Ibid., p. 17. Brown stated that once the war shifted towards the allies, training was sporadic at best, if any at all took place. He also noted an "overwhelming majority of female guards were drafted." If drafted, their status stayed as *SS-Kriegshelferinnen*; if they applied for their position on their own they were "incorporated into the *SS-Helferinnenkorps* ... an added incentive to join" rather than be drafted. The status difference between the two was notable. If the woman applied, she was seen as "more worthy." See Brown, *The Camp Women*, p. 17.

[31] I owe debts of gratitude to Brown and also to Morrison's analysis of the *Aufseherin* trainee program. As did Brown, Morrison also went into great depth in his text about what an *Aufseherin* trainee experienced. See Morrison, pp. 24-26.

[32] Germaine Tillion, *Ravensbrück: An Eyewitness Account of a Women's Concentration Camp* (Garden City, NY: Anchor Books, 1975), 67. Tillion stated that these funds ranged from a general disability fund, membership in the Nazi Labor Front, beverages and food, lodging, and laundry services. Uniforms were provided free of charge.

[33] See Isaac Levy, *Witness to Evil: Bergen-Belsen, 1945* (London: Peter Halban in association with the European Jewish Publication Society, 1995), 11.

[34] Brown explained that women could also be assigned to be *Hundeführerinnen*, women who handled and also trained the camp dogs. See Brown, *The Camp Women*, p. 20.

[35] Nanda Herbermann, *The Blessed Abyss: Inmate #6582 in Ravensbrück Concentration Camp for Women* (Detroit: Wayne University Press, 2000), pp. 109-115. Herbermann, on p. 259, gives a short biography of Tillion. *Aufseherinnen* and *Oberaufseherinnen* would also assist in selections.

[36] The triangles were coloured to identify the status of the prisoners. For example, Jews wore yellow stars, and homosexuals pink stars. Each prisoner was given a coloured triangle that identified his or her race, religion, or sexual preferences. See Ibid., pp. 115-116, and Edwin Gryn and Zofia Murawska, *Majdanek Concentration Camp* (Lublin: Wydawnictwo Lubelskie, 1966), pp. 26-27.

[37] Brown discovered that *Aufseherinnen* whipped one guard for not being harsh enough on prisoners. See Brown, *The Camp Women*, p. 18.

[38] Heike, "Female Concentration Camp Guards as Perpetrators," p. 125.

[39] Tillion, 67. Tillion suggested that married women who had children received more money per month, and occasionally an extra allowance. Besides the guards, it must be noted that there were several other critical female guards at both Auschwitz and Ravensbrück of whom almost not study has done. *Oberaufseherin* Maria Mandl was stationed at Ravensbrück and then Auschwitz, was described by survivors as a "satanic female ... and a sadistic beast." See Herbermann, p. 141 and n.2, p. 141. In 1942 at Majdanek, a woman's camp was set up and several Nazi women who trained at Ravensbrück were sent there as *Aufseherin*. These women included Elsa Erich, former *Oberaufseherin* at Ravensbrück, who later transferred to Majdanek, and several others, including Hermine Braunsteiner, also a subject of my book. For more, see Gryn, pp. 40-41. See also Heike, "Female Concentration Camp Guards as Perpetrators," p. 125.

[40] Schwarz, "SS Aufseherinnen," 34. Note that Schwarz pointed out that no women worked at the following camps: Belzec, Kulmhof, Sobidor, and Treblinka. Women typically guarded women with rare exception.

[41] There were hundreds of other camps where women were employed at but for the purposes of this study, a select few were chosen for analysis simply because it was where the women featured in this book worked or spent the majority of their time from 1939-1945.

CHAPTER IV

FOUR NOTABLE CAMPS

Auschwitz, Bergen-Belsen, Buchenwald, and Ravensbrück

Whenthelastlayersofsubcutaneousfathadvanished,   andwelooked like skeletons disguised with skin and rags, we could watch our bodies begin to devour themselves. The organism digested its own protein, and the muscles disappeared. Then the body had no powers of resistance left. One after another could calculate with fair accuracy whose turn would be next, and when his own would come.[1]

What influence a woman, even without realizing it, can exert on the history of a country and thereby the world! [2]

Auschwitz

The Nazi concentration and extermination camps originated with the planning and development of a concentration camp called Dachau, near Munich, Germany, in March of 1933. Concentration camps were designed as inmate holding facilities and were used as a labor source. Several of the concentration camps also provided the Nazi doctors with human subjects for medical and other experimentation. Prisoners were held in the concentration camps until they were selected for euthanasia or died of disease or illness. The exclusive purpose of the extermination camps was to kill prisoners.[3]

The Nazis not only sent Jews to the camps, but they also sent prisoners of war, homosexuals, the handicapped, mentally ill, physically infirm, Roma, Communists, Socialists, Jehovah's Witnesses, Seventh-Day Adventists, German criminals, dissenters, and others deemed undesirable by the Nazis. The concentration and extermination camps were a highly organized ideological and bureaucratic enterprise of abuse, humiliation, torture, and murder. In some instances, flowcharts were created for the Nazis to follow in order to achieve the maximum output of death.[4] The creation of the Nazi camps was also significant   in that, for the first time in history, a form of technological slaughter was utilized   in Germany, an industrialized nation, to kill people such as the Jews, homosexuals, the mentally and physically disabled, and any other undesirables simply because they existed.

Created under the command of Heinrich Himmler, the concentration and extermination camp Auschwitz (*Oswiecim*) was built in southern Poland between April and June of 1940.[5] Auschwitz remains the largest and one of the most infamous of all the camps, owing to the vast numbers of people interred as well as killed here. Auschwitz was originally used, beginning in 1940, to house Polish and Russian prisoners of war as well as German political dissenters and resisters. Rudolf Höss, a longtime Hitler associate and member of the Nazi party since the early 1930s was appointed *Kommandant* of Auschwitz. By the middle of 1941, Höss received an order from Himmler, as he recalled in his   memoirs:

> In the summer of 1941, I am unable to recall the exact date, I was suddenly ordered by Himmler's adjutant to report directly to the *Reichsführer-SS* in Berlin. Contrary to his [Himmler's] usual custom, his adjutant was not in the room. Himmler greeted me with the following: "The Führer has ordered the Final Solution of the Jewish question. We the SS have to carry out this order. The existing extermination sites in the East are not in a position to carry out these intended operations on a large scale. I have, therefore, chosen Auschwitz for this purpose…you now have to carry out this assignment."[6]

The plan to murder millions of Jews was now official; Höss would be in charge of ensuring that Auschwitz would carry out the orders of the *Reichsführer*.[7] Höss needed to find an area that would accommodate the exterminations near Auschwitz, so he selected Birkenau, where gas chambers and massive crematoriums were built. Other Auschwitz complexes and sub-camps soon opened. During September 1941, the first gassings of Russian prisoners of war   had taken place. The first Jews were gassed in February of 1942. As the war progressed, the need for labor in the camp structure increased, and there was an ever-growing need for women to work as auxiliaries. Women were posted to

Auschwitz soon after the camp opened.[8] Höss had an interesting take on female non-prisoner labor, despite Himmler's own directive that women be treated as equals if they were hired or conscripted by the SS for labor duty.

Höss, a misogynist, was against having women as SS contractors. He felt that they were prone to homosexuality, something he personally viewed as a negative. Further, he felt that women guards were simply unable to maintain personal as well as professional order: "they lacked discipline, were incompetent, were sexually shameless, and were given to lesbianism;" further, he commented that while he "always had a great respect for women in general" that when "in Auschwitz, however, I learnt that I had to modify my views, and that even a woman must be carefully examined before she is entitled to enjoy a full measure

of respect."[9] He was admitting three things here: one, women were not fully, in his mind, up to the task of being equal to men; two, he had to acknowledge his grudging "respect" for women lest they turn in opposition to him and SS men; and, three, that women were needed for work in the camp system so that the Final Solution could be carried out, especially in Auschwitz, the largest extermination camp in the Nazi structure.

By November of 1942, in Auschwitz over 100,000 people were killed, and the numbers continued to rise; by 1944, "more than 600,000 people, about 95 percent of them Jews, poured into the camp."[10] Some prisoners would be selected for work duty, but with the terrible conditions of the camp, thousands did not survive. Prisoners were also subjected to a variety of horrific medical experiments. As with the extension into Birkenau, Auschwitz was constantly enlarged to accommodate the hundreds of thousands of people sent there both to work and to die, since "body disposal was always a problem in Auschwitz

because of the high death rate of the inmates."[11] An estimated one to two million people died in this camp.[12] Auschwitz was liberated on 27 January 1945 by the Russian army.

Bergen-Belsen

Established in 1943, and located in close proximity to the northwest German city of Celle, Bergen-Belsen was constructed as a transit center, but unofficially developed into a concentration camp. As a transit center, Bergen- Belsen was supposed to be a temporary jail, as many of the people taken prisoner by the Nazis were at Bergen-Belsen for only a very short time before being shipped to Auschwitz and other locations. Bergen-Belsen was also designated as a sick camp, which meant that it was "for the use of those sick internees whose death was not immediately required."[13] There was no gas chamber at Bergen- Belsen, but many died while interned there because of disease and horrific labor conditions. Under the command of Joseph Kramer, the camp *Kommandant*, thousands that were interned at Bergen-Belsen were abused, beaten, killed, and starved. Subsequently, Kramer, an experienced commander who had previously worked at Auschwitz, was given the nickname Beast of Belsen for his inhumane treatment of prisoners.[14]

Several *Aufseherinnen* also worked there. Typhus and other diseases were rampant at this camp, hygiene conditions were poor, and many *Aufseherinnen* caught diseases like typhus by being in such close contact with the prisoners. When the Russians began to overpower German troops toward the end of the war, the number of prisoners at Bergen-Belsen increased, which led to even more appalling conditions. One of the best-known victims of Bergen-Belsen was Anne Frank, who died of typhus.[15] The guilt of Bergen-Belsen and its staff was described as follows:

> In respect of Belsen there would not be an allegation that there was a gas chamber or that persons were herded by their thousands to the death but there would be an allegation that every member of the staff of Belsen bore his or her share in the treatment given to the prisoners at Belsen, which they knew was causing and would continue to cause death or injury.[16]

Since there was no gas chamber at Bergen-Belsen, inmates suffered a slow death due to disease or starvation, and often there was no proper disposal of bodies. The conditions at Bergen-Belsen were described as horrific, due to terrible neglect. Bergen-Belsen had several incarnations and also sections. It was first established as a prisoner of war camp, and was then set up as a civilian residence camp. It was also a holding center for sick inmates who could be used for slave labor, or who were in transit to other camps. Finally, it was a concentration camp. The appalling conditions at Bergen-Belsen were a direct consequence of how Kramer and other workers treated the prisoners, having ignored any responsibilities for the prisoners or its personnel. In comparison to other camps, "the conditions at Belsen were caused by criminal and inexcusable neglect coupled with an administrative breakdown, while the conditions at Auschwitz were the direct result of a carefully designed and executed policy of long standing."[17]

The British liberated Bergen-Belsen on 15 April 1945.[18] Bergen-Belsen was one of the first camps liberated by the Allied forces, and served as the location for the Belsen trial, which was later administered by the British government.[19] The forty-five individuals, including nineteen women, placed on
trial at Bergen-Belsen were tried on two counts: war crimes and crimes against humanity.[20]

Buchenwald

Buchenwald, one of the main concentration camps, was built in 1937 near Weimar, Thuringia, east of Frankfurt. Buchenwald was a concentration camp, not an extermination camp, but over 43,000 people, out of an estimated quarter of a million inmates, were killed, or died of abuse, disease, forced evacuations, medical experiments, and starvation.[21]

The *Kommandant* of Buchenwald was Karl Otto Koch, who ran the camp from 1937 until 1941. The camp opened in 1937, the year Koch married Margarete Ilse Köhler, and the newlyweds moved into a lavish estate built on the grounds of Buchenwald where they also began to raise their children.[22] Their estate, known as Villa Koch, was directly across from the entrance of the camp. Frau Koch ordered a special riding hall constructed for her pleasure, and her husband had a zoo built on the grounds.[23]   After Koch was removed as *Kommandant*, the command of the camp was taken over by Hermann Pister. From 1942 until 1945, Pister remained *Kommandant* until Buchenwald was liberated.[24]

From its inception until liberation by American forces on 11 April 1945, hundreds of people died from neglect, starvation, and abuse at Buchenwald. For those that survived, during liberation former prisoners formed groups based on their national origins to provide a means of support for themselves. From 1945 until 1950, the camp served as a prisoner of war camp for the Russians. Thousands of Germans and others were kept prisoner under horrific conditions and many died.[25]

Ravensbrück

Although there were many camps for women, Ravensbrück was one of the first main Nazi camps, and designed for women prisoners.[26] Although camps such as Auschwitz had women's sections, with the very large number of Jewish and other women arrested by the Nazis, it became clear that a women's camp was necessary in order to contain the growing number of female prisoners. Under the directives of Himmler, Ravensbrück was built in 1938 by prisoners from the Sachenhausen camp, in an isolated area outside Berlin called Fürstenberg, in Mecklenburg, incongruously on the banks of a beautiful body of water known as Schwedt Lake.[27] Ravensbrück was a concentration camp but later gas chambers were built where thousands would perish. By May 1939, the first women prisoners were held there. Ravensbrück was also designated the main location for the training of Nazi female recruits; it was here where thousands of camp guards received their training, and it was also here where many women were subsequently employed as *Aufseherinnen*.

The camp had over thirty sub-camps attached to it, and contained thirty- three sections. Although exact figures remain unknown, as many as 3,500, and possibly up to 5,000, women may have been trained as *Aufseherinnen* there. Since Ravensbrück was the largest camp for women, many of the *Aufseherinnen* worked there for years, as the need for guards did not abate. This was because of the

sheer number of prisoners that needed to be   supervised.[28]

The first women prisoners were sent there on 18 May 1939, and the numbers

of female inmates increased tremendously over the next several years.[29] Some of the

most grotesque medical research of the war was performed here, and

women doctors performed several of these terrible experiments. In one such horrific

experiment, bones of Polish women were torn from their bodies in order   to study

their physiological reactions.[30] In yet another, a woman's leg   was

repeatedly cut open and purposely contaminated in order to test new drugs designed

to fight infections.   Pregnant women, in all stages of their pregnancy,

were also experimented on; these experiments included forced abortions,

sterilizations, and operations on their genitalia and female   organs.[31]

Once at Ravensbrück, women who were either hired or conscripted to work

as *Aufseherinnen* were assigned to other *Aufseherinnen,* or an *Oberaufseherin,* for

training.   The training periods varied; some were   given

instructions for a few days while others took months, even up to a year, to train.[32]

Between 1942 and 1945, Ravensbrück had trained over three thousand women as

Aufseherinnen.[33] Once the new workers arrived at Ravensbrück, they underwent an

extensive training course, which lasted anywhere from a few days to over six months.

Indoctrinated in the racist and anti-Semitic policies of the Nazi régime, it was

understood that these SS women workers would uphold the policies of the camps.

During this period, the women trainees were indoctrinated with many racist aspects

of Nazi ideology. They were encouraged to steel their emotions and act out any

aggressions or tendencies towards cruelty that they may have held in check before

against the prisoners.

Once trained, the *Aufseherinnen* would be among the first to meet new

prisoners, usually in the company of a fierce guard dog. Many women who met

prisoners worked with guard dogs, and used the dogs to help control the prisoners.

These women reported to the *Oberaufseherinen* (female head overseer), who in turn

reported to the *Schutzhaftlagerführer* (Protective Custody Camp Leader),

                                   Women as Nazis

who was then ultimately responsible to the *Lagerkommandant* (Camp Commander), the head of the camp.[34] Ravensbrück had the unique distinction of being run almost entirely by *Aufseherinnen*, including the cruel and sadistic chief overseer Dorothea (Theodora) Binz.[35]

One eyewitness, Nanda Herbermann, a German Catholic woman who was arrested for her work with Catholic resisters, described her arrival at Ravensbrück as follows:

> After a few hours' journey, we arrived at the new cross-station, Bahnhof Fürstenberg. Unutterable grief filled my soul. There stood the SS, there stood the female overseers with the trained dogs who would torture us so often in the future. A horror overcame me, body and soul. We were literally thrown into the trucks that were ready for us. Some of us, the little old people and the weak ones, could not make it in so fast. "Old piece of s— t...get up there now or you'll get a lashing!" Our first greeting was of this nature. All my limbs shaking, I climbed onto the truck, and already one of the SS people was grabbing a club and pressing it into the backs of my kneecaps so that I fell to my knees. None of the inmates said a word. Amid so much horror even the most destitute and downtrodden lost their ability to speak. Oh Mother, Mother, how I thanked God that you could not see what was done to your child![36]

Aufseherinnen were employed at many camps other than Ravensbrück. At any camp, conditions were appalling and horribly inhumane. Moreover, some *Aufseherinnen* as well as *Oberaufseherinnen* were personally to blame for the terror and cruelty inflicted on prisoners here.

When questioned about their responsibilities in the camps, several women claimed they were conscripted. However, some admitted that they offered to work in the camps, such as was the case with Binz, who initially volunteered her time. Yet other women stated they were hoping for a better way of life, especially financially, by working at camps such as Ravensbrück.[37] Conscription certainly was a reality for many women and conscripted *Aufseherin* would soon be the majority.[38] By 1943, "the Reich Labor Ministry was empowered to conscript women between seventeen and forty-five years of age."[39] Hundreds of women were then processed through Ravensbrück, and with war losses mounting, sporadic and sometimes no training would be provided to the women.[40] The Russians liberated Ravensbrück on 29 April 1945, one day before Hitler and his wife Eva Braun committed suicide in Hitler's Berlin   bunker.[41]

---

[1] From Viktor E. Frankel, "Dehumanization and Starvation," Chartock, 42.

[2] Blandford, p. 127.

[3] The camp structure, which had nineteen primary camps and thousands of sub-camps, was further summarized in Konnilyn G. Feig, *Hitler's Death Camps: The Sanity of Madness* (New York and London: Homes and Meier Publishers, 1979), pp. 23-37.

[4] Chartock, 208.

[5] Feig, 341.

[6] Rudolf Höss, *Death Dealer: The Memoirs of the SS Kommandant at Auschwitz* (New York: Da Capo Press, 1996), 27.

[7] Höss was not always in charge of Auschwitz, as the *Kommandant* of the camp changed several times from the time it opened until the time it closed. See Laqueur, pp. 39-43.

[8] "The SS Garrison in Auschwitz-Birkenau." See Auschwitz-Birkenau Memorial and Museum   at http://en.auschwitz.org.pl/h/index.php?option=com_content&task=view&id=20&Itemid=17   (9 October 2010).

[9] Roger W. Smith, "Women and Genocide: Notes on an Unwritten History." *Holocaust and Genocide Studies* 8 no. 3, (Winter 1994): 315-334.

[10] Höss, 28. See also Laqueur, pp. 36 and 41.   Note that by 1943, Auschwitz, which had sometimes been referred to as Auschwitz-Birkenau, was broken down into three divisions: Auschwitz I, II, and III. The changes were made to better ensure smooth control and bureaucratic efficiency. The *Kommandants* also changed several times. Note Laqueur, pp. 41-43.

[11] Ibid., 37.

[12] See Emmi Bonhoeffer, *Auschwitz Trials: Letters from an Eyewitness*, trans. Ursula Stechow (Richmond: John Knox Press, 1967), 61. The number of actual dead varies. See also Laqueur, p. 44.

[13] Phillips, xxix.

[14] Laqueur, p. 67.

[15] The editor of *The Belsen Trial*, Raymond Phillips, suggested that the majority of the *Aufseherinnen* who worked at camps like Bergen-Belsen were conscripted. He surmised: "Female SS were employed to administer the women's compounds, to run cookhouses, and do similar work of a minor administrative kind." His analysis ignored the full roles that the women employed by the SS played in the camps. Not all women who worked for the SS did so as an office administrator. His dismissal of their actual roles implied that their roles were not as serious as some might interpret them. Nevertheless, this author's study has shown that many women applied for jobs at the camps, such as in the case of Hermine Braunsteiner, and had a much more active   role than that of a mere secretary. Note too that many were not conscripted, nor applied for a job; *Oberaufseherin* Binz first volunteered for a position in the camps. See Raymond Phillips, *Trial of Josef Kramer and Forty-Four Others (The Belsen Trial)* (London: William Hodge and Company, Ltd, 1949), p. xxviii, and 218.

[16] United Nations War Crimes Commission, *Law Reports of Trials of War Criminals: The Belsen Trial*, 2d. ed. (New York: Howard Fertig, 1983), 9.

[17] Phillips, xxix.

[18] See "Chronology of Laws and Actions Against Jews," in Chartock, 53.

[19] Russian forces took over Buchenwald on 27 January 1945, and made the horrors of that camp public. See United Nations War Crimes Commission, *The Belsen Trial*, p. x.

[20] See Ibid., for the verdicts not covered herein.

---

[21] See Laqueur, 97. Refer also to David A. Hackett, Ed. *The Buchenwald Report* (Boulder: Westview Press, 1995), passim. Note that Laqueur's text suggested that only 239,000 were imprisoned at Buchenwald.

[22] See chapter on Ilse Koch *"Gnädige Frau* - the Gracious Lady and the Mistress of Buchenwald."

[23] For more on the Kochs and their fate, again refer to chapter on Ilse Koch.

[24] Hackett, 59, n 29. Hackett revealed that Pister was tried at the Buchenwald trial, and was sentenced to death. However, Pister was never brought to justice; he died of a heart attack in 1948 while still in prison.

[25] Arthur L. Smith, Jr. *Die Hexe von Buchenwald: der Fall Ilse Koch* (Köln: Böhlau, 1983), 259; reference "Kibbutz Buchenwald," in Chartock, pp. 280-282, and for the day of liberation, see Hacket, 331.

[26] Morrison stated that as early as 1933, a special camp that precluded Ravensbrück was known as Moringen, located near Hanover, and was used exclusively for women prisoners. See p. 11.

[27] Ibid., pp. 11-17.

[28] See also Claudia Taake, *Angeklagt: SS-Frauen vor Gericht* (Oldenburg: BIS, Bibliotheks- und Informationssystem der Universität Oldenburg, 998), p. 30, n. 10. Other estimates are closer to Morrison's. See Morrison, pp. 276-277.

[29] Ibid., pp. 14-17.

[30] Raul Hilberg, *The Destruction of the European Jews* (Chicago: Quadrangle Books, 1961), 603. See also illustration eleven.

[31] Dr. Herta Oberheuser was responsible for many of these experimental atrocities. Reference the chapter on Oberheuser. Note also the eyewitness account of Margarete Buber, who was a prisoner at Ravensbrück. See her *Under Two Dictators*, trans. Edward Fitzgerald (New York: Dodd, Mead and Company, 1946), pp. 251-254.

[32] Morrison, pp. 25-27.

[33] Schwarz, "SS Aufseherinnen," 41. Schwarz notes that Ravensbrück was not the only place where women could train to work as an *Aufseherin*. Women were also sent to Stutthof. See p. 41.

[34] Ibid., 20.

[35] For more on Binz, see my chapter on Binz. The reader must keep an objective mind here as the records at this camp were intentionally (as was the case at many camps) destroyed at the close of the war. Hence, many facts came from survivors, allied soldiers, and, in some instances, the women guards themselves. For more analysis of the number of trainees, see Claudia Taake, *Angeklagt: SS-Frauen vor Gericht* (Oldenburg: BIS, Bibliotheks und Informationssystem der Universität Oldenburg, 1998), 30, and Brown, *The Beautiful Beast*, 3. See also Herbermann, pp. 125 and 140.

[36] See Herbermann, p. 109. Note also p. 13. Nanda was thirty-eight when she was arrested. Her brother Heinz, one of five male siblings who were in the army, wrote to Himmler asking that his sister be released. His request was granted. See again p. 13.

[37] Morrison, 24.

[38] Brown, *The Camp Women*, p. 17.

[39] Brown, *The Beautiful Beast*, 3.

[40] Brown, *The Camp Women*, p. 17.

[41] Laqueur, xxxviii.

CHAPTER V

EXAMINING WHY: SADISM, VIOLENCE, AND IDENTITY

The Group and the Common Enemy

Where was the depravity? Or, perhaps, an overwhelming sense of guilt? Sadism? Bigotry? Hatred? None of these seemed apparent in the psychological test profile. Just the opposite, the psychological profile seemed to indicate an ordinary, rather untroubled person who, although unlikely to be somewhat distant and inflexible in interpersonal relationships, was not bent on the destruction of whole populations of human beings.[1]

Aryan biological superiority was a central part of Nazi ideology, but natural supremacy does not alone explain why so many women became sadists.[2] Could women easily become hardened, violent criminals, capable of committing horrific, sadistic acts? When considering the charges that the *Aufseherinnen* and other women faced at trial, did it really hold true that: "women are typically less violent criminals and therefore less of a threat to the community should they be released" and was it accurate that "the violence they do participate in is often unplanned and frequently of a domestic nature; both are factors a judge may take into consideration, especially as they pertain to the impact imprisonment may have on a woman's family"?[3] Can this be factual when trying to comprehend why so many women (the supposed gentler sex) played active roles in genocide? Was   it because, following female perpetrator's logic, that their crimes were somehow forced upon them due to the fact that they were following orders? Or, that they were conscripted? What about women who volunteered or applied for a job in the camp? Did women view their violent actions in a distorted domestic construct, so that they thought their actions would be somehow held less accountable than their male counterparts?[4] Did their gender make an allowance for their   culpability?

Not necessarily. Certainly, the crimes committed by women in this book were not crimes of a domestic nature nor could they be classified as such. Throughout history, women in power, or with some modicum thereof, could be, have been, and were as violent and sadistic as men, which belies the domestic- oriented theory of the levity of female violence. From the Iceni queen Boadicea, who personally led an army that murdered over seventy thousand male Romans,   to the Japanese Empress Regent Jingo-kogo, who coldly ordered the execution of anyone she perceived as an enemy, to Mary I of England who from 1553 to 1558, ordered the death of hundreds of Protestants in the name of Catholicism, history   has several examples of women who used violence as a means to attain a   goal.[5]

Do most average women have fantasies of being in control? If so, would women use whatever means possible to achieve their desires, including application of masochistic measures and sadistic techniques? What about average women in the context of Nazism? Some women who worked for the Nazis acted   out in barbaric ways because they simply had the opportunity to do so. They made a deliberate decision to exert abuse over helpless   prisoners.

It remains unknown whether women involved with the Nazi party fantasized about torture and murder. Many came from average backgrounds and several blamed their superiors for their crimes, having refused at their trials to accept any personal culpability for their actions. Even more shocking was the level of abuse and depravity the women participated in with regard to the crimes   of the Holocaust. Some of the women involved with the Nazis, like Dr. Herta Oberheuser, purposely used prisoners for medical experimentations. *Aufseherinnen*, such as Elisabeth Volkenrath, took part in selections; Juana Bormann, used her dog as a way to control prisoners; and Hermine Braunsteiner used her feet to inflict abuse. Others such as Irma Grese purportedly used prisoners as a way to support their own sexual deviance.

Of all the women involved with the Nazis, Grese remained one of the most abusive and cruel of all perpetrators, both male and female. Survivor accounts related repeatedly that Grese not only beat prisoners, she sexually abused them as well. Sexual abuse, in one sense, is more humiliating than physical abuse alone; but

both abuses combined and administered by one's own sex were amongst the most

horrifying of all crimes perpetrated by these women. Could Grese's actions, which

allegedly included forcible female-on-female rape, if survivor accounts of her sexual

abuse of prisoners are to be believed, stem from an unknown childhood event?   Or,

was Grese completely normal, but used her position to act out all of   her sick

fantasies? Grese may have suffered from a psychosis known as   *paraphilias*.

Therefore, Grese may have been   like

> some individuals who commit sexual offense who have a normal pattern   of
> sexuality but act out impulsively or opportunistically in a sexually deviant
> manner when under the influence of drugs or alcohol or during stressful
> situations. Other individuals develop a pattern of deviant sexual interests or
> behaviors, also known as *paraphilias*. *Paraphilias* are demonstrable sexual
> fantasies or patterns of behavior that involved nonhuman objects and the
> suffering or humiliation of oneself,   one's   partner, children, or non-
> consenting persons for a period of at least six months. The sexually arousing
> fantasies and urges are recurrent and   intense, and the person who suffers
> from the *paraphilias* has either acted   on the fantasies or suffered serious
> distress because of   them.[6]

When considering women as predators, the absence of scholarship on this

subject proves problematic. Scarcity on the subject might be because "violence is still

almost universally associated with the male and the masculine ... when women

commit violence the only explanation offered has been that it is   involuntary,

defensive, or the result of mental illness or hormonal imbalance inherent with female

physiology."[7] Then again, for women who either made a choice or who were

conscripted, no matter their backgrounds, were their actions that included abuses and

violations against the prisoners really   coerced?

The women who worked as *Aufseherinnen*, doctors, *Kapos*, or who were

married to top Nazi officials, came from different backgrounds. Most women were

conscripted whereas others went willingly into the SS labor force. Many of   the

women, especially the *Oberaufseherinnen*, willingly used various, often hideous

means to control, humiliate, torture, and murder the prisoners that they came in contact with. Not all killed, but most all abused at one level or another. Many women later said that they had no choice. Still, select few women saved people and proved that there was a choice. An example of this was seen with the female guard who saved the life of noted Holocaust survivor Gerda Weissmann Klein. Klein revealed that the woman's physical appearance must have been the reason why she was selected for the job (commenting on the unattractiveness of the guard) but that her looks belied the fact that she was responsible for saving lives of some of the girls under her charge, under great threat to herself.[8]

There does not appear to be many common threads that these Nazi female perpetrators shared. Certainly socioeconomic reasons or forced conscription may serve as a partial comprehension for understanding these women's trigger points for violent behaviors, but personal choice remains the overarching commonality here. Despite claims of *Aufseherinnen* being beaten, whipped, or tortured (which in some rare cases did happen), many more were dismissed for acting too "nice" to prisoners.[9] Guards that were cruel stood out and were rewarded.

The prisoners were the enemies, and for many younger women who went to work as contractors for the SS, they supported Nazi propaganda that advocated elimination of the enemy as well as the expansion of the Aryan master race. Even if they thought otherwise, making any opposing sentiment public amongst their peers was extremely dangerous. Further, in going against Nazi doctrines, these women could have felt that their peers would then consider them enemies of the state. Thus, they would be designated as outsiders, and outsiders disappeared. Scare tactics and propaganda played a key role in asserting the Nazi message of racial superiority and advocated for the necessity of the Final Solution; some women took this to heart, believed fully in the message of Aryan superiority, and sought to do whatever was demanded of them by their *Führer*. Others simply acted out in a way that demonstrated that their aggressions could be rewarded if they acted as men did, and some, like Grese, acted worse than the SS men did.

Girls such as Grese and Hildegard Lächert grew up learning about the need for selectivity in choosing future partners, and the need to ensure that the continuity and purity of the Aryan race endure, lest the Reich fall to the hands of its most virulent enemy: the Jew. Other people defined as undesirable by Nazi eugenic laws were also included as enemies of the German race. Hitler personally ordered that all children be educated in the "laws of heredity, racial breeding, and selection."[10] These children and young adults were led to believe of great rewards should they devote themselves to Nazi tenets and act in service to the state. These women came from all walks of life, and demonstrated anyone could be capable of violence and murder if given agency to do so. Grese, perhaps the most infamous   of all *Aufseherinnen*, came from a family of farmers; Ilse Koch, married a successful (later traitorous) *Kommandant* and used her status as his wife to express power; and the highly intelligent Herta Oberheuser, an SS doctor who   was able to obtain a medical degree, which was still somewhat rare for women at the time, used her medical skills to perform unspeakable acts of vivisection on human beings. These women were responsible for some of the most heinous and horrific crimes under the Nazi régime, a government that advocated violence to maintain civility and order.

Even if violence was encouraged against prisoners, and if violence was   then enacted against guards who were not cruel enough, these women made a choice. In the case of the *Kapo*, perhaps the conclusion that fear of punishment or imminent death made their behaviors more explainable, but for the *Aufseherin*,   the doctor, and the SS wife, a conscious decision to kill, torture, and engage in barbaric psychological as well as physiological cruelty was indeed the case. If these women had been abused before working for the SS, it remains interesting to contemplate whether part of their actions can be blamed on displaced   aggression.

The psychological indoctrination that these women experienced certainly opened that possibility.[11] If women such as Grese and Oberheuser, as well as the other women, became anxious or frightened over the threat of a common enemy such as the Jew, did their apprehension manifest itself into a collective desire to inflict harm on to those weaker than themselves and who could not fight back?

What led women to act like serial killers? Were these women "incapable of the simplest moral judgment?"[12]

Often propaganda and other methods, including peer pressure, were employed to convince women that whatever abuses that they would be engaged in once working in the camp structure were justified; nevertheless, a crucial point to remember was that these women consciously made a choice to do what they did. Certainly, women who were beaten or kidnapped in order to force them to work   as guards or in other positions within the camp structure might not have made a choice based on the concept of free will, but does that excuse their behaviors?   Many defendants at post-war trials claimed that they   were   only   "following   orders"   or otherwise tried to excuse their actions. So what convinced these women to follow orders?

There were several different methods employed by Nazi leaders to ensure that the masses were indoctrinated with hate, including propaganda, which was widely used in film, print media, posters, speeches, and radio programs. Jews   were constantly portrayed as shifty, cunning, miserly, dirty, and capable of terrible crimes against German humanity, including rape, stealing, cheating, and inciting riots.[13] Implied anti-Semitic messages helped the Nazis to find support for their measures against the Jews. Anti-Semitism, wrapped up in official state policy, was used to forewarn Germany of what could happen should the Jews be allowed to take over their country. Constant bombardment of anti-Semitic messages not only helped promote and vindicate measures that were taken against Jews and other undesirables, but was also employed to "elicit hatred against evacuated Jews and in order to prevent any sympathy shown to them."[14] Misinformation became a way for the Nazis to glorify the concept of an Aryan master race, establish anti-Semitism as routine, and create widespread fear amongst the masses so that people would be driven to accept anti-Semitism and other rhetoric that classified enemies of the state as   truisms.

Therefore, with the onslaught of propaganda against the Jews, perhaps the anxiety theory helps explain why so many women that worked for the SS were incredibly violent. Even women imprisoned but who were appointed as a *Kapo* acted appallingly. All prisoners could be and were subjected to cruel and inhumane treatment. One's position in society, racial origin, religion, or familial connections did not guarantee that one would not be sent to a camp for a crime against the Nazi state and subject to possible abuse. For example, a relative of *Reichsführer* (head of the SS and minister of the interior) Heinrich Himmler, Olga, who was German and not Jewish, was sent to Ravensbrück because she had an affair with a Polish officer.[15] Nonetheless, if the ideology of the Nazi régime was one that espoused racial purity, as well as biological superiority, and the need to annihilate a common enemy, certainly

> the forces of common belief contain the equally powerful forces of anxiety, restlessness, and disintegration. Members of the group discover a certain commonness, both conscious and unconscious, that helps them to reassure themselves and see and feel themselves as human beings, to feel pleasant, common positive feelings…these feelings may then give rise to concerted actions and thoughts.[16]

Since some women fought on the domestic front by having babies for the Nazi state, and others worked for the military, some women could do their part for the government in ways previously thought unknown and unallowable to them. In fighting the common enemy by working for one of the largest, most sophisticated, and bureaucratic structures ever invented to control a common enemy, the concentration and extermination camps, women could sometimes, as Irma Grese did, construct their own roles in the régime.

Oftentimes only women of higher socioeconomic status could alter their status. Under Nazism, it does reveal that relegation to the private sphere was not always so tightly controlled if the woman herself wished to alter it, however so slightly, under the guise of serving the Fatherland, and more notably, Hitler, of whom many women were fascinated by. Work, if not forced, could mean service   to the state in an otherwise hyper-masculine, aggressive, and misogynistic government structure. Even if forced, women could construct an agency of power, especially by partaking in criminality or even, more rarely, by saving   lives.

Women who were not employed by the camps as *Aufseherinnen*, but were in a position of power because of who they were married to or because an *Aufseherin* had selected them for a position as a *Kapo*, used various means to   assert their power or to make their presence known. While in the camps, women often resorted to various means to control their prisoners or affirm their authority. Some of the women who were involved with the camps were not physically intimidating, and as a result used various objects to make themselves more fearful to the prisoners. For example, the *Aufseherinnen* Juana Bormann and Irma Grese each used objects to intimidate. Bormann had a large dog, and Grese carried a supposed specially made cellophane whip; other women such as Nazi wife Ilse Koch carried a riding crop, and Ilse Lothe, a *Kapo*, used   sticks.[17]

Can it be argued, however, that despite a common goal to fight an enemy, women do not always have deliberate intentions to hurt others when they perform certain actions? Could certain female life experiences, from birth to adulthood, make women more prone than men to perform actions that have violent consequences even if they suffered no childhood abuse?[18] Would these women,   if not employed by or involved with the Nazi régime, resort to violence on their own? If wartime conditions dictated by Nazism were stressful, and if the stressor was removed, could women obtain a measure of normalcy in their lives postwar? After the war, several *Aufseherin*, including Hermine Braunsteiner, who before she went to work for the SS had wanted to be a nurse and was not known for violence, made attempts at a normal life.

Braunsteiner, who worked at Ravensbrück and other camps, did not resort to any other known act of violence after she was arrested for war crimes in 1945. She married an American soldier, moved to the United States and led a life of   ideal post-war domesticity until she was deported in the 1970s for lying on her entrance papers. She was the first Nazi war criminal to be extradited from the United States. However, before her marriage, Braunsteiner was one of the most brutal of all the female Nazi criminals; her crimes included infanticide, murder, and mass crimes against humanity. Crimes against humanity committed by these women included inflicting physical abuse and torture as to cause certain death.[19]

If the majority of female perpetrators did not lead a life of violence (childhood, familial, or otherwise) before their involvement with the Nazis, what was it about Nazism that led women to such horrible acts of cruelty, sadism, and violence? Within the camp structure, it was acceptable to use whatever means necessary to destroy the Jew and others. Therefore, since "cruelty of this sort involved   coercive relationships," Nazism   subsequently   facilitated   "the

degradation or humiliation of one by another."[20] Conclusions can be   drawn

> thus, if the aims of sadistic violence is to "not only make the victim suffer but especially to humiliate or degrade him, to make him feel helpless or powerless, to 'put him in his place' or 'show him whose boss'...the sadist wishes to make his victim feel ridiculous or small; in the most extreme case, to abuse him in such a way as to destroy his self-respect, break his will, make him give in.[21]

According to Peter Vronsky, an expert on serial killers, violence and sadism are found in women who exhibit the following characteristics: superficiality, self-importance, callousness, apathy, predatory traits, promiscuity, and others, but perhaps even more chilling, Vronsky listed characteristics that any average person could have suffered from, including habitual lying, eating disorders, experience of a broken home, marriage, or abuse somewhere in one's background. These, he argued, are more common in all of us that perhaps people

accept, and certainly these were found in several of the SS female contractors.[22]

Further, he revealed that women have "expert ability to act in a passive- aggressive manner with a carefully crafted persona ... this insidious behavior makes them particularly dangerous ... then their predatory aggression might be truly invisible until it is too late."[23] Once ensconced within the Nazi régime that advocated, encouraged, and allowed violence against the "other," ordinary people could decide to either engage in abuse and torture or not. Following this theory, "ordinary" women could then transform themselves into violent killers simply because they *could*.[24]

Women, who were entrenched in the violence of the Nazi régime, and especially those who worked as *Aufseherinnen*, were put in a position where violence against the enemy was encouraged. Moreover, women who worked for the SS in camps lived with a "self-important consciousness of their superior achievements, rank, and authority, their membership in some prestigious group."[25] Women such as Ilse Koch, who was married to the *Kommandant* of Buchenwald, as well as the female *Kapo* Ilse Lothe, also enjoyed this type of superiority. Perhaps the most important example of this theory was the life of Juana Bormann. Bormann stated at her trial that she went to work for the SS to make more money, but it can also be inferred that she was extremely lonely, sad, embittered, and, perhaps, wanting to belong, looking for something in her life that would make her feel important.[26] Accordingly, working for the SS not only gave Bormann a purpose in life, but gave her a sense of belonging, an identity, and the ability to share in a common goal: eliminate the enemy in the body of the Jew.

The common enemy, these women soon learned, concerned more than the Jew. Gypsies, homosexuals, the insane or deformed, Communists, political prisoners, and anyone else perceived as an adversary of the Nazi state were enemies. Moreover, since these women came from a society that looked down upon them because of their gender, when they were put in a position of relative power, they could in turn humiliate their state-designated inferiors in retaliation for the way society had treated them.[27] It has been further suggested that the Nazis created the camp structure as a war front, and that because of the great "racial war" that the government was undertaking, the women who worked as *Aufseherinnen* could fight on the front lines just as the men were doing at war.[28]

In some respects, knowing what social class the women came from may not matter. For example, Gertrude Tillion, who survived Ravensbrück, and researched the Nazi camp structure, noted that she discovered *Aufseherinnen* came from all levels of society; whether low, middle, and upper, poor, wealthy, strong, and sick, a woman's societal position or physical appearances did not preclude her from working for the SS, as long as her racial background met Nazi requirements. In her investigations, Tillion discovered that before working for the SS as an *Aufseherin*, women held many different jobs, including working as beauticians, clerical assistants, entertainers, housewives, or shopkeepers, and former positions did not mean women were precluded from degrading   inmates.[29]

Humiliation took on many forms. The ideology of the Nazis espoused degrading violence as a means of control and order; certainly several of the *Aufseherinnen* resorted to slaps as an acceptable way to control prisoners.[30] Besides slaps, women used several other sadistic, violent measures against prisoners. Elisabeth Volkenrath, *Aufseherin* at Auschwitz and *Oberaufseherin* at Ravensbrück, threw people down stairs, slammed them against a wall, and beat them mercilessly.[31] Dr. Herta Oberheuser used her medical skills to perform horrific chemical and biological experiments on prisoners. Dorothea (Theodora) Binz, Ravensbrück *Oberaufseherin*, in at least two instances, used a pickaxe on one woman and stomped another to death.[32] Countless women who became involved with the Nazi party simply, more likely willingly, lost sight of what was

right and what was wrong: "The mind of the German, especially that of a National Socialist and member of the SS, was drilled into one particular channel and the broad view of humanity was lost sight of."[33]

---

[1] Irving B. Weiner, *Personality and Clinical Psychology Series: The Quest for the Nazi Personality: A Psychological Investigation of Nazi War Criminals* (Hillsdale, NJ: LEA Publishers, 1995), 9.

[2] Michael Sayers, and Albert E. Kahn, *The Plot Against the Peace: A Warning to the Nation!* (New York: Book Find Club, 1945), pp. 112-115.

[3] Ronald Barri Flowers, *Women and Criminality: The Woman as Victim, Offender, and Practitioner* (New York: Greenwood Press, 1987), 84.

[4] Brown stated that "even sadists like Binz and Grese ... needed a pretext for their activities." The Nazis gave them that pretext. See Brown, *The Beautiful Beast*, p. 56, n. 237.

[5] See "Queen Boadicea, Jingo-kogo, and Mary I" in Guida M. Jackson, *Women Who Ruled*, 2nd ed. (New York: Barnes and Noble Books, 1998), pp. 37-38, 90-91, and 118-119. Boadicea reigned circa 60 A.D., Jingo-kogo 200-269 A.D., and Mary 1553-1558.

[6] See Bradley R. Johnson's "Sexual Violence: The Perpetrator," in Carl C. Bell, Ed., *Psychiatric Aspects of Violence: Issues in Prevention and Treatment* (San Francisco: Jossey-Bass, 2000), 73.

[7] Peter Vronsky, *Female Serial Killers: How and Why Women Become Monsters* (New York: Berkley Books, 2007), pp. 5-6.

[8] *One Survivor Remembers*. DVD.

[9] See Brown, *The Camp Women*, especially pp. 14-20.

---

[10] In the case of Herta Bothe and Irma Grese, the one commonality that these women shared was that they were young, and were educated under the racial policies of the Third Reich. See Bleuel, p. 141. Morrison suggested that the majority of these women came from modest backgrounds. See Morrison, 24. Brown, in *The Camp Women*, found that based on survivor accounts, that the majority of *Aufseherinnen* lacked intellect; note his analysis on pp. 15-17.

[11] Angelika Ebbinghaus, *Opfer and Täterinnen: Fraubiographien des Nationalsozialismus* (Nördlingen, Germany: Delphi Politik, 1987), p. 106-150.

[12] Vronsky, p. 368. Vronsky wrote this in his analysis of Karla Homolka, a serial killer who took part in the murder of her own sister. See his chapter "Sex, Death, and Videotape" pp. 328-369. He also suggested that women who become serial killers, like Homolka, lacked any proper judgment over right and wrong: "her capacity to do the right thing was totally extinct." See p. 368. Lacking proper judgment implied that choice was removed, which was not always the case with the *Aufseherinnen* and other women responsible for genocidal crimes. These women had a choice and exercised their decision by carrying out barbaric crimes against innocent prisoners.

[13] Eric Rentschler, *The Ministry of Illusion: Nazi Cinema and its Afterlife* (Cambridge, London: Harvard University Press, 1996), 152.

[14] David Welch, *Propaganda and the German Cinema, 1933-1945* (Oxford: Oxford University Press, 1983), 291.

[15] Morrison, 84. Many women with famous connections were imprisoned at Ravensbrück despite their familial ties. See Gemma La Guardia Gluck, *Fiorello's Sister: Gemma La Guardia Gluck's Story (Religion, Theology, and the Holocaust)* (Syracuse, NY: Syracuse University Press, 2007).

[16] Glass, 147. Glass suggested that the people who followed National Socialism believed in the Nazi "biomedical vision," because such a belief gave Nazi devotees a form of identity.   Note especially pp. 148-149.

[17] Note that Ilse Lothe allegedly also used her fists to beat prisoners into submission. Refer to the chapter in this book on Irma Grese for more on her use of a whip. At first glance it   was easy to think that a whip was merely that, a whip, but a cellophane whip, or any special construction of any whip by a guard was different. In this camp structure context, creation or adjustment of a common weapon implies specific intent. Special care was taken to use instruments that did more damage and inflicted more pain, with the outcome to extend suffering.

[18] David Shapiro, *Autonomy and Rigid Character* (New York: Basic Book, Inc., 1981), 18.

[19] In-text, passim.

[20] Shapiro, 101.

[21] Ibid., 103.

[22] Vronsky, pp 429-430. However, no one single event, trauma, or marker can be found in all of these women except for perhaps, a large margin commonality, devotion to Hitler.

[23] Ibid., p. 433.

[24] See Browning, passim, for more on men.

[25] Shapiro, 105.

[26] United Nations War Crimes Commission, *The Belsen Trial*, p. 123.

[27] See Tillion, p. 69.

[28] See Brown, *The Beautiful Beast*, p. 32.

[29] Tillion, p. 69.

[30] See especially my chapter on Elisabeth Volkenrath.

[31] United Nations War Crimes Commission, *The Belsen Trial*, 123.

[32] See my chapter on Binz and refer to my chapter on Oberheuser for more on the experiments that Oberheuser led.

[33] United Nations War Crimes Commission, *The Belsen Trial*, p. 132.

PART II: CASE STUDIES OF *AUFSEHERINNEN*

(FEMALE OVERSEERS)

CHAPTER VI

DOROTHEA (THEODORA) BINZ

Volunteer to Vicious Instrument of Death

Certainly it is one thing for a penniless woman to kill a hopelessly insane husband, an invalid child, or a baby that can't be cared for, and quite another thing for a fairly well to do matron to seek out people to murder   for the sake of getting more money and apparently some pleasure from the acts of homicide and butchery.[1]

Many of the women who came to Ravensbrück to work as *Aufseherinnen* were assigned to one of the most merciless of all the *Oberaufseherinnen*, Dorothea (Theodora) Binz. She was a woman about whom Ravensbrück survivor Gertrude Tillion said, "Whenever she appeared somewhere one literally   felt touched by the breath of evil."[2]

Born 16 March 1920 in Dusterlake, Germany, Binz grew up close to the area where Ravensbrück was built, but relatively little was known about her early family life. Sometime in her late teens or early twenties, she worked as a housekeeper, and then she received an apprenticeship in food service, beginning a short career in the food industry. In order to become involved with the Nazi party, and for other reasons that will never be known, in August of 1939, she volunteered for kitchen work at Ravensbrück; Binz was good friends with an *SS- Wächterin* (guard) known only as Frau Mewes, who may have given Binz a lead on a job at Ravensbrück.[3]

She was hired on 1 September 1939. By 1940, Binz was an *Aufseherin* and worked in several areas of the camp. Binz first reported to Johanna Langefeld,

Oberaufseherin. She was then under the supervision of *Oberaufseherin* Maria Mandl, later chief *Oberaufseherin* at Auschwitz, and then once again under Langefeld (who Mandl had replaced for a period). Langefeld left by 1943 and Binz had replaced her at Ravensbrück.[4] Binz never left Ravensbrück. Since she was so adept at handling prisoners, Binz was soon promoted to *Oberaufseherin*, a position she would retain from 1943 until 1945, when Allied forces captured her.[5] Binz apparently was quite beautiful, with long, blond, wavy hair and bright blue eyes, characteristics propagandized by the Nazis as racially "ideal." Ravensbrück survivor Denise Dufournier described Binz as "small and fair, with a childlike face; but wherever she passed at any time the tension and silence were such that the very atmosphere seemed tainted and our hearts even ceased to beat." Other survivors describe her as quite attractive, indeed a contradiction to her true character. Binz's hair was described as shiny, luminous, and having resembled a lion's mane: "*von einer leuchtend blonden Lowenmahne.*"[6]

Eyewitnesses later testified that Binz took her job very seriously, and was one of the most feared guards in all of the camps. The more savage an overseer was, the more likely they would receive notice and perhaps   advancement.[7] Dufournier revealed that it was her impression that Binz was in charge of administering punishment of the third degree.[8] This type of punishment meant flagellation, which Binz often administered. Some survivors testified that Binz would beat prisoners without provocation and would force women to have sex   with her. She also attended beatings of prisoners with her latest male SS lover   and engaged in heavy petting (or light sexual behavior) while prisoners were being tortured in front of her.[9]

Binz, therefore, based on a Nazi interpretation of sexuality, was made out to be a depraved sexual creature. Whether she was bisexual in tendency, unwilling, or even unable to control her sexually motivated sadistic nature, her sexual escapades were notorious. She used her status to fulfill her sexual fantasies; however, there was no way to prove whether these fantasies were hers   or that of her SS superior male lover. With regard to Binz's sexual exploits, rumors abounded about her affairs. One survivor insisted she knew firsthand that Binz had an affair with a camp leader named Edmund Bräuning; she repeated the story that the two lovers watched floggings, much to their own amusement.[10] Binz may have also forced women into prostitution while she was stationed at Ravensbrück. At her trial, Binz testified that she selected female prisoners to be sent to Nazi brothels, and was not unique in taking part in this process, because "although prostitution was officially forbidden by the Nazis, the elite SS guards had set up a network of brothels catering to German soldiers, forced laborers and prisoners, which they intended in part to stamp out homosexuality."[11]

One of the fiercest and most sadistic of all the female guards, Binz was considered the "star character of Ravensbrück," and later reported directly to the commander of the camp, Fritz Suhren.[12] Binz, one of many women with the same responsibilities, was accountable for training many of the women within the camp administration. Indoctrinated with hate, women under Binz were taught to be ruthless killing machines and enjoyed a certain level of autonomy.[13] In Herbermann's memoirs, she revealed that Binz was "known as the most ruthless and sadistic overseer anywhere," and survivors repeatedly referred to her cruelties and "horrifying acts of violence against inmates."[14]

Binz loved to torture and sadistically taunt the inmates at Ravensbrück. Often carrying a gun and a whip with a German shepherd dog at her side, she would occasionally allow her dog to attack prisoners at random. Herbermann related that on one instance in 1942, she received punishment meted out by Binz for lighting a fire in an oven in her barracks simply to keep warm:

> An overseer had to lead me away to the house of horror, to the death house. I was received by Overseer Binz amid many kicks. Two raging dogs, one of them a large breed, jumped at me. One shiver of fear after another ran through me. I was led into a dark cell and the cell door was immediately thrown shut behind me. There I stood in a pitch-dark room, into which no ray of light could penetrate. I could grasp nothing more and was completely at the end of my rope. To think of anything was impossible for me. I suffered a fate worse than death in this hour.[15]

Dufournier also confirmed that Binz usually had an enormous guard dog   at her side, ready to attack. Dufournier further related that Binz, who carried a whip, especially liked to attack the very sick or weak with her whip and/or with   her dog. According to Dufournier, Binz "was so conscientious in carrying out her duties that it was rare for her victims to survive."[16] Binz would also beat female inmates to death sometimes for no reason, and other times would kill inmates for what she conceived to be an offense. Offenses included stealing potato scraps to talking to other prisoners. Binz would even whip women in the face or on the   body for no reason other than Binz did not like the way that they   looked.

In yet another example, Binz, who glorified in the sadistic excesses of   Nazi ideology, was offended somehow by a prisoner who was just working manual labor. Binz forced the woman to lie down on the ground. Binz then proceeded to hack the prisoner to death with a small hand axe. In another instance, Binz was flogging a woman, and, not satisfied with how the woman reacted, stepped on the woman's legs and stomped her to death. Even after the woman appeared dead, Binz rocked back and forth in the woman's blood. The blood covered her boots but Binz, finished with the murder, simply walked away, leaving a bloody trail of footprints. In yet another account of Binz's cruelty, a survivor stated that a group of ten inmates at Ravensbrück refused to take part in medical experimentations, preferring death instead. They, along with a group of 500 women, staged a protest, which Binz attempted to halt. Binz became so frustrated that she ordered death sentences for the ten resisters, and confinement
for the 500 women who helped the resisters hide.[17]

Binz, in an amazing and interesting contradiction to her sadistic personality, during Christmas of 1944, allowed a group of prisoners of Ravensbrück to stage a Christmas party for the incarcerated children. Due   to internal conflicts over arrangements with other prisoners, a group of Polish inmates decided to hold their own party. Surprisingly, Binz grudgingly approved   the second party. On 23 December 1944, Binz and her alleged SS-boyfriend Edmund Bräuning, took the stage to open the party. When several members of the audience, which included several emaciated children, began to cry, Binz ran out   of the room. Did Binz really become overwhelmed with emotion at the sight of children crying? Perhaps the only reason Binz allowed the party to go on was that the SS was afraid of the impending Russian army, and may have wanted to appear caring or sympathetic. It was doubtful that somehow the guards, who also took   part in selecting children for experimentation and gassings, truly felt sorry for the children of Ravensbrück, and were honestly "glad of this seasonal opportunity to   do something for them."[18]

The Russians liberated Ravensbrück on 30 April 1945. Ravensbrück survivor Marguerite Buber related that a few days before the Russians closed in   on Ravensbrück, Binz had led prisoners out of the camp with instructions to report to the nearest Gestapo office for further instruction; Buber related   that   Binz's instructions were largely ignored.[19] Binz was taken captive shortly thereafter and was tried in a British court. During an interrogation, Binz testified   to having personally shot over two hundred Polish prisoners.[20] Binz stood trial for multiple war crimes at the Ravensbrück trial, which took place in Hamburg, Germany. She was sentenced to death by hanging, and was executed on 2 May 1947.[21]

---

[1] Ann Jones, *Women Who Kill* (New York: Holt, Rinehart and Winston, 1980), 129.

[2] Tillion, 68, and Brown, *The Beautiful Beast*, p. 32. For another description of Dorothea (Theodora) Binz, see *"Aufseherinnen"* in Isa Vermehren's *Reise durch den letzen Akt: Ravensbrück, Buchenwald, Dachau: Eine Frau berichtet* (Hamburg: Christian Wegner Verlag, 1946), pp. 72-73.

[3] Herbermann, 141. In trying to uncover Binz's first encounter with Ravensbrück, Vermehren explained how she might have found her position. See Vermehren, 72.

[4] Brown, *The Camp Women*, p. 17 and 19.

[5] Vermehren, 72. See also Ravensbrück survivor Wanda Póltawska, *And I Am Afraid of My Dreams* (London: Hodder & Stoughton, 1987), for a description of Binz. Note also Brown, *The Beautiful Beast*, p. 3, n. 127, for another brief description of Binz. Note also Morrison, p. 231.

[6] Dufournier, 18. For the hair description, see Vermehren, p. 72. See n. 170 in this book for how beauty and cruelty contradicts people's preconceived notions of character.

[7] Brown, *The Camp Women*, p. 19.

[8] Dufournier, 18.

[9] Tillion, 59.

[10] Morrison, 117.

[11] See for quote Reuters and Haaretz.com. "Secrets of Nazi camp brothels emerge in German   exhibition."   http://www.haaretz.com/news/secrets-of-nazi-camp-brothels-emerge-in-

german-exhibition-1.225307 (19 September 2010) and also for more on the Binz brothel testimony, "JUSTICE Will Be Served, Human Rights: HR Laws." http://hrlaws.blogspot.com/2009/02/4nazi-germany-forced-prostitution-rape.html   (19   September 2010).

[12] Tillion, 68.

[13] Irma Grese was one woman who trained under Binz. For more on Grese, refer to her chapter in this book and see also Brown, *The Beautiful Beast*, passim. Brown suggested that it was hard to gauge how much Binz's sexual, sadistic excesses influenced Irma Grese. He also noted that both Binz and Grese enjoyed showing off their power in a very sexual manner. See Brown, *The Beautiful Beast*, pp. 33-35.

[14] Herbermann, p. 141, n. 3.

[15] Ibid., 142.

[16] Dufournier, pp. 18-19.

[17] Ibid., 18, and Tillion, 69. Tillion, on p. 83, related this interesting story about Binz. See pp. 82-83. See Brown, *The Beautiful Beast*, p. 35, for more on the axe incident.

[18] Morrison, pp. 233, 267-269, and especially p. 270.

[19] Buber, 314.

[20] Tillion, 7.

[21] Brown, *The Beautiful Beast*, 33, and Tillion, 141.

CHAPTER VII

JUANA (JOHANNA) BORMANN

Sadistic Instrument of Torture and Death

Luckily for men, the monstrous women were exceptional.[1]

Helena Kopper in her deposition stated that you [Juana Bormann] were the worst hated person in the camp, that you were in charge of the clothing store and always had a large dog with you which you set on the prisoners.[2]

Juana (Johanna) Bormann was born on 10 September 1893 in Birkenfelde, East Prussia. She never married. At her trial, Bormann stated that she went to   work for the SS to make more money, but it can also be inferred by her actions   that she was extremely lonely, embittered, and, conceivably, looking for something in life that would make her feel important, which the SS provided.[3]

Bormann was also a lot older than many of the other *Aufseherinnen*. Slight in stature, Bormann, was over fifty at the time of her arrest, was not an attractive woman, and did not physically appear, at least in her court photos, to fit the Nazi feminine ideal, like the blond-haired, blue-eyed, healthy, and stout Irma Grese   did. Before she was employed as a guard, Bormann had worked for an insane asylum. While employed at the asylum, Bormann only made 15-20 marks per month, per her testimony at her trial. Evidence has suggested that she was involved with the T4 program. However, it remains unproven whether she indeed had anything to do with the euthanasia of the insane for the T4   program.[4]

Bormann became part of the SS as a civilian employee in March 1938 in order to increase her income. Once she went to work in the camp system, she   made more than 150 marks per month, considerably more than she had made at other jobs.[5] She was initially assigned to work at Ravensbrück as a kitchen helper, and later became an *Aufseherin*. She was known for her cruelty and propensity for violence, often applied by her dog. On 15 May 1943, Bormann was assigned to work at Auschwitz. While there, she probably took part in selections for Dr. Josef Mengele, the Nazi doctor responsible for some of the most gruesome medical experiments of the Holocaust, but Bormann denied these charges at her trial. Bormann was then sent to the Birkenau detachment, where she stayed until December of 1943. Another assignment led her to Budy, a detachment of Birkenau. While at Birkenau, Bormann was assigned to work as a *Kommando* (commando), and took part in selections, although she denied this at her trial.[6]   She was finally sent to Bergen-Belsen, where, according to her own words, she   was put in charge of looking after the camp pigs. She used her status to engage in barbaric abuses; these included beatings, whippings, and savage torture against prisoners who tried to steal the pig's food.[7] Dogs continually provided her a way to express her power over the innocents. While employed at the camps, Bormann used her "pet" dog to attack prisoners.

Several female survivors related horrific accounts about Bormann and her sadistic use of her dog or dogs. Numerous accounts existed that corroborated the fact that Bormann continually used a dog to punish prisoners. In her defense, Bormann stated at her trial that she had purchased a dog as a pet, and only kept   the animal as such. She also stated that she had given her dog away, and had not had him while she was working at Budy, but that she only took the dog back once it fell ill. She stated that she certainly did not use the animal for any attacks against prisoners under her care, despite the fact that five different survivors testified to the contrary at her trial. She was said to have set her dog on a menstruating prisoner in *Appell*, although Bormann asserted repeatedly, despite survivor testimony, that her dog was only a pet, and was not an official SS-trained
dog, nor was she ever granted permission to use her dog at work.[8]   She emphatically denied that she had ever let her dog attack anyone. Many horrifying accounts came from female prisoners who witnessed Bormann's use of her dog to

hurt inmates; dogs were actually encouraged as a tool for the women guards by Himmler himself:

> It was, in fact, Himmler's own idea to "arm" women with dogs instead of guns because the dogs would frighten women more than men. A woman with a dog was worth two guards. As allied air attacks over Fürstenberg increased in 1943, Himmler feared uprisings in the camp, and ordered that the dogs be used "like wild beasts" to suppress any sign of revolt and "trained to savage to death everyone except their handler".[9]

A survivor testified at Bormann's trial that Bormann not only allowed her dog to attack a prisoner, but that Bormann encouraged the dog to masticate a prisoner to death.[10] Still another survivor testified that while Bormann was passing a female prisoner in Birkenau, she attacked the prisoner by "clasping her by the hair." She then threw the prisoner on the ground, and "while she was lying on the ground you [Bormann] let the dog go and bite her so severely that she was a mass of blood. She said that after a doctor had examined the woman there was no movement from the body."[11] Dog bites were common and were widely feared by the prisoners. As Himmler wanted, dogs and female guards terrorized prisoners from the moment of arrival to throughout their stay at camp:

> On arrival it was these "raven women" with their snarling attack dogs who met the new prisoners as they spilt out of cattle trucks at Fürstenberg station to a cacophony of barking and female cries of "Achtung, achtung". Any who fell were set upon by the dogs. And the sinister howling of the dogs accompanied each dawn roll call, when prisoners stood petrified as dogs encircled those who fainted. One of the camp's SS doctors, Gerhard Schliedausky, gave evidence after the war about the treatment of dog bites in the camp hospital. "These bites were more frequent in the spring when the dogs were in season and more agitated. "I remember cases of very serious bites of the chest, legs and arms," he said. He also recalled one dog called Prince, who was the most feared dog in the camp. A French prisoner-doctor talked of women bleeding to death from dog bites.[12]

In another instance, Bormann was assigned to a group of women who were forced to stand in a group and repeatedly hit the ground with a pick. When Bormann decided that she did not like the way that a small group of women was working, she gleefully set her dog on the women. For some unknown reason, she then noticed an eighteen-year-old inmate named Regina. Bormann ordered her dog to attack Regina, and the dog proceeded to tear Regina's legs apart. Regina, who suffered massive blood loss from the attack, was covered with open sores   and bites, which were never treated. The wounds became infected and Regina passed away from the injuries Bormann's dog inflicted on   her.[13]

Numerous survivors also cited that although they had not actually seen Bormann set her dog on prisoners, they had heard repeatedly how brutal Bormann was and how she always used her dogs to cruelly attack prisoners. Another survivor testified that she had witnessed, again and again, that when Bormann was not satisfied with production from an inmate work detail, she would set her dog   on the prisoners. The dog became an outlet of Bormann's agency of   power.

Bormann apparently reveled in setting her dog on any prisoner she was not satisfied with. Yet still another account existed of a female prisoner who was so badly bitten all over her body by Bormann's dog, she died of her wounds within days of the sadistic attack.[14] In one more example, while strolling   alongside another work detail, Bormann, according to a trial witness, once again became dissatisfied with what she was observing. An inmate had sat down, as she was   too ill to stand up any longer. When Bormann approached this inmate, another prisoner stepped forward to state that the fallen woman was too ill to work and asked for leniency. Instead of granting leniency, Bormann smashed two teeth   out of the requester's mouth, and then set her dog on her, causing, once again, fatal injuries.[15]

According to survivor testimony, Bormann would also sadistically beat and torture the female inmates, often at a whim, and without any provocation.   She would force the women to exercise for hours at a time and sometimes knocked women's teeth out for "crimes" that included stealing rotten root vegetables. Bormann denied this at her trial. A twenty-year-old Greek Jewish woman testified that Bormann was a sadistic, brutal woman, who showed no mercy on anyone.[16] Many other inmates testified, citing multiple instances, that

Bormann would beat a prisoner, for such infractions as stealing a scrap of food. Survivors also testified that Bormann would use a "rubber truncheon" for inflicting beatings, and, if she did not have this object handy, would use her fists. Bormann stated at her trial that although she had slapped the ears of prisoners she supervised, she never hit anyone hard enough to loosen teeth.[17] Bormann, who would sometimes assist in selections, according to a survivor who saw his sister being selected by Bormann, often forced women to strip naked before coercing them to perform strenuous calisthenics.[18]

The British captured Bormann in April of 1945. Several *Aufseherinnen* like Bormann, before being transferred to prison, were forced to remove bodies from lorries into mass graves.[19] Bormann, after a brief period of imprisonment, stood trial at Lüneburg, near Bergen-Belsen, for war crimes. Her trial began on   17 September 1945 and lasted until 17 November 1945. The prosecution argued that there was more than sufficient evidence to prove that Bormann beat prisoners without provocation, and also proof that Bormann had assisted with   selections.

With regard to selections, Bormann allegedly pointed to certain prisoners who caught her eye, and would say, "this one looks quite weakly, she can be   taken away as well."[20] Survivors who witnessed Bormann's abuse also   reiterated that she had used her dog as a means to control and punish prisoners. When the subject of her dog came up at her trial, Bormann again asserted that her dog was only a pet. Bormann then stated that she had no idea she was being arrested, as she had left her dog behind at Bergen-Belsen, and would not have done so had she known she was being taken into custody.[21] Bormann also stated that she loved dogs, and would have never used the dog against anyone.

Her defense counsel, Major A.S. Munro, of the R.A.S.C. (Royal Army Service Corps), in defense summation, stated that there was widespread confusion over what type of dog Bormann allegedly had, and that witnesses, in their "eagerness to accuse somebody" exaggerated claims against Bormann and her dog.[22] Munro also argued that Bormann had led a miserable life before working for the SS.   He stated Bormann only became involved with the camps because she needed more money and desperately wanted to feel a sense of belonging. He asserted that because Bormann was so slight physically and very frail, she could never have beaten anyone with rubber truncheons or other items, as alleged by survivors.   He also used her age as a way to excuse her allegiance to Hitler and   the SS. Further, Munro, who tried to repeatedly gain sympathy for Bormann by   his admission that she often had no choice but to occasionally slap an inmate,   stated "it was not surprising that *Aufseherinnen* at these camps had sometimes lost patience in what must have been a very difficult task indeed to control."[23] He further argued that Bormann was not responsible for selections, and that the survivors had mistaken Bormann's role when prisoners were led away for execution. Munro argued that Bormann had not selected prisoners, but may have been walking by the same area where selections were going   on.[24]

Bormann was found not guilty of committing war crimes at Bergen- Belsen, but was found guilty of war crimes while at Auschwitz. Bormann received a sentence of death by hanging, and was moved from her prison at Lüneburg to a prison in the city of Hameln, Germany to await execution. The night before her death, Bormann stayed up passionately singing Nazi songs along with other female Nazi criminals. Bormann was executed on 13 December   1945, and was buried in the grounds of Hameln prison.[25] The fate of her dog was unknown.

---

[1] Jones, 140.

[2] Fyfe, 208.

[3] United Nations War Crimes Commission, *The Belsen Trial*, p. 123.

[4] Fyfe, 211. See Appendix II for more on T4.

[5] Ibid., 206.

[6] Ibid., 208.

[7] United Nations War Crimes Commission, *The Belsen Trial*, p. 44.

[8] Ibid., 209.

[9] Sarah Helm, "The Nazi guard's untold love story." *The Sunday Times*. http://www.timesonline.co.uk/tol/news/world/europe/article2181914.ece (19 September 2010).

[10] United Nations War Crimes Commission, *The Belsen Trial*, for the testimonies of witnesses Rozenwayg and Sunschein.

[11] Ibid.

[12] Helm, passim.

[13] Phillips, pp. 670-671, for the testimony of Rachela Keliszek.

[14] Fyfe, 209.

[15] Ibid.

[16] Phillips, pp. 668-669, for the testimony of Alegre Kalderon.

[17] Fyfe, 209.

[18] Phillips, 675. Refer to the testimony of survivor Yilka Malachovska.

[19] See Ibid., facing page 256, "SS Women Removing Bodies from Lorries Into A Communal Grave."

[20] United Nations War Crimes Commission, *The Belsen Trial*, p. 113.

[21] Phillips, 212.

[22] Ibid., 527.

[23] Ibid.

[24] Ibid., 528.

[25] Ibid., pp. 642-644. Note also Brown, *The Beautiful Beast*, pp. 86-89, for more on the last days of Bormann, Grese, and Volkenrath. Brown also, in his research for his text on Irma Grese, visited the Hameln prison. While there, he discovered several interesting things. The bodies of Bormann, Elisabeth Volkenrath and Irma Grese, along with ten other male SS, were exhumed and moved to an undisclosed location in a nearby cemetery. The exact location remains undisclosed for several reasons.

CHAPTER VIII

HERTA BOTHE

Not Responsible?

The camp commandants were fully aware of the nature of the work they were doing; their identification with the work, its emotional force, and their personal motives set them apart from others and explain their readiness to work in the camps. Most of them served in the camps without feeling any revulsion.[1]

Herta Bothe was born on 8 January 1921, in Teterow, Mecklenburg. Bothe came of age when the power of the Nazi party was rising, and she would have been exposed to the ideologies espoused by Hitler and the National Socialists. Little is known about her social class or her family life. She may have had problems with literacy, and could have viewed working for the SS in the camp structure as an upward socioeconomic move.[2] Bothe held different jobs, which included working as a domestic until she decided to train as a nurse. Her nursing training lasted for a very short period until she went to work in the camp structure.

In either September or October of 1942, Bothe was conscripted to work as an *Aufseherin* at Ravensbrück. During her training at Ravensbrück, she was taught to manage a *Kommando*. She stayed at Ravensbrück for over a week before being sent to Stutthoff, near Danzig.[3] She stayed at Stutthoff for two years, until July 1944, when she was sent to Bromberg. Bothe stayed at Bromberg for six months, and in January 1945, was forced to evacuate the area along with other camp personnel. Bothe, along with other Nazi personnel, marched for six weeks until they reached Bergen-Belsen.[4]

Bothe initially worked in the bathhouse for a few days until February 1945, when she was then assigned to the wood *Kommando*, a position she held until the British army captured her in April 1945.[5] While in charge of the *Kommando*, Bothe supervised about sixty prisoners. Male and female prisoners were both used for slave labor purposes in the wood *Kommando*, and Bothe was one of the few *Aufseherin* assigned to the duty alongside a male SS guard. She denied at her trial having carried any weapons to help her control the prisoners, but did admit to using her hands to slap any prisoner who attempted to steal. However, numerous survivors testified that while the prisoners were carrying their meager food rations, Bothe shot at them for sport.[6] Part of Bothe's duties was to ensure that wood was delivered to the kitchen and other areas of the camp where wood was needed.[7] Bothe shared sleeping quarters with other *Aufseherinnen*.

While Bothe was employed at Bergen-Belsen, several survivors relate that she beat inmates with her fists and pieces of wood for minor infractions such as stealing scraps of food or wood. At her trial it was related that when she was first assigned to the bathhouse at Bergen-Belsen, she beat a naked woman with a "rubber truncheon," certainly inflicting grave harm and pain.[8] Bothe admitted that while working in the wood *Kommando*, where part of her duties included securing wood from the forested areas surrounding Bergen-Belsen, that she would beat or slap prisoners for stealing, but denied ever using extreme force or objects other than her hands to punish people. The British arrested Bothe along with Irma Grese and several other *Aufseherinnen* in April of 1945. Bothe's trial began on 17 September 1945, and lasted until 17 November 1945.

At her trial, Bothe continually asserted that all *Aufseherinnen* were instructed not to punish people themselves, but to always report any crimes committed by prisoners.[9] She however, maintained that she did not always report the actions of the prisoners, and instead slapped them, arguing that after a few slaps that they did not disobey orders again. Still, many survivors argued to the contrary.

One survivor alleged that Bothe beat a Hungarian Jew named Eva to death with a block of wood for reasons unknown, and yet another teenage prisoner stated he saw Bothe shoot two prisoners to death, again, for reasons that he could not personally ascertain. Her defense at her trial reminded the court that several witnesses also testified that Bothe never carried a pistol, nor was she known for doing so, and that the testimony of the teenager, seventeen-year-old Wilhelm Grunwald, the main deponent against Bothe, should be ignored.[10] The same witness claimed that on one occasion he also saw Bothe shoot several prisoners.   He stated that she shot them because the women who were carrying bins of food scraps stopped to rest, which infuriated Bothe to the point where she allegedly   shot these women to death.[11]

Bothe also allegedly beat a woman for stealing turnip peels, which was a beating so severe that the woman died from the injuries. After Bothe realized the woman was dead, she ordered some of the women inmates to remove and dispose of the body.[12] Bothe further related at her trial that she had a major problem with prisoners stealing from her *Kommando* unit, but that when she was able to catch the thieves in the act, the only punishment she meted out was a minor slap on the face with her hands, and then would set about to try to recover the stolen   items.

Bothe asserted further that once the prisoners received a "box on the ears," for the most part they stopped stealing from her unit. Bothe and her defense attorney, Captain J.R. Phillips, of the British Royal Regiment of Artillery, argued that Bothe was never in a position of authority while working in the *Kommando*, and as such, could not mete out punishment for any infractions. Phillips also pointed out to the court that other eyewitnesses for the prosecution were not only mistaken in their identification of Bothe, but had given the court   erroneous testimony.[13] Bothe, in her defense, continually insisted that she had   only followed orders given to her by her male SS superiors.

Other survivors stated that Bothe was responsible for beating several female prisoners to death with wood, her fists, and was quite possibly, responsible for shooting or injuring people with a pistol, facts that Bothe strongly denied at her trial. Another worker at Bergen-Belsen, Ilse Lothe, testified against Bothe. Lothe stated that she knew firsthand that Bothe was guilty of mistreating several prisoners.[14] Bothe insisted that the SS men told her what to do and she only followed orders.

During closing remarks, the prosecution cited numerous survivor accounts that related Bothe's cruelty and inhumane measures used against prisoners, including one incident where Bothe beat a woman to death with her bare hands.[15] The prosecution also reminded the court about evidence that demonstrated Bothe abused prisoners with her hands, and had used rubber hoses to beat prisoners.[16]

Her defense attorney Phillips maintained that Bothe was only twenty-four when captured, and had arrived to work at Bergen-Belsen when conditions had already disintegrated. Thus, her attorney argued, Bothe could not be held responsible for the conditions of the camp. Concerning the beatings, it was argued that while such treatment was cruel and unusual, it did not, at least in the case of Bothe, lead to murder.   Therefore, Phillips argued, Bothe could not be   held in the same regard as Irma Grese or Juana Bormann, whose actions indicated that they were personally responsible for at least the death of one or more inmates. Moreover, Phillips stated that Bothe had grown up under the Nazi régime, and having been educated under conditions espoused by the Third Reich,
that she could not entirely be blamed what had happened at Bergen-Belsen.[17]

Bothe was found guilty of committing war crimes at Bergen-Belsen, and for these crimes, she received a sentence of ten years in prison. She was released   on 22 December 1951, having served only six years.[18] Bothe later married, changing her name to Lange.   Much later in her life she gave interviews where   she discussed her time in the camps as an *Aufseherin.* She denied being entirely responsible for her actions, and believed that had she not acted in the way that she did that she would have been a prisoner as well. Her life went largely unnoticed until 2009.

After *The Reader*, a fictionalized account about a female camp guard, was made into a film starring Kate Winslet, interest in female guards rose. Bothe in particular became a focus of *The Sun*'s Chief Features Writer Oliver Harvey. For his article on Nazi women guards, Harvey interviewed Maurice Philip Remy, a Munich filmmaker. Remy claimed to have interviewed Bothe shortly before her death. Harvey revealed that Remy informed him that:

> she (Bothe) had never been properly taught to read or write. Bothe didn't even seem aware of her role in the Holocaust. She grew up in a poor family and was working when she was a child. To become a guard was probably a great opportunity for her. She had horrible memories of the concentration camps but no capacity to make sense of her role in them.   She had no remorse. She couldn't understand she had done something wrong. She felt she was a victim. In an interview nine years ago, Bothe said: "Did I make a mistake? No. The mistake was it was a concentration
> camp, but I had to go to it otherwise I would have been put into it myself. That was my mistake.[19]

Harvey argued further that because of her devotion to Hitler and the Nazis, Bothe consciously made the choice to do what she was accused of in the camps.[20] However, other investigators have argued that some women did not have a choice in the matter because they were conscripted to work in the camps. Nonetheless, even if forced, *Aufseherinnen* did not always have to mimic the behavior of brutal male (and female!) guards, nor did they have to make the decision to behave they way that they did without provocation.

Still, some women guards did receive punishment if they were viewed by their fellow guards as not punitive enough; despite this and other conclusions drawn, Harvey's analysis of Bothe was critical in that it further validates that in light of her total lack of personal accountability for her crimes, Bothe's prison sentence   was light in comparison to what her victims   endured.

---

[1] Segev, 217.

[2] Oliver Harvey, "A 'kind, sweet' granny hiding an evil secret" in *The Sun* http://www.thesun.co.uk/sol/homepage/showbiz/film/2259283/Kate-Winslet-plays-an-evil-Nazi-guard-in-her-Oscar-nominated-film-The-Sun-reveals-the-real-life-story-behind-the-character-she-plays.html?print=yes (21 February 2009)

[3] Phillips, pp. 385-386.

[4] Ibid., 387.

[5] Ibid., 388.

     Women as Nazis

---

[6] Harvey.

[7] Phillips, pp. 386-387.

[8] Ibid.

[9] Ibid., 389.

[10] Phillips, pp. 389 and 565.

[11] Ibid., 665, for testimony of Wilhelm Grunwald.

[12] Ibid., pp. 387-388.

[13] Ibid., pp. 388-389. For more on defense summation, see Ibid., pp. 564-565.

[14] Ibid., 565, and note my chapter on Ilse Lothe.

[15] Ibid., 388.

[16] United Nations War Crimes Commission, *The Belsen Trial*, p. 116. Instead of fully showing remorse for her crimes, Bothe was more deeply concerned about contracting a disease from the corpses when Allied forces made the *Aufseherinnen* move bodies.

[17] Ibid., p. 124.

[18] Fyfe, pp. 642-644.

[19] See Harvey, passim, and Heike, "Female Concentration Camp Guards," passim.

[20] Harvey stated, in his conclusion, that: "Hitler's army of women killers did have a choice." See Harvey.

CHAPTER IX

HERMINE BRAUNSTEINER

The *Aufseherin* Who Almost Got Away

Unlike the SS men, a sizeable percentage of who fell into that universal category of true physical misfits, bowlegged, slope-shouldered, etc., the *Aufseherinnen* were, in general, stout, strong, and healthy women.[1]

Hermine Braunsteiner (Ryan) was born on 16 July 1919 in Vienna, Austria, and was raised a Roman Catholic. Her conservative family came from a working class background; her father was employed as a butcher as well as a driver and her mother as a laundress.[2] Braunsteiner was blue-eyed, blond-haired, and by Nazi Aryan standards, very attractive.   After attending school, she found work in a brewery and then as a domestic servant; later, she found employment at Heinkel Aircraft Works.[3] However, Braunsteiner desperately wanted to study nursing, but for reasons unknown, was either unable to or was not successful in nursing training.[4]

She then spent a year in England, and later returned to Austria, where an acquaintance told her about jobs at Ravensbrück.[5] Braunsteiner applied for a position as an *Aufseherin*, was hired in August of 1939, and after a period of selective training, began work at Ravensbrück. She became an *Aufseherin* when she was still in her late teens.   Between the ages of twenty and twenty-two, she   was promoted to the rank of *Oberaufseherin* at Ravensbrück.[6]

On or about 7 October 1942, Braunsteiner was sent to work at Majdanek, which was an extermination and prisoner-of-war camp. Majdanek was near Lublin, where Ilse Koch's husband, Karl Otto Koch, was   supervisor.[7] Braunsteiner was sent to Majdanek because a section of the camp had just been established for women. Thus, several *Aufseherinnen* like Braunsteiner who had worked at Ravensbrück and other camps were sent to help set up the new   ward.[8]

Within a few months, Braunsteiner and other *Aufseherinnen* may have supervised anywhere from six to eleven thousand women.[9] Braunsteiner's duties may have included supervising female inmates for roll call, watching over them while they worked, and, quite possibly, assisting in selections. She was known   for "whipping women for not sewing on their prison numbers correctly" among other cruelties.[10] Her actions against prisoners escalated, and it remains unknown if she ever received reprimands for her actions. She was, however, rewarded for her service. In 1943, she received the *Kriegsverdienstkreuz II Klassen* (War Merit Cross, Second Class); which begs the question if her cruelty was known, was she rewarded for that as well?[11]

Braunsteiner may also have administered various punishments as "allowed" under SS rules and regulations, but her actions escalated in barbarity. She took part in selections, shot prisoners, and murdered babies and children. Any infants who arrived with their mothers at Majdanek were immediately put to death, and women who were in charge of processing incoming female inmates   may have supervised these murders.   Known for her cruelty, she whipped and   beat prisoners without provocation. She threw children onto trucks going straight into the gas chambers.[12] The majority of young children were also   routinely murdered; exceptions were rarely made for those who were strong enough to work. While at Majdanek, Braunsteiner was referred to by some survivors as the stomping *Kobyla*, or mare, an allegory about her use of boots to stomp on prisoners.[13]

Braunsteiner stayed at Majdanek until March of 1944. She was sent back to Ravensbrück, where she stayed for a few months until she fled as the Soviet armies advanced. She was known to have escaped to Vienna, where she   remained for some time.[14] Braunsteiner remained at large in Austria until Allied forces captured her towards the end of 1945.[15] She was then transferred to various prisoner of war camps, and remained under arrest until the British, who had interned Braunsteiner until 1949, released her to Austrian authorities.[16]

She was then tried in an Austrian court for war crimes at Ravensbrück (but not Majdanek), which included infanticide and murder.[17] She received a sentence of three years in prison, and received an assurance by the Austrian government that she would not be tried for war crimes in Austria for the rest of her natural life.[18] After her release from prison in 1950, and while staying in Austria working in food service, she met an American engineer by the name of Russell Ryan.[19] They fell in love, and first moved to Canada, where they were married in October 1958. The couple then moved to New York in April 1959 using falsified displaced persons papers for Braunsteiner.[20] Russell Ryan found work as a contractor and they made a decision to have her apply to become a citizen of the United States.

Braunsteiner applied for American citizenship in 1962, but did not comply with the requirement that she disclose her war crimes conviction on her application. Braunsteiner became an American citizen in January of 1963.[21] In 1964, Braunsteiner was living with her husband in Maspeth, New York, and by all accounts they had a very happy marriage and were accepted in the community, but kept largely to themselves.[22] In an article dated 14 June 1964, a reporter by the name of Joseph Lelyveld from *The New York Times* first broke the story of Braunsteiner's past, setting off an international discussion about Nazi war criminals.

Simon Wiesenthal, Holocaust survivor and famed Nazi hunter, had provided Lelyveld with leads on her whereabouts.[23] Earlier that year, Wiesenthal became aware of Braunsteiner when he was in Israel, where he met with three Holocaust survivors from Majdanek who had brought her to his attention. They enquired whether he had heard of the stomping mare; he had not and he set out to find her.

Based on evidence he uncovered shortly after she had become an American citizen, Wiesenthal was able to track Braunsteiner down. He found her living a quiet, unassuming life as a housewife, well-liked by her neighbors and respected in the community. Wiesenthal further discovered that while Braunsteiner was tried and found guilty for some of her crimes committed, she   was not specifically charged with crimes at Majdanek, a critical point.[24] This omission by prosecutors meant that she could be retried for crimes she executed while at Majdanek. The piece from *The New York Times* initially received little attention, but the furor continued to grow in the survivor community and elsewhere that such a criminal could be living an "ordinary" life. Wiesenthal tirelessly tracked down survivors who offered to come to the United States to testify against Braunsteiner.[25]

In 1971, because of the publicity and public outrage over her crimes at the concentration and extermination camps where she had worked, combined with survivor testimony that very publicly detailed her murderous actions, the American government began procedures to revoke her citizenship. The official reason for revoking her citizenship was that she had failed to disclose on her citizenship application that she had been guilty of war crimes in the camps. Braunsteiner fought against extradition throughout 1972. When neighbors, friends, and associates (in one case, even a child, who recalled she made him pancakes with sugar) were interviewed by reporters, all said that they could not believe the meticulous, kind, caring housewife who was known for her pretty
home and delicious cooking could be a brutal guard.[26] It would require many years to get Braunsteiner extradited from the United States to West Germany.[27]

In 1973, an extradition warrant was issued for her arrest by the West German government on the charge of murder. Braunsteiner argued that she could not be extradited because she was an American citizen, but the judge assigned to her case, Chief Justice Jacob Mischler, refused her claim against extradition.[28] Mischler also denied any other defense her counsel argued for against extradition. Although she continually contested extradition, Braunsteiner was sent back to West Germany to stand trial in August of 1973, and became the first American citizen to be extradited for offenses committed while employed in the   Nazi concentration and extermination camps.[29] Her second trial for war crimes began   in 1975, in Düsseldorf, West Germany, which became known as the Majdanek   War Crimes Trial, and would last over five years.[30] Sixteen defendants would be tried, including men and several other *Aufseherinnen*. All mounted a vigorous defense, and one *Aufseherin* defendant died during the   trial.[31]

Braunsteiner's defense continually attempted to argue her case. Part of the defense's argument stemmed from the fact that Braunsteiner was Austrian, not German, and could not be tried legally in a West German court. The court dismissed her argument, because when Germany took over Austria in 1938 in the *Anschluss*, Braunsteiner had technically become a German citizen, and   had therefore acted for the Nazi government when she worked as an   *Aufseherin*.[32]

Countless survivors related their interactions with her, and further testimony was introduced to show that not only had Braunsteiner murdered prisoners of all ages, but also, quite like Irma Grese and Dorothea (Theodora)   Binz, she had enjoyed kicking and stomping on people with her thick leather boots. She crushed the necks of some prisoners, and kicked to death others. Braunsteiner also   hung people, including children, may have taken part   in selections, and apparently took great pride in her murderous   actions.[33]

She was also found to have used horrible and cruel means to control or abuse inmates without provocation on the part of the prisoners.[34] At one point,   her husband moved to West Germany to be with his wife. He remained devoted to her throughout the trial and beyond, continually protesting her innocence: "My wife, sir, wouldn't hurt a fly."[35] When the trial, which lasted until 1981, was finally over, Braunsteiner was found guilty of murder. The Simon Wiesenthal Center summed up her trial this way:

> In 1975 Braunsteiner-Ryan and eight other former female camp guards were made to answer for themselves in the Majdanek trial in Düsseldorf. She was charged with "collaborative murder in 1,181 cases   and being an accessory to murder in 705 cases". The trial wore on for almost six years, until Braunsteiner received two consecutive life sentences in 1981. Due to lack of evidence, only three of the nine charges   of the indictment resulted in a verdict.[36]

The West German courts sentenced her to life in prison.

She did not serve out life in prison. Braunsteiner was sent to a prison hospital on 24 April 1990, and remained there until she was released in 1996 due   to "compassionate" reasons, since she had developed diabetes. The stomping mare, who used her feet to maim and kill, had both of her legs amputated due to diabetes complications.[37] She died on 19 April 1999 in Bochum, Germany.[38] In an interview published in 2001, Simon Wiesenthal, the man responsible for finding Braunsteiner, revealed some new information about her, stating   that

> Hermine Braunsteiner was responsible for the death of many hundreds of children in a concentration camp ... six or seven months ago, the judge informed me that she had become so sick that he must relieve her from prison, and do you know what had happened? She had lost both her legs. Her American husband bought an apartment in Düsseldorf so he could see her in prison twice every week, and now he has the apartment and the wife that could not walk. So![39]

---

[1] Tillion, 69.

[2]   "Hermine   Braunsteiner   Ryan,"   from   the   Simon   Wiesenthal   Center http://motlc.wiesenthal.com (29 December 2001).

[3] Douglas Martin, "A Nazi Past, a Queens Home Life, an Overlooked Death" *The New York Times.* http://www.nytimes.com/2005/12/02/international/europe/02ryan.html (19 September 2010).

[4] Brown, *The Beautiful Beast*, p. 19, n. 84.

[5]   "Hermine   Braunsteiner   Ryan,"   from   the   Simon   Wiesenthal   Center http://motlc.wiesenthal.com/ (29 December 2001). The author of this essay from the Simon Wiesenthal Center suggested the reason for her transfer was that Braunsteiner, who was trained under *Oberaufseherin* Maria Mandl, had a terrible disagreement with Mandl sometime after completion of her training. Thus, Braunsteiner was transferred to Majdanek.

[6] See Cosner, 18, and "Hermine Braunsteiner Ryan," in Wistrich, pp. 215-216. Brown's records dispute the change in rank. See Brown, *"The Camp Women,"* p. 201.

[7] For more on Majdanek, see Laqueur, p. 409.

[8] See Gryn, pp. 40-41.

[9] Ibid., 42.

[10] Martin, passim.

[11] Brown, *"The Camp Women,"* p. 201.

[12] Harvey, passim.

[13] Gryn, pp. 42-43.

[14] Martin, passim.

[15] "Hermine Braunsteiner Ryan," from the Simon Wiesenthal Center.

[16] Martin, passim.

[17]   Simon   Wiesenthal   Archives. "Some   Significant   Cases: Hermine   Braunsteiner." http://www.simon-wiesenthal-archiv.at/02_dokuzentrum/02_faelle/e05_braunsteiner.html   (1 August 2010).

[18] Cosner, 18, and "Hermine Braunsteiner," Robert S. Wistrich, *Who's Who in Nazi Germany* (New York: Routledge, 1995). The German website "Justiz und NS-Verbrechen" contained some valuable insight about Braunsteiner and others.   Refer to "Verfahren Lfd. Nr.   869," http://www.jur.uva.nl/junsv/brd/files/brd869.htm (13 November 2001)

[19] Martin, passim.

[20] Ibid., and Brown, *"The Camp Women,"* p. 201.

[21] See Cosner, 18, and "Hermine Braunsteiner," Robert S. Wistrich, *Who's Who in Nazi Germany* (New York: Routledge, 1995), pp. 215-216.

[22] Martin, passim.

[23] "Hermine Braunsteiner Ryan," from The Simon Wiesenthal Center.

[24] Ibid.

[25] Ibid.

[26] Martin, passim.

[27] Simon Wiesenthal Archives. "Some Significant Cases," passim.

[28] "Hermine Braunsteiner Ryan," from The Simon Wiesenthal Center.

[29] Harvey, passim.

[30] Cosner, 18.

[31] Alice Orlowski, who served at four different camps as an *Aufseherin* and also as a *Kommandoführerin*, died during the trial. See Brown, *"The Camp Women,"* p. 185. [32] See "Hermine Braunsteiner Ryan," from The Simon Wiesenthal Center. [33] Martin and Harvey, passim.

[34] Cosner, 18. See also my chapters for more on Binz and Grese.

[35] Harvey, passim.

[36] Simon Wiesenthal Archives. "Some Significant Cases," passim. Wiesenthal was appalled that several of her co-defendants received sentences from acquittal (one) to a few years in prison.

[37] "Städteerichte-Hermine Braunsteiner-Ryan" http://www.free.de/lotta/archiv/LOTTA-Nr.1/Staedte.htm (13 November 2001).

[38] Martin, passim, and Simon Wiesenthal Archives. "Some Significant Cases," passim.

[39] Refer to Simon Hattenstone, "The Nazi Hunter" in *The Guardian* http://www.smh.com.au/news/0111/01/world/world13.html (29 December 2001). Wiesenthal's work led to the creation of the Office of Special Investigation, a branch of the Department of Justice. It would be this office that would continue to root out Nazi criminals in the United States. This office, after combining with the Domestic Security Section, is now known as the Human Rights and Special Prosecutions Section. See The United States Department of Justice, http://www.justice.gov/criminal/hrsp/. For how Braunsteiner was the first Nazi criminal to have her American citizenship revoked and was then deported, see also US Attorney's Bulletin, Vol. 54 No 01, Office of Special Investigations, www.justice.gov/usao/eousa/foia_reading_room/usab5401.pdf-2006-02-14 (1 April 2009).

CHAPTER X

ELISABETH VOLKENRATH

Nightmare Creature

It was easy to prove the guilt of the nightmare creatures who wielded the whip…they were caught in the midst of their murders and on the scene   of their crimes…unhappily, their crimes cannot be obliterated with   them.[1]

Elisabeth Volkenrath was born on 5 September 1919, at Schönau, near Badlandeck, Silesia. By the age of twenty, she had married. Her husband worked for the SS.[2] After her marriage, Volkenrath worked at a beauty shop as a hairdresser. In 1939, Volkenrath was called up for national service, and was sent   to work in a munitions factory.   By 1941, she was conscripted for active duty for work with the SS. She asserted at her trial that she had no alternative but to train as an *Aufseherin* at Ravensbrück.

It was at this camp where she received her initial instruction in prisoner control. She understood her training to indicate she was to use any means necessary to control or otherwise subdue the prisoners, under the direct order of Himmler. Of her employment with the SS, Volkenrath said that "I never actually became a member of the SS; we merely wore the uniform and became   supervisors at concentration camps."[3] Volkenrath's statement was correct; women could not join the SS but could work for them.

Volkenrath was assigned to an outside *Kommando* at Ravensbrück, where she was in charge of making sure prisoners did not escape.[4] By March of 1942, she was sent to Auschwitz I, where she supervised prisoners sent to the tailor workroom.[5] She was transferred to the Birkenau section of Auschwitz, where she handled the screening and distribution of packages that were delivered to the camp. Volkenrath also took care of distributing bread to prisoners. At some   point in 1943, Volkenrath was discharged from package duty, which was then assigned to *Aufseherin* Irma Grese.[6] After working in Birkenau, Volkenrath was sent back to Auschwitz I, where she stayed until 18 January 1945, when she was sent to   work at Bergen-Belsen.[7] She would hold a total of three positions, *Aufseherin, Rapportführerin*, and, after arriving at Bergen-Belsen, was promoted to *Oberaufseherin*.

Volkenrath arrived at Bergen-Belsen on 5 February 1945, and was appointed *Oberaufseherin*. She became sick within days of beginning her new job, and was sent to the hospital. She was unable to return to work for over a month. When she returned to work, Volkenrath again went to work as an *Oberaufseherin*, supervising several *Aufseherinnen*. Volkenrath was later accused of heinous, nightmarish crimes while she was at Auschwitz and at Bergen-Belsen. From abuse, torture, and participating in selections, although the latter she would adamantly insist that she took no part in (she argued at her trial she simply observed, and kept order), her crimes were atrocious and deliberate in   nature.

Volkenrath was suspected to have routinely selected people for the gas chamber, a task she was observed to have enjoyed, although she vehemently denied this at her trial. She argued that the *Aufseherinnen* had no choice but to be present at selections so that order could be kept. Volkenrath was alleged to have beaten women with rubber truncheons. She was also accused of slapping women senselessly (which she did admit to), and beating some women so severely with her fists that they died of the abuse. Volkenrath was also believed to have stripped a woman naked and then participated in her beating, while male guards looked on. "Making sport" was another forced activity that the *Aufseherin* took part
in; it was this activity that Volkenrath participated in as well as supervised.[8] She
was not alone in the camp. Volkenrath's sister also worked at Auschwitz in the laundry, and went by the name of Weinniger. It is not known whether this was Volkenrath's maiden name or her sister's married name. It was not known what, if anything, her sister thought of Volkenrath's work as a vicious guard. Auschwitz survivor Gertrud Diament claimed she knew Volkenrath, and stated that she knew

Volkenrath's maiden name to be Milan. Diament also asserted she saw Volkenrath take part in many selections.[9] Volkenrath took great pride in her supervisory role and was respected by many of her fellow *Aufseherinnen*. She and Irma Grese were both at Auschwitz, and at Bergen-Belsen both served as *Oberaufseherin*.

Because of her position as *Oberaufseherin*, Volkenrath enjoyed a certain status among the women who worked for the SS. She was in charge of supervising several women, and may have achieved a sense of satisfaction knowing she was responsible for overseeing some of the daily activities at the camps where she worked. While Volkenrath was at Auschwitz, she observed not only selections, but also took part in severe punishments inflicted on prisoners by the *Aufseherinnen* she supervised.

She also either participated in or observed an *Aufseherin* being whipped for breaking rules, which may have included assisting prisoners in smuggling letters out. Volkenrath could not abide any infractions, and was notorious for following the rules of the camps in which she worked. Numerous eyewitness accounts exist that proved her personal cruelty and murderous actions towards prisoners. When later confronted at her trial with her numerous crimes, as a way to escape culpability for some of the charges she was accused of, Volkenrath claimed she had typhus for several weeks in 1942 (lasting until December of that year) while she worked at Auschwitz. Her defense was that because of her numerous sicknesses, she could not have been responsible for the crimes she was
being accused of, especially at Auschwitz.[10]

Auschwitz eyewitness Josephine Singer revealed that when Volkenrath was supervising workers in the tailor workroom, she saw her throw a woman down a flight of stairs. Singer also claimed she witnessed Volkenrath abuse and beat several people.[11] Survivor of both Auschwitz and Bergen-Belsen, Lidia Sunschein also witnessed Volkenrath's abuse many times. Sunschein stated that when Volkenrath was working in the parcel department at Auschwitz, she witnessed Volkenrath beating people up who were thought to have stolen from the department. Sunschein, while on the stand, admitted that she did not know Volkenrath by name.

She stated that she simply could not identify her as either Volkenrath or Weinniger, but Sunschein asserted that she recognized Volkenrath's face as the woman responsible for many beatings in Auschwitz.[12] Survivor Etyl Eisenberg claimed that she witnessed Volkenrath going into the prisoner's barracks, without warning or provocation, and "take food and clothes from women. She [Volkenrath] was very cruel and made a habit of beating them and pulling hair."[13]

Hilda Loffler, another Auschwitz survivor, stated that she witnessed Volkenrath inflict horrible abuse, sometimes with her bare hands, on prisoners that resulted in many deaths. Loffler also asserted that Volkenrath would purposely abuse, beat, and starve people in order to bring about their death in the most cruel manner possible. Volkenrath argued that it was necessary to slap the prisoners because they attempted to take parcels and bread that was not theirs.

Survivors, however, said that slapping was the least of the abuses Volkenrath committed with her hands. She was alleged to have punched many women in the face, sometimes until they collapsed.[14] Erika Thuna, who survived Auschwitz, stated that she had witnessed Volkenrath continually abuse and assault women who were forced to go on parades; the parades could also mean the forced *Appell* or the march for selection.[15]

Katherine Neiger, who also survived Auschwitz, claimed that she had seen Volkenrath brutally thrash a young female prisoner who was caught stealing vegetables. The prisoner was terribly sick, but Volkenrath forced her to kneel for hours holding the stolen vegetables above her head. When the prisoner could no longer kneel, Volkenrath became enraged and beat the woman so severely that the prisoner lay unmoving for hours. Neiger also said that Volkenrath took a stick and whipped her in the face because Neiger had left her coat undone.[16] Alexandra Siwidowa, yet another eyewitness, claimed she had seen Volkenrath beat many people to death with a variety of objects.

Siwidowa said she saw Volkenrath "beat many women internees with a rubber truncheon. On seventy or eighty occasions she beat people into unconsciousness."[17] The testimony of Edith Trieger, another survivor, matched Siwidowa's testimony.[18] Another survivor of Auschwitz named Zlata Kaufmann alleged that she had seen Volkenrath not only beat people causing their deaths,   but had seen the *Oberaufseherin* personally take part in selections. Kaufmann said that she had also witnessed Volkenrath stomping on prisoners and slamming them against walls.

Kaufmann also stated that she knew Volkenrath had taken part in selections because women Volkenrath had picked out were sent to Block 25 at Auschwitz, which was the block where women were held immediately before being sent to the gas chambers. [19] There were so many claims against Volkenrath from women like these that "the allegations against her [Volkenrath] were so numerous that the authorities stopped collecting further evidence at an early state of the enquiries."[20]

When the British liberated Bergen-Belsen in April 1945, Volkenrath was taken prisoner. As with several other *Aufseherinnen* and *Oberaufseherin* who were arrested, the British ordered the women to clean up and properly bury some   of the bodies; Volkenrath may or may not have taken part in body disposal. The women were then first sent to the *Wehrmacht* (German Armed Forces) Tank Training School, a few miles away from Bergen-Belsen. After a short period,   the *Aufseherinnen* were then taken to a prison at Lüneburg, Germany.[21] Volkenrath was charged with two counts of war crimes at both Auschwitz and Bergen- Belsen. Her trial began on 17 September 1945, and lasted until 17 November 1945.[22]

When questioned about her guilt, Volkenrath admitted to almost nothing. She denied all of the survivor claims, denouncing them as lies. During the cross-examination by prosecution at her trial, Volkenrath denied the allegations that Ravensbrück was where "SS women were taught to beat and ill-treat prisoners   and that at that place you [Volkenrath] were taught that the only way to keep prisoners in order was to beat them and ill-treat them until they were frightened to death."[23] She did admit to "making sport" or forcing some prisoners to exercise,   or stand at attention for long periods, but failed to admit to any knowledge about selections or what the gas chambers were used for. Trial proceedings noted that while at Auschwitz and other camps, Volkenrath   was

> comparatively young. She was the head *Aufseherin* and responsible for the actions of those under as well as for allocating her duties…she, too,   was ruthless. Kicking and beating, she casts her shadow over the whole story of the lives of the wretched internees. Her defense was mainly a flat denial of everything that was said about her.[24]

The prosecution further reminded the court that Volkenrath had been present at several selections, but that her claim that she did not know what the selections were for, or where the people who were selected were going, was false. The court was also reminded of testimony which claimed in yet another instance   of cruelty and abuse, that Volkenrath was so upset over two escapees, that she   gave orders to starve over six hundred prisoners for three   days.

The prosecution then reminded the court that everyone on trial, whether "doctor, the *Aufseherin*, or the *Lagerführer*, is equally guilty of murder of these people, because he or she knew precisely what they were selecting, what was going to happen, and where those chosen were going."[25] In summation,   a prosecutorial statement directed at Volkenrath's guilt was equally damning: "Do you seriously think that Volkenrath, who had enough intelligence to become an *Oberaufseherin*, did not know?"[26]

Volkenrath's defense attorney, Major A.S. Munro, of the R.A.S.C. (Royal Army Service Corps), who also defended Juana Bormann, stated in Volkenrath's defense that the court should consider her youth, and the fact that she did not want to become involved with the SS, but had no choice when she was conscripted. Moreover, Munro argued, Volkenrath's position as *Oberaufseherin* was not as important as the prosecution alleged. Munro reminded the court that as an *Oberaufseherin*, Volkenrath's main role was to supervise the *Aufseherinnen*, and that as this type of supervisor Volkenrath had very little administrative power within either Auschwitz or Bergen-Belsen, at least until late 1944, when Maria Mandl, former *Oberaufseherin* fled, leaving Volkenrath as her *de facto* replacement.[27] Volkenrath herself stated, "I have always been very strict, but have never murdered anyone. I have boxed the ears of girls if they did anything wrong."[28]

Volkenrath also stated that she was only following orders, including that given by *Lagerführer* Maria Mandl, and also by direct orders of Himmler. Volkenrath also claimed that *Kommandant* Kramer, who was in charge of Belsen when she was there, had instructed her to "make sport" with the prisoners. Sport again meant several things, including forcing the prisoners to do strenuous exercises, and she argued that the male SS guards forced her to make the prisoners do these exercises.

Volkenrath also sought the court's sympathy by stating that she had tried to let Kramer know just how bad conditions were in Bergen-Belsen, and, in terms of punishing prisoners, tried "not to forget that I was a woman and a human being."[29] In an unusual step, Volkenrath also said that Rudolph Höss, a senior Nazi official who was once head of Auschwitz, was to blame for all the crimes committed at Auschwitz. She then stated that Heinrich Himmler, *Reichsführer* (Head of the SS) was responsible for all of the crimes committed in all concentration camps.[30]

Volkenrath would not admit to many of the charges brought against her. She did grant that she had forced prisoners to stand with their hands above their heads during one particular *Appell*, but that she was ordered to do so, and at no time ever treated prisoners with disrespect until immediately instructed otherwise. She argued that the less intelligent prisoners would be slapped, but that she had no choice but to do so less chaos erupt in the camps she was at. When continuously confronted by the prosecution for her crimes, she attempted to blame the SS men, or insinuate that the *Aufseherinnen* were only following orders.

She also avoided answering questions that would require her to say the word selection. Rather she inferred that she supervised and/or took part in parades, the outcomes of which she was not made aware of, nor could she have possibly known. Her argument was that she was "on duty" and therefore had no choice but to attend the parades. It seemed incredulous that she could believe that such a defense would work, in light of the numerous survivor and photographic testimonies against her. Volkenrath also claimed that she did not take part in selection herself, but that she merely accompanied the male SS so that she could help keep order among the prisoners who were going to their death.[31]

Volkenrath was found guilty of war crimes at both Auschwitz and Bergen-Belsen, and was sentenced to death by hanging.[32] Volkenrath was scheduled to hang on 13 December 1945. Volkenrath was moved from the prison at Lüneburg to a prison in the city of Hameln to await execution.[33] On the eve of her execution, Volkenrath sang Nazi songs.[34] Volkenrath was the first of the *Aufseherin* scheduled to die. The British executioner Albert Pierrepoint conducted her execution the morning of 13 December.[35] She was buried in the courtyard of Hameln prison.[36]

---

[1] "Belsen and Dachau," *New York Times* (15 December 1945): 16 (L).

[2] Phillips, 718. Volkenrath related that she had not seen her husband for quite awhile at the time of her arrest.

[3] Ibid., 719.

[4] Ibid., 217.

[5] See chapter four, the sub-section "Auschwitz."

[6] Brown, *The Beautiful Beast*, 41.

[7] Fyfe, p. 213.

[8] Ibid. "Making sport" was forced, laborious exercising as punishment for even a minor "infraction" such as menstruating while at *Appell*, or for anything that the guards may have perceived as a slight.

[9] Phillips, 218. See also p. 659.

[10] Ibid.

[11] Ibid., 613.

[12] Ibid., pp. 116-120.

[13] United Nations War Crimes Commission, *The Belsen Trial*, p. 26.

[14] Ibid., 30.

[15] Ibid., 35.

[16] Ibid., 31.

[17] Ibid., 34.

[18] Ibid., 35.

[19] Ibid., 28. See also Phillips, 670.

[20] Phillips, xlii.
[21] Brown, *The Beautiful Beast*, pp. 66-67.
[22] Phillips, 642.
[23] See Ibid., 217.
[24] Ibid., xlii.
[25] Ibid., pp. 597 and 613.
[26] Ibid., 599.
[27] United Nations War Crime Commission, *The Belsen Trial*, p. 123.
[28] See Phillips, p. 719.
[29] Ibid.
[30] Ibid., 720.
[31] Ibid. See also p. 528.
[32] Ibid., 644.
[33] Brown, *The Beautiful Beast*, pp. 82-83.
[34] Ibid., pp. 86-87.
[35] Ibid.
[36] Ibid., 87.

CHAPTER XI

IRMA GRESE

The Angel of Death

In my experience, the matrons were cruel, more vicious (sadistically vicious) than any SS man. These women, who, as I read later, ranged from baronesses to countesses to prostitutes, were the most vicious. You rarely found SS men who played games with their dogs in which the point was for the dogs to get the prisoner's derrieres, but the matrons did.[1]

Irma Grese, the Beautiful Beast, or Angel of Death, as some survivors of Ravensbrück and Auschwitz depicted her, was one of the most infamous as well as one of the cruelest of all *Aufseherinnen* and *Oberaufseherinnen*. Irma Ilse Ida Grese was born on 7 October 1923, in Wrechen, near Mecklenburg, Germany. Her parents, Alfred and Berta, who had two other daughters and two sons, were dairy farmers, and the Greses were a farm working family.[2] Soon after discovering Alfred had had an affair, Berta committed suicide in January 1936 by drinking poison.[3] Albert remarried three years later.

Undoubtedly, her mother's suicide had an effect on the young Irma Grese. Blond-haired, blue-eyed, and by Nazi contemporary standards, quite beautiful, Grese came of age at a time when Nazi power was rising. By the time Hitler moved towards absolute power in 1933, Nazi indoctrination had reached all levels and areas of Germany. Daniel Patrick Brown, the leading expert on Grese, asserted that she was, already by the age of 9 or 10, deeply influenced by Hitler and the Nazis. Propaganda, Brown further argued, played a key role in forming the young girl's tendency to support Nazism: "Certainly her receptiveness to Hitlerian ideology was apparent from this point forward."[4] The Nazis, specifically because of their susceptible makeup and lack of a fully developed psychological, individualized, and fully formed personality, especially targeted children.[5]

Special programs were also instituted for German youth; children were especially indoctrinated in Nazi ideology and Grese was part of this group of children who were exposed to Nazism at a very early age.[6] Grese wanted to join the BDM but her father refused to let her or any of her siblings take part in any Nazi-directed activities; her sister Helene also wanted to take part but only Irma was successful at circumventing total parental authority concerning voluntary involvement with the Nazis.[7] Her mother died in 1936, and Alfred Grese later remarried.

Did the suicide of her mother and father's remarriage have an effect on her? Hypotheses have emerged, but it remains unclear whether the death of Grese's mother had any effect on her as far as her future criminal career with the Nazis was concerned. Grese's younger sister Helene, when questioned about any connections to Irma's crimes with her mother's early death, refused to answer.[8] At Grese's trial, Helene described her sister as an intimidated, scared young girl: "In our schooldays when, as it sometimes happen, girls were quarreling and fighting, my sister never had the courage to fight, but on the contrary she ran away."[9]

In 1938, Grese left school and held various jobs. Her sister Helene said Grese worked in agriculture beginning when she was 14.[10] She worked as a dairy farmhand in Fürstenburg and then as a shop girl in Luchen.[11] In 1939,   she attempted to find a job as a nurse (which she would later state at her trial was her preferred career choice) but had to settle for an apprenticeship as a nurse's aide at Hohenlychen hospital, an SS recuperative infirmary. Grese worked as a nurse's aide for over two years, and early in her career, was exposed to vivisection performed on prisoners from Ravensbrück.

She soon left Hohenlychen, perhaps because she did not succeed in her attempts to nurse patients. She was given a lead on a job as an *Aufseherin* by the Nazi doctor Karl Gebhardt, whom she had met at Hohenlychen. Gebhardt, whose assistant was Dr. Herta Oberheuser, gave Grese information about a position at Ravensbrück, the main concentration camp for women that was somewhat close   to her home. Grese jumped at the chance, but was not old enough to become an *Aufseherin*.[12] Disappointed, she sought another job, and found one as   a   dairy machine operator. She stayed at the dairy for over a year. Grese stated at her trial that she was conscripted as an *Aufseherin*, but evidence also exists which showed that while at Hohenlychen, she made several important contacts, including one   that led her directly to Ravensbrück; therefore the implication was that she sought the job as an *Aufseherin* voluntarily because of Gebhardt's encouragement, and   was not conscripted.[13]

By the summer of 1942, Grese was looking for a better post and, following up on the leads provided to her by Gebhardt, got the job at Ravensbrück as an *Aufseherin*, subsequent to her completing training. As Grese claimed at her trial, she felt that the German government attempted to prevent her from becoming a nurse, so she had no choice but to work at a camp.   Again, she stated   at her trial that the government conscripted her to work in the camps but her later testimony, as well as that of her sister Helene, verified that she went to work at
the camps of her own volition.[14]

The facts alone do not support Grese's claim that she was conscripted. Rather, she volunteered for the position of *Aufseherin*.[15] Albert Grese, once he found out where his daughter Irma was working in 1943, had a terrible fight with his daughter, and may have beat her for taking part in SS activities. Helene Grese revealed that her sister never returned to the family home after this fight. Helene also revealed that she wanted to join the BDM along with her sister, but their   father absolutely refused to allow the girls to get involved.[16] Grese herself also stated at her trial that the Nazi government "sent me to Ravensbrück concentration camp although I protested against it."[17] However, Helene revealed   at her sister's trial that her sister had always wanted to be a part of the SS society, and had joined an SS-led organization that allowed women voluntarily once she turned eighteen, purportedly against their father's expressed wishes. New scholarship by Daniel Patrick Brown, who kindly shared his research with me in a conversation, suggests that her father knew.

Grese was not conscripted for service in the SS; a case can be made for the fact that she was the one solely responsible for making the decision to work there, not the Nazi government. She could have taken another route, like many other German women, which was to get married and bear as many children as possible for the Third Reich. This life did not appeal to her, for reasons that may never be fully known. Nevertheless, some hypotheses have emerged, with most relating to the fact that a young woman with seemingly no other opportunities open to her, took the one position that seemed the most promising. The job allowed her, however on the periphery, to be involved with hospital personnel that she had met. In addition to the medical world, Hitler also held a fascination for her, as did the allure of working with the SS. Perhaps Grese just simply wanted to work as a guard, since the SS provided her with a way to alter her socioeconomic status without any college education or marriage.

Nazism and employment in the SS hierarchy offered her a way out of her everyday life and the chance to make something of herself in the world. Nazi propaganda, such as, "We are the first. We must succeed. We will succeed and Germany will live forever," may have appealed to a young, impressionable woman like Grese.[18] Propaganda such as this might have given her a sense of camaraderie or unity and a chance to participate in the new Nazi government. As contractors for the SS, the heady power implied in their status as cohorts of the elite men's group must have been incredibly compelling to a young woman with restricted socioeconomic opportunities, although not all women who worked for the SS had such limitations.

Perhaps the truth lies somewhere in this hypothesis: the chance to work at a facility, close to home, where she would be exposed to a medical environment may have appealed to her. Moreover, despite her father's warnings, the Nazi party remained a strong attraction for her. Grese was hired at Ravensbrück in July 1942, and was quickly admitted to the training program for *Aufseherinnen*.

After training for a short period, Grese became an official *Aufseherin* and her pay was fifty-four Reichsmarks a month.[19] Grese would retain the distinction of being one of the youngest of all the *Aufseherinnen* with status, authority, and relative autonomy as compared to other women who worked for the SS.[20] She was recognized by Maria Mandl, *Oberaufseherin* at Ravensbrück, and was seen early   on as a guard who was not only useful to the SS machine, but could easily be promoted. This was relatively rare for a female SS contractor and especially for   one as young as Grese. She continued to rise in rank and was given more tasks. At one point in her career as an *Aufseherin*, Grese was in charge of over eighteen thousand prisoners. It was her cruelty to innocent prisoners as well as her resolute, almost devotionally juvenile commitment to Nazi tenets that made her notorious amongst everyone in the camp structure.[21]

She would stay at Ravensbrück until March of 1943, when she left for the Birkenau (she was specifically assigned to *C-Lager* in Birkenau) camp at Auschwitz, replacing another *Aufseherin*, Elisabeth Volkenrath, as mail censor.[22] More men were being sent to the eastern front, and women were needed not only   to replace these men, but also because the killings increased exponentially in the extermination centers.[23] Grese stayed at Auschwitz Birkenau until January of 1945. Mandl was one of her supervisors there, as was Margot Drechsel, a *Rapportführerin*. While there, Grese supervised close to thirty thousand female prisoners.[24] It was during her stay at Auschwitz that she "was responsible for murdering perhaps as many as thirty prisoners a day."[25] In January of 1945, she was then sent back to Ravensbrück for a short period of about eight weeks, and by March 1945, was finally assigned to the camp at Bergen-Belsen. This last camp was under the command of Joseph Kramer, the "Beast" of Belsen. While at Bergen-Belsen, Grese was appointed to the positions of *Arbeitsdienstführerin* (SS Labor Control Officer) and *Rapportführerin*. She would also be promoted to that   of *Oberaufseherin*. Throughout her career, she was known as a   sadist.

Grese's career as an *Aufseherin* was full of depravity, horror, extreme cruelty, forced bisexuality, and murder. She always wore a crisp, clean uniform, and usually carried a pistol and a whip. The whip was allegedly custom-made for her out of cellophane, and when questioned about her use of the whip as a means to gain a promotion, Grese replied, while not acknowledging her use of the whip, "When I carried a whip I was not promoted at all."[26]

However, Grese herself admitted to "making sport." She also admitted to striking prisoners, and forcing them to kneel for long periods of time. She stated that she had a "whip which I used consistently whenever necessary."[27] At her trial, in a twisted attempt to justify her brutal actions, she revealed how she came   to use her whip:

> In the beginning I did not use anything at all, but later on, when the crowds in Camp "C" became larger, then a great deal was stolen and prisoners did not obey my orders, even when they were quite light orders. Every day there were complaints of things stolen in the kitchen, and I put two Aufseherinnen in charge and gave them orders to keep their eyes open and whenever they found somebody on the spot who stole anything, to   give them a good thrashing. In the beginning every prisoner had two blankets, but when the crowds became bigger I had to see that everybody got a blanket and therefore each prisoner only got one. We found they had cut up all those blankets and made all sorts of things out of them - shoes, jackets, etc. I gave strict orders that everything which had been made out   of blankets was to be returned at once, but I got nothing at all, so then I ordered the control of all the blocks and also personal searches of the prisoners. On those occasions I used my whip.[28]

Her attempts at explaining the use of the whip demonstrated how her sense of   logic was completely distorted. She did not accept responsibility for her actions; instead, she blamed the prisoners whom she felt caused her such provocation that she had no choice but to beat them into submission. She had many tools for "control" purposes. Grese also liked to wear heavy leather boots, which she used when she kicked, stomped, and tortured inmates.[29]

She did not, based on her own testimony, carry a rubber truncheon as many of the other *Aufseherin* did, although survivors stated otherwise. Grese's violent nature did not always sit well with other *Aufseherinnen* and even with SS men, as some saw her actions as beyond the scope of what they considered "appropriate;" however, this remains factually incorrect in the respect that if Grese (and others) were seen as interfering, or overstepping their boundaries, they were somehow worse than the protesting perpetrators.[30] Not everyone saw Grese   as a camp "enemy." She used her youth and sexual attractiveness as a way to   make connections in the camps. Grese did have many lovers while working in the camp structure, including SS men and perhaps women as well. While she was at Auschwitz, she became deeply involved with Dr. Josef Mengele and worked alongside with him during many selections.

Based on the Darwinian concept of survival of the fittest, selection was an appalling process in which men were separated from the women, young from the old, children from their parents, and the ill from the healthy, and were immediately murdered by means of bullets or poison gas. The prisoners who survived selection who were not shot, gassed, experimented on, poisoned, beaten, or otherwise tortured, instead fell victim to abuse, disease, death via manual labor/exhaustion, and starvation. Men, and women such as Grese, perpetrated much of the abuse. [31]

Survivors testified at Grese's trial that during one selection led by Mengele, they witnessed Grese beating people into unconsciousness who tried to escape from either the selection or the work lines in order to join their loved ones. Survivor Ilona Stein testified at Grese's trial that she had witnessed Grese assisting Mengele in the selection of thousands of prisoners. If anyone tried to escape, Stein related, Grese would chase the prisoner herself, and beat the   escapee senseless. She would then drag the person back to the selection lines.[32]   In other instances, when prisoners tried to run away from the lines, Grese would point them out to male SS guards who would then shoot the inmates. Other witnesses from Auschwitz asserted that Grese would shoot prisoners who tried to   escape.[33]

A number of survivors portrayed Grese as one of the cruelest women they had ever encountered at the camps. Eyewitnesses said that they had observed   Grese punishing people who tried to help anyone picked for selection. Survivors claimed that if Grese saw anyone trying to assist prisoners marked for a selection line, she would pull those people aside.   As punishment, she would then beat the helpers senseless, sometimes inflicting fatal blows with her whip and boots.[34]

Aufseherinnen like Grese were trained to work with SS men like Dr. Mengele in every possible aspect of prison management, including camp administration. Their duties also included processing prisoners to assist or take part in experimentations, as well as the aforementioned selections. This also included stern orders not to associate with the prisoners. Violation of this order could mean severe punishment or even death for both the *Aufseherin* and prisoner.[35] They were also shown how to prevent escapes and how to administer punishment.

Many women were assigned to work with certain *Oberaufseherinnen*, in a form of internship, in the hopes of gaining a higher position in the hierarchical structure of the camps.[36] Some women were in positions of power within the camp, and supervised other female camp employees in addition to prisoners. Many were also responsible for the administration of the camp itself, though on a relatively small scale in comparison to the men. Grese was promoted rapidly, and was even assigned to be in charge of a men's compound at Auschwitz.[37]

Witnesses at her trial continually testified that Grese, following the example of her supposed mentor Binz, would beat, whip, kick, sadistically physically and/or sexually abuse female prisoners, sometimes under order and other times of her own volition.[38] Grese, who again was known to use her dog on prisoners, had another nickname given to her by survivors; it was perhaps appropriate that her victims depicted the self-styled post-war "Hollywood star" as the "angel" of death.[39] She was given this unusual nickname because of a combination of her attractive and supposed perfect physical "Aryan" features, as well as her willingness to put women, and men, to death without any hesitation.

Several survivors and witnesses related that they personally saw Grese assist in many selections at the horrifying Auschwitz/Birkenau camp. Many prisoners considered this camp a living hell, and where Grese "truly earned her notorious reputation."[40] These testimonies asserted that while at this camp, Grese allegedly raped several female prisoners, physically abused many others, and took part not only in selections but outright murder for minor infractions. In 1945, she was then sent back to Ravensbrück and was finally assigned to Bergen-Belsen.

While at Bergen-Belsen, she was given the position of *Kommandofüherin* (chief commander), and *Arbeitsdienstführerin* (SS Labour Control Officer). With her promotions, Grese's cruelty and sadistic tortures increased.

Grese was responsible for many horrific beatings and several murders at the camps where she worked. At her trial at Bergen-Belsen, several survivors related their experiences with her. Survivor Ilona Stein recounted at Grese's trial:

> Whilst I was at Birkenau, an SS woman named Irma Grese was responsible for many beatings, one murder, and sending people to the gas chamber…what I speak of I speak of to my own knowledge. In July 1944, I was working in the kitchen at Birkenau when I saw a woman, whose daughter was in the adjoining camp, go to the dividing wire in order to speak to her daughter. Grese, who was passing by on a bicycle, immediately got off, took off her leather belt, and beat the woman with it. She also beat her on the face and head with her fists, and when the woman fell to the ground, she trampled on her. The woman's face became black and blue…the woman was in the hospital for three weeks suffering from the effects of this beating.[41]

Grese would state that when confronted with a prisoner, depending on the infraction, she would have no choice but to use physical treatment. Moreover, she stated she would beat whatever part of the body was easiest for her, with walking sticks, whips, or her hands.

Survivors claimed that if she did not like the way that some prisoners performed their duties, Grese would force the inmates to kneel for hours at a time, while holding unbearably heavy stones over their heads, a fact she denied at her trial.[42] Incredibly, she would also assert that she had even tried to assist some of the Jews that were in her charge.[43] When a prisoner committed a minor infraction, Grese would also force prisoners to engage in "sport" which was extreme exercise, or perform very strenuous slave labor until they collapsed. When they could no longer comply, she would beat, kick, and whip them until she was satisfied that they had suffered enough.[44] Grese formed unusual friendships with some of the prisoners. Grese befriended one prisoner, Magda, and their acquaintance developed into an abnormal, interdependent relationship.

Despite the differences in their positions, Grese used Magda as a sounding board for her choice in unwilling female sex partners, and even used her as a distraction when she grabbed and allegedly raped women in the camp.[45] Grese regularly beat her charges at Birkenau with horrific force; in one instance, Grese felt a prisoner acted inappropriately and Grese beat her so badly she lost several teeth. However, Grese never beat Magda in this fashion. Despite their relationship, Magda acknowledged that Grese was a vicious, sadistic woman.[46] What remains challenging to deconstruct was how prisoners saw through her cruelty and commented on Grese's physicality.

Even more surprising, Grese was apparently so beautiful that several of the prisoners remarked in depositions and interviews that they were always struck by how attractive Grese was, in spite of her monstrous cruelty.[47] Grese also befriended another inmate named Nina, surprisingly because Grese felt Nina looked a lot like her. It came to Grese's attention that Nina resembled her, and Grese sought Nina out on several occasions to act as a lookout while Grese allegedly sexually abused women. Grese would also use female prisoners to satisfy her own sexual, sadistic fantasies. She apparently raped women at will, with Nina acting as a guard. For her service to Grese, Nina was rewarded with extra food and special attention.[48]

Grese managed to shock even those prisoners who had already witnessed incredible depravity. While she was at Birkenau, where she may have been in charge of anywhere from 18,000 to 30,000 prisoners, Grese became pregnant and needed medical assistance.[49] She found a female Jewish doctor named Giselle Perl, and Grese demanded that Perl, although she was Jewish and it was against Nazi law for her to do so, examine her and perform an abortion.[50]

Perl also related that Grese would often come to her medical quarters and watch her examine female prisoners. Perl stated that Grese especially "relished whipping well-developed young women on the breasts … Grese would eventually become sexually aroused just watching the women suffering."[51] Perl, who was horrified at the abysmal and psychologically disturbing behavior of Grese, observed her become very aroused when Grese saw the infected breasts of her whipping victims being lanced.[52] Described as "one of the most beautiful women I have ever seen ... yet, Irma Grese was the most depraved, cruel, imaginative sexual pervert," Grese's violence and perversions knew no boundaries.[53] From whipping women's breasts, achieving "orgiastic spasms" when viewing women experiencing horrific pain, to demanding an abortion performed on herself (against SS rules), her career as an *Aufseherin* and her crimes against humanity eclipses even imagined horrors in the camp structure.[54] Further, Perl and other survivors noted that while assisting with selections, Grese beat people who resisted in any way, large or small, using her fists, baton, whip, or her dog. Once again, the use of a dog becomes an extension of the women's own deconstruction of SS hyper-masculinization as interpreted into a power agency that the women themselves controlled.

Like Juana Bormann, Grese also had a dog while at the various camps where she worked. She would strut around the camp with her trained guard dog, and would not hesitate to set her dog on anyone whom she did not like, or who was pointed out to her by her subordinates.[55] She would then punish women during roll call by making the prisoners stand for long periods, and would then let her dog attack the prisoners at random.[56] Hanka Rozenwayg, a Polish survivor of Bergen-Belsen, testified:

> In July 1943, whilst at Auschwitz, I was employed digging ditches outside the camp. Whilst so employed I laid down my shovel for a rest, and Lothe, who was in charge of my working party, saw me. I saw her go to the woman SS guard, and I heard her ask the SS woman to set her dog on me. I recognize this SS woman as No. 2 on photograph Z/4/2. I did not know her name, but have since been told that it was Irma Grese. Grese set her dog on to me and as a result I was bitten by the dog on my right shoulder. I still have a scar on my shoulder where the dog bit me. I was made to continue working and I had to dress the wound myself after I had returned to the block.[57]

Concerning the outcome of Grese's dog, a British soldier later related that after Grese was taken prisoner, he was so disturbed by the dog, and what the dog may have assisted Grese in doing, that he "had to save one bullet because he wasn't   too keen on Grese's Alsatian being around."[58]

In addition to the use of the dog, other survivors testified that Grese would beat inmates in the face and on their bodies with rubber truncheons, often leaving the woman to suffer unaided. Other *Aufseherinnen* would beat women to a bloody pulp, but Grese stood out to many survivors because of her extreme cruelty that seemed to know no boundaries. Grese would punch or beat women in the mouth until their teeth would fly out of their mouths, or until their jaws broke, for no reason and without any provocation. A survivor named Margaret related that Grese beat her so hard she lost several teeth; the reason was that Grese heard

Margaret laughing during an *Appell*.[59] Violence against prisoners without any provocation was typical for Grese, as it was for other *Aufseherinnen*; Grese, however, stands out as one of the most horrible of the women guards.

Still another survivor named Gitla Dunkleman testified that while at Bergen-Belsen she witnessed Grese, whom she termed "the worst of the women

SS," force prisoners to parade, and if anyone fell out of line because of illness and/or weakness, she would beat the prisoner until she drew blood.[60] Yet another trial witness, Gertrud Diament, who was at both Auschwitz and Bergen-Belsen, testified that Grese's favorite habit was to beat women until they lay on the ground, utterly helpless. Grese would then kick them with her hard leather boots until she saw blood flowing from their wounds.[61]

The British liberated Bergen-Belsen and captured Grese on 5 April 1945.[62] After her capture, Grese stood trial at Belsen along with forty-four other defendants.[63] It was later revealed that she had stayed at Bergen-Belsen because   of a love affair with a married SS officer. Grese and other prisoners were sent to the *Wehrmacht* Tank Training School, a few miles away from the Bergen-Belsen camp.[64] The Bergen-Belsen trial began on 17 September 1945, and lasted only two months. During her trial, she became a media sensation because of her youth and beauty.

Western media sensationalized Grese, and many articles called attention to her youthful attractiveness. Implications can be drawn that people had a hard time accepting that women who were so young and pretty could commit such heinous crimes. Certainly no such articles appeared about Bormann, which further implied ageism by the media and superfluous conjecture based entirely on Bormann's looks. If a guard looked cruel, she must then be cruel. If a guard was attractive, how could she be responsible for such horrible crimes? Survivor Gerda Weissmann Klein certainly felt that one female guard she had come in contact   with must have been cruel because the woman "barked ... literally barked" when instead the *Aufseherin* was responsible for saving her life. [65] Grese was the visual (but certainly not aural) opposite of a barking, unattractive guard.

Articles appeared in major periodicals with titles such as "Belsen Girl Guard Blames all of SS," and "Woman Guard Accused Again," which called attention to not only her gender, but her youth, her clean pressed uniform, blond sausage-like curls, big blue eyes, and bright countenance.[66] Some trial   observers further noted that Grese again stood out among the other defendants, which was "accentuated by the fact that the women sitting on either side of her 'traversed the range from ugly to repellant'."[67] For example, when citing her trial testimony, one journalist led an article with "Lueneberg, Germany, Oct 5 (UP)-All members of the SS (Elite Guard) were equally guilty of murder, *blond* Irma Grese, an SS guard, declared in statements today" and include the descriptive "a three-part confession by the *pretty* 21-year-old guard, often called the worst of the SS-women."[68]

Clearly, the fact that Grese was young, blond, and attractive weighed heavily on the minds of journalists who were present at her trial. Grese herself spent time ensuring that her hair looked nice and that she presented as an attractive a figure as possible. This may have been because of her personal self- vanity, but certainly the fact that an SS man with whom she had allegedly had an affair was also on the stand with her could have played a role. Repeatedly, Grese, who paid careful attention to her hairstyle and personal hygiene, even while in prison, drew attention because of her huge blue eyes, curly blond hair, and personal demeanor, was referred to as a girl with a "pretty blond head."[69] Beauty could not save her from the guilt from which she was so complicit. Her trial testimony further indicated that she alone made the decision to act the way that she did; Daniel Patrick Brown, the first to write a biography on Grese, argued that it was Grese's own words that played right into the hands of the prosecutorial team, helping to convict her own fellow guards. [70]

Grese herself stated that as far as any guilt she may have had, she blamed the "dead Heinrich Himmler, Gestapo Chief, for brutal treatment of internees at the camps," but did admit that she, along with all of the SS, held responsibility for some crimes.[71] When cross-examined by Colonel Backhouse, he asked: "Your sister [Helene Grese] said that when you were a little girl you were frightened to stand up for yourself, and you ran away to avoid a fight. I now suggest to you that you found it great fun to hit somebody who could not hit back?" Grese replied with one word: "No." Backhouse may have been on to something when asking her this question. Working for the SS as a contractor gave Grese the agency to act out then against anyone who she then might have reconstructed as the bullies from her past. When questioned at her trial about being the worst SS woman in all of the camps, Grese replied with, "Yes, they say so. They are all lying. These people exaggerated and made an elephant out of a small fly."[72]

When asked about her rapid promotions, which may have been based on her ability to process prisoners with total indifference and distinct cruelty, since she went from a small town dairy farm girl to a woman in charge of tens of thousands of prisoners, Grese replied with "that has nothing to do with the dairy."[73] Grese, to escape some culpability for her criminal actions, also claimed that she initially worked as a telephone operator in the *Blockführer* room at Auschwitz, and, consequently, was not guilty of some charges brought against her; however, at her trial, the prosecution reminded the court that a woman was never allowed that duty.[74] Grese's own testimony suggested that while at

Auschwitz, she had purposely used roll calls as a means to cruelly torture and sadistically beat prisoners.[75]

Grese, like Elisabeth Volkenrath and Juana Bormann, was also housed in a prison in the city of Lüneburg. The prosecution, in summation, reminded the court that by her own admission, Grese had agreed to several of the charges brought against her, which included beatings and corporal punishment.[76] Her defense attorney Major I.S.W. Cranfield of the British Honourable Artillery Company reminded the court that Grese was very young when her biological mother died, apparently to invite sympathy for her, and perhaps even try to explain why she made the decisions that she did to work for the SS, engaging in criminal acts that defied description even to the veteran attorneys.

Cranfield also argued that Grese had grown up poor, since her father was only a farmer, and it was implied that because of her familial socioeconomic status that caused her so much personal turmoil that she was rendered very vulnerable. He noted that she had also received little education because of her low social status, had been susceptible to Nazi indoctrination, and what the party had to offer a poor, motherless girl like Grese (despite the fact that she had, from all accounts, a decent stepmother in her father's second wife). Cranfield further argued that Grese had had no choice when she went to work as an *Aufseherin*, as she was conscripted.[77] Cranfield had attempted to argue that Nazism, not Grese herself, was responsible for what she did while employed by the SS. Despite these arguments by the defense, Grese, a "sadist of the first rank" was found guilty of committing war crimes at Bergen-Belsen (including having whipped 18,000 women), and guilty of war crimes while at Auschwitz.[78] She received a sentence of death by hanging.

Grese was moved from her prison at Lüneburg to a prison in the city of Hameln, Germany.[79] The night before her death, she allegedly sang Nazi songs with Elisabeth Volkenrath and Juana Bormann.[80] After eating a last meal, Grese was led to her execution, requesting that her death be as quick as possible. After Elizabeth Volkenrath was hanged, Grese was next. As she was led to the gallows, and after placing her lips on a cross, Grese gave one last command of *schnell* (quick);

she was executed on 13 December 1945, by the British executioner Albert

Pierrepoint.[81] Grese, along with several other prisoners, was buried in the grounds of

Hameln prison.[82]

---

[1] This quote was taken from the testimony of Susan Cernyak-Spatz, in Koonz, 404.

[2] Taake, p. 50, Morrison, pp. 8-9; for Irma Grese's own testimony, see Phillips, 248.

[3] Brown, *The Beautiful Beast*, pp. 13-14.

[4] Ibid., p. 14, n. 66. Brown related a key point towards understanding why young girls such as Grese develop into the sadistic killers that they became; he stated that Grese, who was a rather shy girl, when an adult, the "Nazi system afforded her the opportunity to vent her frustrations on the unfortunate inmates under her command." See Ibid., p. 15, and 15, n. 71.

[5] Ibid., p. 14, n. 66.

[6] Gudrun Schwarz, "Forgotten Perpetrators: Women in the SS" (paper presented at the United States Holocaust Memorial Museum, Washington, DC, 9 January 2001), 3.

[7] See Phillips, pp. 247 and 615.

[8] Morrison, pp. 9-11.

[9] Phillips, 247.

[10] "Helene Grese." Bergen-Belsen Trial Documents at BergenBelsen.co.uk. http://www.bergenbelsen.co.uk/pages/Trial/Trial/TrialDefenceCase/Trial_036_Grese.html (1 August 2010).

[11] See Brown, *The Beautiful Beast*, p. 19.

[12] See Ibid, p. 26. Helene Grese, Irma's sister, provided much of this information at her sister's trial. See also "Helene Grese." Bergen-Belsen Trial Documents. Note also Edgar Lustgarten, *The Business of Murder* (New York: Charles Scribner's Sons, 1968), 86. See also Judge Walter B. Beals and United States Government, *The First German War Crimes Trial: Chief Judge Walter B. Beals' Desk Notebook of the Doctor's Trial, Held in Nuremberg, Germany, December, 1945 to August, 1947*, ed. W. Paul Burman, 2 vols. (Chapel Hill, NC: Documentary Publications, 1985), pp. 125 and 127, and refer also to my chapter, "Herta Oberheuser."

[13] Ibid., pp. 19-27, for an outline of Grese's life between 1939 and 1942. On p. 27, Brown did not decide on way or another in terms of whether or not Grese voluntarily went to work for the SS or was conscripted; instead, he argued, "her behavior in the camps is of greater consequence than how she arrived there."

[14] Lustgarten, 92.

[15] Brown, *The Beautiful Beast*, pp. 27-28, and p. 27, n. 124 and n. 126. Brown revealed here that Grese was conscripted, but not as an *Aufseherin*, but rather as a *Flakhelferin*, which was a female anti-aircraft auxiliary; Grese tried to train as a nurse again, but, as Brown stated, this failed and she had to fall back on any opportunity open to her. The *Aufseherin* positions were more appealing to her than the *Flakhelferin*, or, perhaps, as Brown further suggested, she had no other choice but the SS. See Ibid., pp. 28-29, and p. 29, n. 132.

[16] See Phillips, pp. 247 and 615.

[17] Ibid., pp. 248.

[18] Segev, 74.

[19] Brown, *The Beautiful Beast*, 38.

[20] Phillips, 248.

[21] Ibid., xli.

[22] Ibid., 253 and see also Brown, *The Beautiful Beast*, 41. On p. 56 of the same text, although Mandl supervised her, Brown mentions that Binz was "Grese's alleged mentor."

[23] Brown, *The Beautiful Beast*, pp. 39-41.

[24] Phillips, pp. 246 and 615. For more on Drechsel, see Brown, *The Beautiful Beast,* where Brown noted on p. 58, n. 243, about Margot Drechsel, *Oberaufseherin* and *Rapportführerin.* Drechsel's name was deconstructed by prisoners as "Dreschelke" as Brown illustrated. This twist on her name was used to describe guards for whom the prisoners could not remember their names. See specifically Ibid., p. 96, n. 375. Two stories existed at the time of this writing concerning her fate. One has her being hung by the Soviets, where yet another asserted that Dreschel escaped at the end of the war and was never held accountable for her crimes, which rivaled the other guards found throughout this study. See Ibid., p. 96.

[25] See Brown, *The Beautiful Beast,* p. 56 for the quote, and note also p. 61-63.

[26] Phillips., pp. 249 and 259. Refer to the whip testimony found on p. 259. The whip may or may not have also had beads attached to the ends. Survivor testimony varied on the exact kind of whips Grese used. See also "Irma and the Whip," *Newsweek,* (11 October 1945): 3e.

[27] Fyfe, 713.

[28] "Helene Grese." Bergen-Belsen Trial Documents.

[29] Phillips, pp. 255-256. Note that Brown pointed out that its important to note that at her trial, Grese did say that the man in the end accountable was Himmler; but that "I supposed I have as much guilt as all the others above me." See Brown, p. 84, and p. 85, n. 340.

[30] Brown, *The Beautiful Beast,* pp. 46-49.

[31] For a brief biographical description of Mengele, see Laqueur, p. 419.

[32] Fyfe, 747, for the testimony of Ilona Stein, and for more on Grese's willingness to beat people who tried to escape selection.

[33] Phillips, pp. 257-259. Brown argued, and I agree, after reviewing her testimony numerous times that it was indeed Grese's own testimony that helped prove her guilt. Her defense attempted to convey that survivor testimony was not entirely reliable in the sense it was not clear what they had actually witnessed; therefore it was implied hearsay, albeit eyewitness, testimony could not be relied upon. See Brown, *The Beautiful Beast,* pp. 80-85 for his excellent explanation of course proceedings and how Grese's own words harmed her.

[34] Ibid., 673, for the testimony of Klara Lebowitz.

[35] See Tillion, 70.

[36] When Grese was first employed as an *Aufseherin,* she was assigned to Dorothea (Theodora) Binz and numerous accounts portray Binz Grese's mentor.

[37] Phillips, 248.

[38] Refer to my chapter for more on the depravities of Binz.

[39] Brown, *The Beautiful Beast,* 39.

[40] Ibid., 41.

[41] See Fyfe, 747.

[42] Phillips, 673, for the testimony of Klara Lebowitz.

[43] Fyfe, 711.

[44] Phillips, 260.

[45] For more on Magda, reference Joy Erlichmann Miller, *Love Carried Me Home: Women Surviving Auschwitz* (Deerfield Beach, FL: Simcha Press, 2000), 139.

[46] Ibid.

[47] Ibid., pp. 36 and 106. Grese was also referred to as the "Belle of Auschwitz, Angel of Death, Blond Angel of Death, Blond Angel of Hell, or the Beastess of Belsen." See Cosner, pp. 62-23.

[48] Ibid., 36, "Nina."

[49] See Cosner, 62, for estimates on how many prisoners Irma Grese supervised at Auschwitz.

[50] Brown, *The Beautiful Beast,* 52.

[51] Ibid., 48.

[52] Smith, 323.

[53] Carol Rittner and John Roth. *Different Voices: Women and the Holocaust* (St. Paul, MN: Paragon House, 1998), p. 116.

[54] Ibid., p. 117.

[55] Phillips, pp. 255-256.

[56] Erlichmann Miller, 36.

[57] Fyfe, 746. For more on Lothe, refer to chapter in my book.

[58] Brown, *The Beautiful Beast*, 64.

[59] Erlichmann Miller, 106.

[60] Phillips, 661.

[61] Ibid., 660.

[62] Ibid., 248. See also Cosner, p. 63.

[63] See Ibid., xxiv.

[64] Brown, *The Beautiful Beast*, pp. 73-74.

[65] *One Survivor Remembers*. DVD, and n. 170.

[66] "Belsen Girl Blames all of SS," *Newsweek*, 7, no. 2 (6 October 1945), and "Woman Guard Accused Again" *New York Times*, 28 September 1945, 8 (L).

[67] Brown, *The Beautiful Beast*, 70.

[68] "Belsen Girl Guard Blames all of SS," *Newsweek*, 7, no. 2 (6 October 1945). Emphasizes mine.

[69] "Irma and the Whip," passim.

[70] Brown, *The Beautiful Beast*, p. 81.

[71] "Belsen Girl Guard blames all of SS," and "Irma and the Whip," passim.

[72] Phillips, 259.

[73] Ibid.

[74] Phillips, pp. 246 and 615.

[75] United Nations War Crimes Commission, *The Belsen Trial*, p. 114.

[76] Ibid.

[77] Ibid., p. 123.

[78] Jane Potter, "Women in War and Peace." *The Routledge History of Women in Europe since 1700*, edited by Deborah Simonton (London and New York: Routledge, 2007), p. 285.

[79] Brown, *The Beautiful Beast*, pp. 82-83.

[80] Ibid., 86. For more on Nazi songs, refer to Eberhard Frommann, *Die Lieder der NS- Zeit: Untersuchungen zur Nationalsozialistischen Liedpropanganda von den Anfängen is zum Zweiten Weltkrieg* (Köln: Papy Rossa, 1999).

[81] Fyfe, pp. 642-644.   For more on her last minutes, see Cosner, p. 63. See also Brown, *The Beautiful Beast*, p. 93.

[82] Ibid., p. 87.

CHAPTER XII

HILDEGARD LÄCHERT

Blutige Brigide: Bloody Bridgette

It will have blood they say, blood will have blood.[1]

Hildegard (Hilde) Lächert was born on 19 February 1920.[2] An illegitimate child, her father was a metal worker and her mother's profession remains unknown.[3] Her exact identity may be confused with other *Aufseherinnen* with similar last names.[4] She was believed to have spent time with the BDM, then in various Nazi women organizations. Lächert had an affair with a man employed by the Luftwaffe and then with a member of the SS. She first became pregnant at age eighteen and had two children from these relationships. It was believed that at   least one parent assisted with raising her children once she went to work as an *Aufseherin*.[5] Lächert found out about the position as an *Aufseherin*, most likely from an advertisement or through a friend. She applied in late 1941 or early 1942, and was hired.

Lächert was first sent to Ravensbrück. In 1942, she was transferred to Auschwitz. By 1943, she was on maternity leave. After her leave, her exact status was unclear, but by 1944, she would finally be sent to Majdanek, where she earned the nickname "Bloody Bridgette." Prisoners gave her this name because   she liked to whip prisoners across the face until blood was drawn. It would be at   the two latter camps where her most notorious crimes took place, and for which   she would be sentenced to two separate prison terms totaling twenty-seven   years.

Survivors related at her trials that Lächert was notorious for her cruelty. She conducted *Appell*, and would order "sport." She did so when she felt that prisoners were acting, according to her interpretation of how Nazi victims should act, "inappropriately" so that she could restore "order". She would beat prisoners with her fists, and also whipped them mercilessly until she saw blood. Like Bormann, Lächert also used her dog on prisoners as a special instrument of horror. Her dogs would attack anyone on her direct command. Prisoners recoiled in horror when Lächert would approach with her dog. As a mother, the idea that she could extend her cruelty to children seems to the normal mind impossible, yet she did.[6]

She was known to have thrown children into trucks, and was said to have assisted with selection, overseeing women being selected for either labor or death at all of the camps where she worked. *Aufseherinnen* such as Lächert routinely helped SS doctors with supervising female prisoners chosen for selection for either the gas chambers or to be used for labor. A word from the *Aufseherin* could influence the end result for the prisoners, which was life or death. It is not meant to imply that all *Aufseherinnen* exerted such influence, but numerous survivors testified that Lächert, who was especially known for her cruelty, was able to influence male SS, whether guards or doctors, in choosing prisoners for life or death. Indeed, many also testified that Lächert was directly responsible for killing dozens of people. This further asserts that these women "had extensive

scope for action despite the male-oriented hierarchy in concentration camps."[7]

Survivors, who referred to her as a sadist, commented on how Lächert had special hatred for Jewish children, and showed them no mercy. Jutta Scharf testified that it was almost impossible for her to comprehend how a woman close to her own age could be such a brutal perpetrator.[8] When describing her interpretation of Lächert, Janina Latowicz said that she had "animalistic bloodlust". Survivor Henryka Ostrowska also testified about Lächert's penchant for continuing beatings and whippings until blood flowed from her victims.[9]

Did the camp structure provide Lächert with a sense of control and autonomy denied to her in life outside of the camp structure? What was the incentive or primary factor for her cruelty? Quite possibly, since from such an early age her pregnancies and socioeconomic status offered her no way out of her life, it can be thus theorized that the camp structure gave her agency to express,   and extend onto innocent victims, her anger at how her own life was   unfolding.[10]

The Polish government at the Auschwitz trials (November to December 1947) tried her first. The prosecutor, when addressing the court concerning both Rudolf Höss (also tried at Auschwitz) and those who worked under him, asserted that the men and women who worked in the camp structure were "all essential   cogs in the Nazi killing machine; a machine that functioned smoothly   only because of their zeal, brutality, and total disregard for human life."[11] Lächert denied all charges against her and attempted to construct a defense that she was conscripted for duty; consequently her argument, however implied, centered on   the fact that she was forced to act the way that she did because of male authority who ordered her to do so. Her defense attorney also raised questions about Lächert's guilt and that she had been a victim of mistaken identity. Lächert was sentenced to fifteen years in prison.

She would be retried, and this time it would be for crimes committed while at Majdanek. At the third Majdanek trial (26 November 1975 to 30 June 1981), where she was tried alongside of Hermine Braunsteiner, she was accused   of being an accomplice to the murders of dozens of people and also for having taken part in selections. Witnesses for the prosecution cited that Lächert had taken part in selecting children for immediate death in the gas chamber. According to eyewitness testimony, this was a task that she apparently greatly enjoyed. This contradicts Lächert's own role as a mother. At first, one would think that a mother of two young children could not possibly want to kill any human beings, especially children. Nevertheless, survivors testified that Lächert saw any Jewish child as the enemy, and an enemy she fully believed that she was tasked with destroying, to her alleged immense delight. She would be found guilty of actively taking part in selections, and also for being a joint accessory to the murder of at least a hundred people. She was sentenced to twelve years in prison.[12] Despite whatever claim Lächert made that she was only following orders, it remains an undisputed fact that she killed; Daniel Patrick Brown found a quote from   a

German journalist concerning the Majdanek trials and Lächert's testimony: "after all, no one ever ordered her to turn her dog loose on pregnant women or to drown babies in latrines."[13] Lächert made a choice, as did the other *Aufseherinnen* who chose to kill, in that she exercised her own free will. Lächert died in 1995, having spent almost her entire adult life as a war criminal.

---

[1] Attributed to William Shakespeare.

[2] It was not clear where she was born. Some sources cite Berlin, others the country of Austria. See also Abraham J. Edelheit and Hershel Edelheit. *History of the Holocaust: A Handbook and Dictionary* (Boulder, CO: Westview Press, Inc., 1994), p. 198 and Ann Taylor Allen, "The Holocaust and the Modernization of Gender: A Historiographical Essay." *Zygmunt Bauman: Volume II, Part Three, The Holocaust*, edited by Peter Beilharz (London: Sage Publications, Ltd., 2002), p. 151.

[3] Michael Mann, *The Dark Side of Democracy: Explaining Ethnic Cleansing* (Cambridge: Cambridge University Press, 2005), p. 255. Mann discussed the lack of data to ascribe "motive" for the *Aufseherinnen*, but recent scholarship has sought to redress that omission.

[4] See Brown, *The Camp Women*, p. 163. Brown pointed out that a Hildegard "Lecher or Lächert is supposed to have murdered Jewish women in Bozen. After a Frau Lächert spent some time in custody in 1974, the file was officially closed due to Lächert's death in 1995." See p. 163. This woman may or may not have been the subject of this chapter; a "Bloody Bridgette" was known to have worked in Ravensbrück, Majdanek and Auschwitz.

[5] Mann, p. 255. Alexander V. Prusin also reminds us that the *Aufseherinnen* were neither Nazis nor SS, as they were "paid as contractors." See: Alexander V. Prusin, "Poland's Nuremberg: The Seven Court Cases of the Supreme National Tribunal, 1946-1948." *Holocaust and Genocide Studies* 24, no. 1 (spring 2010): p. 22, n. 28. See also Allen, p. 151. It can be assumed that the parent (s) took on raising the children once she was imprisoned, but no proof exists of this that has been made public.

[6] "Hildegard Lächert." *Lächert und ihre Aufgaben in Majdanek.* http://www.gymnasiumbethel.de/Schulleben/projekte/2ekge/majdanek/Portraets/ostrowska/laecher t_in_duesseldorf.htm

[7] Heike, "Female Concentration Camp Guards as Perpetrators," p. 139.

[8] "Hildegard Lächert." *Lächert und ihre Aufgaben in Majdanek.*

[9] Ibid.

[10] Allen, 151.

[11] Prusin, 11.

[12] "Third Majdanek Trials." Jewish Virtual Library http://www.jewishvirtuallibrary.org/jsource/Holocaust/WarCrime40.html (1 September 2010).

[13] Brown, *The Camp Women*, p. 11.

CHAPTER XIII

MARIA MANDL

Der Sadistisch Tier: The Sadistic Beast and Queen of the Realm of the Dead[1]

> You could see haughtiness and pride on the face of every SS woman. We were told everyday that we were nothing but numbers, that   we had to forget that we were human beings, that we had nobody to think   of us, that we would never return to our country, that we were slaves, and that we had only to work. We were not allowed to smile, to cry, or to pray. We   were not allowed to defend ourselves when beaten. [2]

Maria Mandl (Mandel) was born 10 January 1912 in Münzkirchen, Upper

Austria. She was one of the most notorious of all of the *Aufseherinnen*, yet has

remained a guard little studied. She joined the Nazi party at the age of twenty-six in

1938, the same year that she went to work for the concentration camp system.[3]

After working as an office clerk, she was believed, like many of the other women

who worked as SS contractors, to have responded to a recruitment poster for

Aufseherin. Described as "tall, blond, and impeccable" Mandl was a woman who

had a "fanatical admiration of beauty and love of music."[4] She was also "credited

with a special way of striking women, the first blow making the women's nose bleed"

as well as being able to shatter the jaw of a prisoner at whim.[5] In recollecting Mandl,

other survivors and eyewitnesses commented on her "wonderful golden blond" hair

as well as her "china-blue eyes."[6] Mandl's physical countenance resembled an

Aryan ideal, but as survivor Fania Fénelon noted: "her face without a trace of makeup

(forbidden by the SS), was luminous, her white teeth large but fine. She was perfect,

too perfect. A splendid example of the master race: top-quality breeding material so

what was she doing here instead of reproducing?"[7] Mandl did not marry nor did she

have children.[8] Instead, her work and the Nazis became her *de facto* family unit.

After leaving her office job, Mandl trained as an *Aufseherin* and was assigned to work with several other female guards at Lichtenburg concentration camp, a former castle. By May 1939, she was sent to Ravensbrück where she reported to *Oberaufseherinnen* Emma Zimmer and Johanna Langefeld. While she was at Ravensbrück, Irma Grese came to the attention of Mandl. Mandl encouraged Grese and also played a part in getting the young Grese promoted,   then transferred: Mandl "had been in charge of *Aufseherin* training when Grese completed her instruction."[9] Mandl had replaced Johanna Langefeld, Ravensbrück *Oberaufseherin*, for a period, and then by 1942, was sent to Auschwitz-Birkenau with Zimmer.[10]   At this camp Mandl had at least two lovers and kept a horse for her own personal pleasure sport.[11] Survivors have helped to construct a vivid portrait of this cruel woman whose barbarities equated her with any male counterpart.

Ravensbrück survivor Herbermann was a German Catholic woman whose status defined her as "Aryan." Herbermann resisted Nazism, was arrested, and sent to Ravensbrück. Herbermann was forced by the SS to work as a *Kapo*. Herbermann said that based on her firsthand encounters with Mandl, of whom she described as an "infamous demon," she felt that gender did not play a role in separating the guards in terms of cruelty. [12] Herbermann discussed Mandl in a   comparative   fashion,   especially   when   recalling   Ravensbrück   SS-*Obersturmbahnführer* Max Kögel, of whom she already referred to as "the most vulgar of inhumane monsters that one can possibly imagine."[13] She said of Mandl that "equal to him in this rank was the Overseer (later Chief Overseer) Mandl, a satanic female who naturally got along particularly well with the commandant."[14] Herbermann, who said that "it was characteristic that only the overseers who were the most brutal were quickly promoted," further related a specific account with Mandl.[15]

Herbermann, who supervised 397 prisoners at Ravensbrück, had allowed a small fire in her block for warmth. Kögel discovered this and reported her to Mandl. Mandl questioned Herbermann in a brutal manner, but Herbermann told

Mandl she had permission for a small fire. Many prisoners could not even fathom speaking back to a guard. Herbermann said she "dared to bring up all of this" and for her tenaciousness, Mandl sent her to detention in solitary confinement after giving her "two cracking smacks."[16] In relating this interaction with Mandl, Herbermann repeated her opinion about Mandl, placing Mandl once again in equal status to the male officer: "Chief Overseer (*Oberaufseherin*), who was quite equal [she was referring again to Kögel here] to the commandant in vulgarity and meanness."[17] Herbermann may not have realized she had done this, or, perhaps, her egalitarian analysis was intentional.

Nevertheless, this comparative biographical deconstruction illustrated that the prisoners themselves saw no gender dissimilarity in terms of how the guards and officers interacted with prisoners; perhaps, then, the reader should also not make any blatant distinctions along constructions of gendered agency when it comes to analysis of SS female contractors, volunteer or not. Mandl took part in many cruelties at the camps where she worked. In one example, she observed a camp prisoner doctor inspecting the vaginas of young women for "embryos and valuables, both of which meant death."[18] In one incident, Mandl commented on how pleased she was that one young girl subjected to the vaginal inspection was a virgin.[19] Her work also included selections.[20] She was personally responsible for numerous deaths, possibly as many as 500,000, and the vagaries in her personality make her an especially disturbing character study, especially as revealed by Richard Newman, music critic and historian, with his account of survivor Fania Fénelon. Fénelon, when recalling Mandl,

> related a tale of ringleted Polish toddler who arrived at the camp with his mother, destined for the gas. As Mandl strode through a crowd of women and children awaiting their turn in the "shower," the little boy ran up to her. Instead of kicking him away, she bent to pick him up, covered his face with kisses, and carried him off. For a week she took him wherever she went, giving him chocolates and dressing him in fresh blue outfits daily, the finest from the piles of confiscated children's clothing. Then, suddenly, the child was gone. Mandl had personally delivered him to the gas chamber, honoring her Nazi loyalties above any human feeling. The

> SS were trained in such "incorruptibility," the vaunted Nazi hardness, and learned to exercise extreme cruelty without mercy.[21]

Like this little boy, Mandl liked to have "pet Jews," who, in essence, she would treat as her toys, disposing of them at her own personal whim. She "adopted" other Jewish children for a short period, and then sent them to their death. Mandl possessed a contradictory nature. After a selection, or abusing someone, she would give another prisoner extra rations or demonstrate some form of kindness.

In one account, survivor Cordelia Edvardson related how a young girl approached Mandl, something no one dared to do lest they suffer Mandl's wrath. The girl told Mandl that she was hungry, and Mandl sent her to the supply office to get a can of food, which was unheard of in Auschwitz where countless innocents perished daily because of starvation.[22] Despite this random act of supposed altruism, Mandl was noted more for her barbarity and extreme cruelty. She also enjoyed setting her dogs on prisoners so that the inmates would run towards the electrified fences, killing them.[23] If any prisoner looked at her and she interpreted the glance as an insult, the prisoner would disappear. She would send people to their death for any reason, whether they were designated for selection or not. Death continually surrounded her.

Mandl's close work with Mengele led a survivor to construct a unique, and horrifying "twinned" description of the pair as "Mengele and Mandl, Mandl and Mengele, the blond camp commandant Maria Mandl in Auschwitz-Birkenau and the dark-haired Dr. Mengele, who carried out the selections. The King and Queen of the realm of the dead."[24] Mengele carried out horrific experiments on twins. The survivor constructed Mandl and Mengele as twins, albeit fraternal, but yet completely intertwined by a shared umbilical–like death cord. This interpretation of the two provided yet another account that further blurred, if not completely removed, gendered distinctions in terms of actions and accountability for appalling crimes against humanity and mass murder. Mandl's own personality shifts from 'evil queen' of Auschwitz to a shocking quasi-benevolent mother figure, however transitory and at her complete and total whim, further demonstrated the illogical, as well as the twisted psychology behind Mandl's logic as well as her day-to-day thought processes.[25] Deconstructing Mandl's passion for music and her devotion to the women's orchestra at Auschwitz provided continued analysis into her psyche.

Mandl loved classical music. During her term as *Oberaufseherin* at Auschwitz-Birkenau, she was able to indulge her passion. By 1942, there had been two men's orchestras, and in the spring of 1943, a women's orchestra was established. Mandl and Franz Hoessler, SS-*Obersturmführer*, began the women's orchestra at Auschwitz, where works by composers such as Mozart to Schubert were played.[26] Prisoner Zofia Czajkowska was its first conductor. Music would be played "at roll calls, to accompany official speeches, to welcome transports, and   at hangings."[27] The music calmed both the prisoners and the guards, albeit momentarily, as "even the particularly cruel Maria Mandl seemed to be a human being once again" but once the music stopped or the attention of the guard was brought elsewhere, the calm ended and the cruel behaviors once again emerged.[28] Playing for the orchestra for many prisoners could mean survival. Often other prisoners would bring to the attention of guards like Mandl other inmates who had musical talent in the hopes that their lives could be saved.[29]

Mandl played a key role in the women's orchestra, for which "there is no accurate record of the exact number of women in the orchestra at any given time."[30] Alma Rosé replaced Czajkowska in August of 1943. Rosé was a "violin virtuoso" and was "the niece of Gustav Mahler," the famed composer.[31] Rosé, who was born in Austria, had a successful career as a musician before being captured by the Gestapo in 1942. She was sent to Auschwitz in 1943, where she came to the attention of Mandl and Hoessler. Rosé's lineage, coupled with her talent, gave her a different status and, since the "SS treated Rosé with respect,   often referring to her as Frau Alma," she was able to use her status in the camp to save many lives, since "from the beginning, Rosé was the protégé of Hoessler and Mandl.[32] The women in the orchestra also dressed differently from the other prisoners. They were called "Mandl's Mascots" or "Mandl's Pets" and as

"Mandl's pets, the girls in the orchestra wore a special uniform for concerts: dark blue skirts, some pleated; white blouses; black stockings; and jackets of … prison material."[33] Women orchestra members were even allowed to keep their hair, since "Mandl wanted us to look pretty" a survivor related.[34] However, just because the SS as well as the female guards enjoyed the music, did not mean that prisoners received a respite from random acts of cruelty or selections. Guards would listen to the music as if they were attending a concert as an event, and then would immediately leave to select prisoners for the gas chambers or would engage in random acts of violence.[35] Despite doctor intervention, including even on the part of Mengele himself (for him to have personally reviewed her case spoke of Rosé's status), Rosé died on 4 April 1944, at 4:00 a.m.[36] Mandl, "who was deeply attached to Alma, mourned openly. The day Alma died, Mandl came to the Music Block and announced that the orchestra women could visit the Revier to bid farewell to their leader. The invitation was unprecedented at Birkenau."[37] Mandl's public display of grief at Rosé's death was very rare for any SS figure. Mandl moved on, and was later rewarded for her service to the Nazis.

During the spring of 1944, Mandl received a Military Cross of Merit Second Class for service to the Nazi state; for the female guards, this was indeed a high distinction.[38] In November 1944, she was sent to a subcamp of Dachau, Mühldorf. From there, in May 1945, she went on the run, and made it back to Münzkirchen. She was arrested on 10 May 1945 by American authorities. They turned her over to the Polish authorities the following year to be held for trial.[39] Mandl was tried as part of the Polish Supreme National Tribunal (Najwyzszy Trybunal Narodowy or NTN), where she was charged with war crimes and crimes against humanity; "indictments against them consisted of two general charges: that of membership in both a criminal organization [the SS] and in a crimination association [the concentration camp system], and more specifically, that of genocide with the tragedy of the European Jews" the center focus.[40]

The prosecution's case was facilitated by the testimony of Höss, and also survivors themselves. The prosecutorial team was able to make a case against the

SS and guards that demonstrated "regardless of whether they escorted the victims to the gas chambers, pushed them aside, or pulled the switch that injected gas into the airtight chamber, they all were essential cogs in the Nazi killing machine."[41] Therefore, Mandl was equally culpable in her guilt and no allowances were made for gender. Under examination, Mandl denied that she had guilt for any deaths; instead, she argued, "she had treated prisoners fairly and had beaten only those who had violated 'discipline'."[42] This came from the woman who was believed to have signed off on orders sending 500,000 people to their deaths in the gas chambers.

Her defense team denied any charges against her that led to any accusation of murder, and, while "her attorney acknowledged her official position" he "challenged the accusation that she had taken part in selections."[43] The challenge   to charges against her concerning selections centered on the fact that only SS doctors carried these out. Further, he argued that Mandl, like "a number of guards, the   defense stressed that their clients were 'simple individuals of limited intelligence ... who blindly and obediently carried out superior orders'."[44] The defense that Mandl was somehow simple and only carried out commands given to her belies eyewitness testimony, as well as statements given by the American armed service personnel who, when interrogating her, found her to be of high intelligence.[45] Mandl, like the majority of her male co-defendants, was found guilty of "membership in criminal associations and groups and of shared intent to commit mass murder" and sentenced to death.[46] Mandl was given a sentence of death by hanging and was executed on 18 January 1948.[47]

---

[1] The term comes from p. 64 in survivor Cordelia Edvardson's *Burned Child Seeks the Fire: A Memoir* (Boston: Beacon Press, 1997).

[2] Vivien Spitz, *Doctors from Hell: The Horrific Accounts of Nazi Experiments on Humans* (Boulder, CO: Sentient Publications, 2005), p. 147.

[3] Prusin, p. 12.

[4] Richard Newman and Karen Kirtley, *Alma Rosé: Vienna to Auschwitz* (Portland: Amadeus Press, 2000), p. 326.

[5] Ibid. Newman and Kirtley complied an outstanding biographical portrait of Mandl in chapter 17 titled "Mandl's Mascots," providing one of the first and most accurate accountings of Mandl. Newman and Kirtley also note that Mandl's birthplace was not too far from Hitler's. See p. 226.

[6] Fania Fénelon and Marcelle Routier, *Playing for Time* (Syracuse: Syracuse University Press, 1997), p. 30. Note that Gabriele Knapp said that when she reviewed Fénelon memoir along with the recollections of other orchestra survivors, that Fénelon's "memory, as it was with many concentration camp survivors, applied specific forms of self-censorship and selective recall. Fénelon's co-author turned her memories into a semi-autobiographical novel. The other musicians believe that Fénelon's rendition of what happened in the women's orchestra, namely their daily struggle to stay alive, was, among other things, not authentically told." See Gabriele Knapp, "Music as a Means of Survival: The Women's Orchestra in Auschwitz." *Feministische Studien* trans. Katherine Deeg, Anette Bauer, and Liana Curtis. vol. 1 (1996): p. 26, n. 1.

[7] Ibid.

[8] Newman and Kirtley discuss how Mandl loved children but was especially "cruel toward newborn babies and their mothers." See Newman, p. 226.

[9] Brown, *The Beautiful Beast*, p. 56, n. 234.

[10] See Brown, *The Camp Women*, pp. 17, 173 for mentions of Mandl, and also note p. 16 for discussion on recruitment efforts at Ravensbrück. See p. 17 for reference on how Grese thwarted Mandl's authority concerning limitations on the use of turpentine to clean uniforms. See also Brown, *The Beautiful Beast*, p. 38, n. 168 for more on the turpentine story. Refer to Herbermann, p. 141, n. 2 and also p. 195. Also note Morrison, passim. See Heike, "Female Concentration Camp Guards as Perpetrators," p. 124 for discussion on Lichtenburg, and then pp. 126-132 for a biographical portrait of Langefeld. After Langefeld left the second time, Binz replaced her. For a brief mention of Zimmer, who was fired in 1943, for reasons Heike asserted was either because of her age or her alcoholism, see Herbermann, p. 195, and 195, n. 1. See also Heike, " ... *da es sich ja lediglich um die Bewachung der Häftlinge handelt ...*" *Frauen in Konzentrationlagern Bergen-Belsen, Ravensbrück* edited by Claus Füllberg-Stolberg, et al (Bremen: Edition Temmen, 1994), pp. 221-240.

[11] Newman, p. 326.

[12] Herbermann, p. 195.

[13] Ibid., pp. 140-141.

[14] Ibid., p. 141.

[15] Ibid.

[16] Ibid., p. 142.

[17] Ibid., p. 141.

[18] Edvardson, p. 68.

[19] Ibid.

[20] Spitz, pp. 124-125, for the testimony of survivor Vladislava Karolewska, who related that she was told by Mandl that she was not going to be sent to labor detail; instead, Karolewska stated she was selected for experimentation by the SS doctors.

[21] Newman, pp. 326-327. Newman related other accounts about Mandl that noted her kindnesses towards one survivor, which he indicated were indicative of "the deep split in the Nazi personality." He referred to the story of Zippy, a prisoner who was on the receiving end of Mandl's kindness when she became ill with period pains. Mandl showed her kindness by letting her rest until the pains subsided; in contradiction to the typical guard response, such as seen with Juana Bormann, who used her dog to maul a menstruating prisoner. See the chapter on Bormann in my book.

[22] Edvardson, p. 72.

[23] Ibid., p. 73.

[24] Ibid., p. 64.

[25] "SS Female Overseers in Auschwitz." DEGOB: National Committee for Attending Deportees. http://degob.org/index.php?showarticle=2018 (20 October 2010).

[26] Knapp, "Music as a Means of Survival," p. 28. Knapp detailed the composers and pieces, which were "over 200 pieces typical of the contemporary tastes of the time." See Ibid., p. 29.

[27] "Female Nazi War Criminals." http://www.capitalpunishmentuk.org/nazigirls.html (3 November 2010).

[28] Brown, *The Beautiful Beast*, p. 58.

[29] Stephen Moss, "Memories of Auschwitz." *The Guardian*. (13 January 2005).

[30] Knapp, "Music as a Means of Survival," p. 27.

[31] Ibid., p. 28.

[32] Ibid., p. 29. Knapp revealed how the women had a different barrack. See also Newman, pp. 250-251.

[33] Newman, p. 251.

[34] Ibid. Newman related how Rosé was able to negotiate, with Mandl, everything from a chance to take a nap, to extra margarine, or parcels that could contain food or other items. See Ibid., pp. 260-261.

[35] Ibid., p. 266.

[36] Ibid., p. 302; note also pp. 299-301.

[37] Ibid., p. 302. The funeral and autopsy were also unprecedented for a prisoner. Some survivors maintain that the SS brought flowers and wreaths while others dispute such accounts. Subsequent treatment and disposal of Rosé's body were not entirely ascertained. See Ibid., p. 303-324. What was certain was that Mandl did indeed mourn for Rosé.

[38] Prusin, p. 12.

[39] See "Maria Mandl." *The Jewish Virtual Library*. http://www.jewishvirtuallibrary.org/jsource/biography/mMandl.html (31 October 2010), passim. See also Ulrich Herbert, Karin Orth, and Christoph Dieckmann, *Die Nationalsozialistischen Konzentrationslager: Entwicklung und Struktur* (German Edition) (Göttingen: Wallstein, 1998), p. 816. See also pp. 806 and 819, as well as passim for more on *Aufseherinnen*.

[40] See Prusin, p. 10 for the quote and for NTN background, especially pp. 1-2, as well as passim.

[41] Ibid., p. 11.

[42] Ibid., p. 13.

[43] Ibid., p. 14.

[44] Ibid.

[45] See "Maria Mandl." *The Jewish Virtual Library*. She was also reported to   be "dedicated to her work." Footage of Mandl can be seen (silent) at: *March of Time* (outtakes) Krakow scenes; War Crimes Trial: "Butchers of Auschwitz." Story RG-60.0983, Tape 917. Steven Spielberg Film and Video Archive at USHMM. http://resources.ushmm.org/film/display/main.php?search=simple&dquery=Auschwitz&cache_file =uia_qcezwC&total_recs=123&page_len=25&page=1&rec=5&file_num=1467   (1   November 2010).

[46] Prusin, p. 15.

[47] Note that there are varying accounts of her execution date. Brown, in *The Camp Women*, p. 173, gave 2 December 1947 as her execution date, when other sources state the January 1948 date as the more accurate. See also Prusin, p. 15. See www.yadvashem.org for "The Auschwitz Trials: Historical Focus" by Naama Shik, who asserted Mandl was the first to be hung.

PART III: *ANDERE FRAUEN* (OTHER WOMEN): *EINE FRAU, EINE KAPO, UND EINE ÄRZTIN* (A WOMAN, A BLOCK COMMANDER, A DOCTOR)

CHAPTER XIV

ILSE KOCH

Eine Gnädige Frau, The Gracious Lady and Mistress of Buchenwald

[Ernst] Blanck testified that Ilse Koch said to her husband concerning an inmate: "Karl, that dirty Jew just looked at me." Colonel Koch beat the inmate severely. [Kurt] Leeser worked in the pathological laboratory and testified that a fellow inmate, one Josef Collinette, had been killed for his tattoo. He first saw the skin on Collinette alive and next saw it detached in the laboratory. He saw a lampshade of human skin in the laboratory. A deposition by [Ignatz] Wegerer was admitted into evidence. He deposed that Ilse Koch kicked an inmate into a ditch, and kicked him repeatedly. He further deposed that he worked in the pathological ward, and that a lampshade was made for Ilse Koch while he was there, as well as a pocketknife case and cases for manicure instruments.[1]

It was April 11, 1945, when 19-year-old American soldier Abner Ganet stepped inside the barracks guardroom of Buchenwald. The concentration camp was eerily silent. His eyes were drawn to several lamps with delicate shades, painted with beautiful butterflies and birds. Ganet moved closer to the lamps, drawn by the contrast between their beauty and the grim surroundings. Then Ganet and his three battle- seasoned comrades ran outside to vomit. The lampshades were made of stretched human skin. His 1st Infantry Division rousted four Nazi women hiding in another building. A pretty blond woman said the lamps were   hers, showing no remorse or shame. "I took my .45 out, and I cocked the pistol and I was going to shoot her," Ganet said. "My company commander said, 'You can't do this. If you do, you're as bad as she is.'" He lowered the gun from her head. Two weeks later, the woman was tried and hanged, Ganet said.[2]

Margarete Ilse Köhler was born in Dresden on 22 September 1906. Besides her parents, Ilse, as she was more "affectionately" known, had two brothers, and grew up in a lower-middle class environment.   Her father, a factory foreman, was a social democrat, but her family was not overtly political.[3] She finished secondary school, trained in accounting, and then worked as a secretary for several companies.[4] As she was quite good-looking, with reddish blond hair and large, expressive eyes, men were attracted to her; she would never be short of male company even during her marriage. She once dated a man named Fritz Schaeffer, but with whom she broke up when she met her future husband, a man with, in Ilse's mind, better prospects.[5]

By 1932, she was involved with the Nazi party and desired to become a member in order to bring her closer to Hitler and Nazi associates. She applied for party membership on 1 April 1932, and was accepted a mere month later on 1 May. Her father was known to have commented to her that it was good that she was involved with the rising Nazi power structure, as he felt "you must be part of the time that you are alive in."[6] It remains doubtful that patriarchal approval would have lent itself to supporting the monster that she later became once she was ensconced in the camp structure.

By 1934, she had become involved with the National Socialist party and worked at Sachenhausen camp as a secretary. This was where it was believed she had come to the attention of SS-Officer Karl Otto Koch, who was nine years older than her.[7] Koch, who was born on 2 August 1897, was the son of a local government bureaucrat, fought in World War One and was awarded an Iron Cross second class. He was an avowed anti-Semite and anti-Communist, and before he became a member of the SS in 1931, was a hooligan and known embezzler, a crime for which he was arrested, and spent some time in jail. He joined the Nazi party, and Koch quickly established himself as a devoted member of the party. He received a number of posts, each escalating in authority. Koch trained at Dachau and was believed to have first reported to Theodor Eicke, the commander of the *Totenkopfverbände* (SS Death Head Special Units) and the head inspector of the camps.[8]

Koch considered Eicke his personal mentor, and certainly through Eicke Koch was able to nurture relationships all the way up to Himmler; most of these relationships proven to be quite fiscally beneficial. He worked at Columbia House, and then Sachenhausen. At Columbia House, where he reported to Eicke, he was taught extreme torture methods. Koch would also order prisoners to bark at him like dogs just for amusement. He engaged in numerous brutalities, and would jump at any chance to degrade prisoners. He was involved with the SA overthrow in early 1934, and may have also been involved with the death of Ernst Röhm. Koch was known to have taken part in, or at least have overseen, a particular hideous event. He ordered prisoners to dig holes where they were then told to stand in, with only their heads sticking out. These men were partially buried alive as trucks were then run over their heads, in a grotesque obstacle course.[9]

Koch also was trained in, and took part in, beatings on the "little horse." The "little horse" or the whipping horse was very similar to a gymnasium bench. Prisoners were bent over, face forward, over the bench where then whippings and beatings across the lower back and buttocks would occur. These beatings were also referred to as the "kidney" beatings. After she met Koch, Ilse attended some of these beatings and was said to have "showed considerable satisfaction" at the punishments.[10] Eicke wanted men like Koch to serve as guards because he felt that men like him who could show no sympathy towards the "enemy" prisoners were necessary.[11]

Eicke viewed Koch as someone worthy of promotion, and Koch was reliant on Eicke for his rather rapid, upward mobility in the SS structure. Eicke had coordinated, with Hitler's direct knowledge, for a new camp near Weimar. This camp was very near where Johann Wolfgang von Goethe lived, and right next to his favorite oak tree (the famed Goethe *eiche* where the author spent much time under). It was called Buchenwald, or German for birch wood. At the entry of Buchenwald, Eicke, who was influential in the design of the camp, had a sign constructed that read *Jedem das Seine* (to each his own). Eicke would also promote Koch to head the new camp after Jacob Weiseborn, who lasted a few months as *Kommandant*, was removed and sent to another camp, Flossenbürg.[12]

In 1937, Koch was appointed Camp Commandant at the Buchenwald concentration camp.[13] He would run the camp from 1937 until 1941, when he was removed from his post in late 1941 or early 1942, when he was then transferred to Majdanek.[14] Ilse played a key role in her husband's career as camp *Kommandant*, and, once married, she used her position as his wife to pursue her own cruel, atrocious goals.

Associates of the couple felt that Ilse had pursued Koch relentlessly and assumptions can also be drawn from the fact that it was Koch's personal and professional connections that lent to his attractiveness. Ilse used Koch's connections for her own advancement, and encouraged a committed relationship, understanding fully well that as a wife of a major SS officer, she could alter her own status and agency *vis-à-vis* the marriage. After a three-year courtship, the Kochs planned to be married and applied for permission. After receiving permission (all SS marriages had to be approved, as it was not only an SS rule, but all marriages in Germany at that point had to receive government permission), on 25 May 1937, they married in a SS-marriage ceremony at Sachenhausen concentration camp. The couple moved into the Villa Koch, a palatial manor home built on the grounds of Buchenwald. From 1938 to 1940, the couple had two children in quick succession, Artwin and Gisela who were all born at Buchenwald. Koch's son from a previous relationship, Manfred, also lived with the Kochs until he was sent away to boarding school. Koch loved the boy and doted on him, but Ilse intensely disliked Manfred. She favored her children with Koch over him and was believed to have pushed her husband into sending his son away.[15] Koch, who was not viewed as a domicile family man once Manfred was sent away and once he was married to Ilse, pursued his own career and his own personal wants knew no boundaries. He engaged in numerous affairs and may have caught a sexually transmitted disease as a result.[16]

Koch, a brutal sadist, was extremely corrupt, and certainly influenced his wife to engage in the same type of behaviors. He was also cruel and violent. It was at this camp where "inmates were used in pseudo-scientific experiments in which they were injected with infectious diseases or equally deadly vaccines."[17] He not only used the inmates at Buchenwald as an end to his own selfish means, he also stole from the Nazis by selling various items for personal profit. He loved to flaunt his status and wealth, as did Ilse. They had a zoo built adjacent to the camp and promoted the idea that Buchenwald was a great place to raise their   young family. Ilse was certainly closely involved in her husband's command of   the camp, witnessing and even encouraging abuse of prisoners. Moreover, Ilse   had a vested interest in maintaining pseudo-directive of the camp as she profited handsomely from ongoing embezzlement of camp riches   herself.[18]

Ilse, who spent thousands on clothing, furs, and jewels, was given a Mercedes with a chauffeur. She had numerous photographs of herself and took great pride in material possessions made possible by ill-gotten gains from the camp. The couple loved to entertain, and their family photograph albums reflect this. Their home was elaborately decorated, and they moved amongst the upper societal classes nearby Buchenwald. She loved to stay up late drinking, and would sleep in, preferring her servants and nanny to take care of the children. Evidence would later emerge that she took cognac with her coffee, and had problems with alcohol that would increase as the day went on. Her afternoons were spent shopping, horseback riding, or having tea with titled ladies and society women. Witnesses at her trials would testify that in addition to leading a glamorous public life, within the camp structure her life was different, and it was she who allowed this reconstruction of her "wifely" role. Ilse also took pride in assisting her husband with running Buchenwald, and often watched when roll calls took place,   or when sport was issued. She seemed to glorify in the more sadistic aspects of sport, and was believed to have reported prisoners for any perceived infraction of camp rules. She would deny all charges made against her and always insisted she was just a woman in charge of her family, nothing less, and nothing more, despite

numerous accounts that contradicted her.[19]

For the next several years, the Kochs ran Buchenwald, although again, repeatedly at her trials Ilse would maintain that she was just a wife and mother, and insisted she had had no actual part in the management of the camps. Evidence to the contrary emerged from actual Nazi records, which referred to her possibly being an *Aufseherin* first at Ravensbrück. It was at Buchenwald, where she allegedly held the title *Oberaufseherin*.[20] Ilse employed several prisoners at the Villa Koch; their duties included taking care of the Koch children to bringing the mistress coffee in bed and taking caring of the family dog.[21] Throughout her stay at Buchenwald, several inmates referred to her as the *Kommandeuse*, or Mrs. Commandant.

Witnesses would claim "Ilse Koch and her husband sort of ruled together" lending itself to the theory that Ilse herself altered her agency as a SS wife, quite outside the normative behavioral construction of SS wives; critical, however, remains the fact that she was allowed to do so, which further suggests Koch permitted his wife to reinterpret her role, with the two emerging more of a corrupt partnership rather than a typical SS male/female married relationship of the time.[22]

Ilse was known as the bitch of Buchenwald, or *die Hexe von Buchenwald* (witch of Buchenwald).[23] However, Kurt Dietz, survivor and former valet for Karl Otto Koch, related that she preferred that all prisoners address her as *gnädige Frau* (the gracious lady).[24] The gracious lady, known for receiving expensive gifts from her husband's friends, spent her days riding horses in a specially built riding hall. Ilse, who kept an immaculate home, thanks to the endless supply of servants at her disposal at Buchenwald, amassed an incredible collection of both contraband food and expensive wines. It was these same servants who lived in fear of her wrath.

Since Ilse had problems maintaining such a large household, Karl Koch's stepsister, Erna Raible, moved in with the Kochs to help take care of the children.[25] Even with extra help, Ilse took full advantage of her status as the wife of the camp commandant. She constantly demanded special treatment from her servants, allegedly liked to take baths in costly wine, and was suspected of having several affairs.[26] Dr. Waldemar Hoven and Hermann Florstedt, both members of the SS, were supposed lovers of Ilse, according to Kurt Dietz, who knew both Kochs.[27] She was seen as a woman who glorified in her position, and who flaunted her sexuality.

Certainly, construction of her identity was viewed as barbaric and "unnatural" by those who hated her, and especially by the courts that would try   her. How did her behavior differ from male SS? Were depictions of her character exaggerated because of her gender? Whatever constructions of Ilse emerged while she was at Buchenwald and up until her death, the image of a woman with such power and influence, even if constrained within the boundaries of the camp structure, crossed gender barriers of identity and ruled her "unnatural", lending to hyper-sexualization of her character.[28] Her abuses cannot be entirely disputed, as too many eyewitness testimonies exist. Moreover, her savage cruelty knew no boundaries.

She also would order her dog to attack on command if she viewed anyone as a "threat" to her. If laundry was not done properly, or if someone spoke to her out of turn, these people would be executed. Anyone who looked at her askance would meet the same fate. She once threw a prisoner's hat away from him, knowing that whatever move he made he would be shot, and witnesses testified   she took great pleasure in events such as these, laughing at prisoners. Ilse was a rabid anti-Semite, and called Jews "swine" and had absolute derision for anyone not fitting the Nazi "ideal." [29]

Several survivors from Buchenwald related that Ilse, who allegedly took several SS men, including SS doctors such as Buchenwald physician Waldemar Hoven as her lovers, enjoyed flaunting her sexuality and used her attractiveness as a weapon of abuse. Without provocation, she would not only abuse prisoners verbally, she also purposely wore provocative clothing in order to provoke and taunt prisoners. Ilse enjoyed lying down in the gardens of Buchenwald, wearing sheer clothing meant to entice male prisoners.[30] She would report any male prisoner for simply just glancing at her. In one instance, she intentionally wore a short dress and walked by a group of male prisoners. When she caught a male prisoner briefly looking up her dress, she beat him in the face with her riding crop.[31] On one occasion, she caught a group of hungry male prisoners picking fruit and the horrific whippings they received at her behest were quite severe for their crime.[32] Her crimes increased and she was believed to have engaged in embezzling from the camp for her own profit. Her husband's crimes began to mount as well, and they included ordering murders of camp personnel, to "hiring out camp laborers to civilian employers, racketeering in food supplies and, in general, running the camp for his own personal profit."[33]

Rumors about activities at Buchenwald began to raise suspicion about Koch's corruption, but the case came to almost nothing early in 1941, since the first "investigation had failed to bring conviction when a parade of witnesses categorically supported Koch's plea of innocence."[34] Accounts continued to emerge about the couple, and after Koch's execution, focused on Ilse's own abuses of prisoners. Eyewitnesses would later state the rumors as fact. Witnesses at Ilse's trials stated that they knew firsthand that there "were two lamp shades in the lounge of the accused, said to have been made of human skin. One appeared to have tattoos on it. The accused had a photo album, a briefcase, book covers, and a pair of gloves made from tattooed skin."[35] However, the skins, documentation and preservation of the same may not have been Ilse's undertakings.

SS doctor Erich Wagner wrote his dissertation, *Ein Beitrag zur Tätowierungsfrage* about tattoos and criminality. He complied albums of photos of prisoner's tattoos, and it was believed that Ilse took a special interest in his work; this may have been nothing other than she was having an affair with him and feigned an interest in his theories. Prosecutorial witnesses at her trial stated that Ilse was so obsessed with Wagner's work that she had asked her husband to kill the prisoners of whom Wagner had photographed, but Nazi officials vehemently denied that she had had anything to do with this or the skinning of anyone for such purpose.[36] Heads of prisoners were also shrunk and kept as trophies; it was alleged that Ilse kept a shrunken head as a memento as a grotesque paperweight in her home, which she would deny vehemently. However, accounts of her coveting skin and having men killed for tattoo trophies did not   abate.

Another survivor gruesomely related, "Frau Koch had a lady's handbag made out of the same material [human skin]. She was just as proud of it as a South Sea island women would have been about her cannibal trophies."[37] Koch seemingly did not interfere with his wife and her interactions with the prisoners,   no matter what boundaries her assignations crossed. Moreover, once he left Buchenwald, Ilse may have felt that she was free to carry on her affairs with whomever she wished.[38]

Her husband, however, provided her with the agency that she needed to extend her own power at Buchenwald, and certainly it was under his authority that led her to being appointed *Oberaufseherin* at Buchenwald.[39] She oversaw the arrival of prostitutes from Ravensbrück to work at the Buchenwald camp brothel, and also supervised twenty-two *Aufseherinnen* who guarded the hundreds   of   female prisoners. Ilse was viewed as a cruel, sadistic woman whose violence knew no boundaries. By 1941, Koch's dealings with inmates and fellow SS, along with his involvement in everything from alcohol trafficking, extraordinary gifts for his wife, illegal food sales, and embezzlement of property confiscated from prisoners, created deeper suspicion from his Nazi superiors. His misappropriation of material goods against the Nazi government would eventually lead to his downfall. Complaints about Koch and his viciousness also began to be too many to ignore, as had been done in the past, sometimes with direct orders   from Himmler.[40]

Koch's brutality in handling prisoners while he was stationed at Buchenwald was so infamous that when transferred to another camp near Lublin, Poland, known as Majdanek, Himmler would refer to the camp as Koch-Lublin.[41] Although, early on in Koch's career, Eicke may have been the intermediary and protected him from his enemies; with Eicke gone to the eastern front and Koch's illegal activities seemingly increasing unabated, it was inevitable that he would   get caught and found guilty. Koch was already under investigation for some time, as was his wife, under direct orders from the top Nazi command. After Karl's transfer, Ilse stayed behind and another investigation into the Kochs commenced. Both were under investigatory arrest. Ilse stayed at the Villa Koch until the summer of 1943, when she moved to Ludwigsburg with her children.[42]

By 1943, the SD's financial offices ordered the case against Koch (which was first brought about a few years prior) reopened. The man appointed to look into Koch's machinations was Konrad Morgen. Morgen was a lawyer who began investigating Koch for criminality, and who would be the undoing of the Kochs. Koch was being investigated for a number of crimes, including ordering the murder of camp doctor and a hospital attendant who had taken care of him for a sexually transmitted disease. By 1943, Koch had made so many enemies no one could protect him. His former mentor, Eicke, was killed in February 1943 when his plane was shot down at the eastern front. Koch's crimes were numerous, and his biggest mistake was his ongoing lying and stealing from the SS. Morgen found evidence that Koch had "embezzled 100,000 marks" and also found "proof of murder."[43] Morgen tried to report his findings of Koch's numerous crimes, but found supervisors reluctant to pursue prosecution against a chief SS officer and camp commandant.

Finally, Morgen was able to somehow get a telegram to Himmler, who gave Morgen what he was looking for: permission to prosecute both Koch and Ilse.[44] Koch would be arrested by the Gestapo and tried for embezzlement, forgery, and noncompliance with Himmler's policies. The Nazi court found Ilse Koch not guilty, but her husband was sentenced to death twice. Koch had, in his long career as an SS man, stolen from the Nazis. Koch's many crimes against the Nazis included his embezzlement of camp goods. For example, instead of turning over property looted from prisoners, he had used the goods for his own personal profit, including gold from the teeth of prisoners. He had also ordered the murder of two German medical personnel who had treated him for a sexual disease. Koch was sentenced to death and was shot by the SS on 5 April 1945 days before Buchenwald was liberated. Appropriately, his body was burned in the crematoria at Buchenwald.[45] After her husband was executed for crimes against the Nazi régime, Ilse moved her children into a hotel. She then went to Erna's home with her children, where she complained about her husband and how she failed to escape with a gold chess set.[46] While staying with Erna at Ludwigsburg, she met many American soldiers and perhaps she felt herself free from   arrest.

Unbeknownst to her, she had already been under investigation: "In February 1945, just a few months before the liberation of Buchenwald concentration camp, American Intelligence issued a confidential report on the crimes of Ilse."[47] Initially, Ilse had no idea about the American investigation. Deluded by her own perception of her sexual attractiveness, her ego did not accept that she could ever again be linked with the crimes of her husband, especially by the Americans who seemed to pay her so much attention. Was this because the SS had found her innocent once before of crimes in Buchenwald and she felt that she could not be held culpable by anyone else, especially the Americans? She did not escape closer scrutiny, however. A Buchenwald prisoner

had recognized her and led to even closer scrutiny by American officials. One American soldier asked her if she had been at Buchenwald, which she denied, but the soldier did not desist and asked her eldest son some questions. Ongoing enquiries and a raid on her home led to the discovery of her photograph albums and other evidence, including her Nazi party membership card, all of which led to

her eventual arrest.[48]

On 30 June 1945, she was accused of war crimes, by the American military courts in Dachau. Ilse later went on trial for war crimes and   mass   atrocities committed at Buchenwald before an American military commission. She would be the only female defendant at the trial, which was known as the "Dachau Court Trial."[49] During her incarceration, she became pregnant, and her advanced state of pregnancy during her trial remained a source for conjecture as   to who the father may be. She had been guarded by several different American soldiers, and was kept in isolation. Josef Kirschbaum was an interrogator who had direct access to Ilse, as had a few other men. However, it remains unknown who had sexual relations with her while she was kept in confinement. A story about a former lover digging a tunnel to get to her to engage in sexual relations has been unproven and seems quite unlikely, given how closely the prisoners were guarded. Could she have been raped or was it consensual? Ilse herself refused to reveal who she had sex with or how she became pregnant. In April 1947, exactly two years after Buchenwald was liberated, she was sentenced to life in prison.[50]   On 29 October 1947, she gave birth to her fourth and last child, Uwe, who was given her maiden surname, and was immediately taken away from her.[51] Was Ilse really guilty of all of the crimes that she had been charged with and found guilty of?

Ilse's own defense was that she was completely innocent, nor did any camps ever employ her; she merely happened to be married to a camp commander who was an important figure in the SS hierarchy. Ilse's actual role at Buchenwald, she would argue, was sometimes confused with that of an *Aufseherin*.   Although she was referred to as a witch and a bitch, she stated that was never an *Aufseherin*, nor was she ever in a position of actual authority. Her only role, her defense argued, was that of an SS-*Frau*, or wife of an SS officer, which allowed her some measure of power, and perhaps allowed her to indulge any cruel or sadistic desires she may have had. However, one witness testified that in 1941, "he [Buchenwald *Kommandant* Koch] issued an order to the effect that orders by her were to be

obeyed to the same extent as if he had given them.[52] At her first trial, the court

found that although she had not been employed by any Nazi organization, "whatever

she did in connection with the camp and its inmates she did as a volunteer."[53] Hence,

the

> military authorities saw fit to charge her with the greater crime of being a principal in the operation of the Buchenwald concentration camp. The prosecutor presented ample evidence to prove that charge. It is agreed by everyone concerned that the charge was proved.[54]

Morgen, the same SS lawyer who led an investigation into the Kochs, was

threatened by an American prosecutorial team to testify that Ilse had indeed taken part in skinning and using skins for personal objects. Morgen refused. He stated repeatedly that she was simply not guilty of the skin charges. He did tell the American administrators interrogating him that Ilse was a criminal, but he had proven himself that she was not responsible for the skins or for any objects made out of skins. The Americans said they would give him over to the Russians and then when this warning did not work, allegedly beat him continuously; the thrashings also failed to convince Morgen to state otherwise about Ilse. Morgen persevered, and the Americans relented.[55]

There were numerous questions surrounding witness testimony and "misstatements and misapprehensions," which led American judicial authorities to inquire about her trial and whether or not she had received fair treatment. Subsequently, there was an investigation ordered by General Lucius Clay, Military Governor of Germany, into Ilse's trial.[56] This inquiry was led by one Homer Ferguson of Michigan, and it took place from June to November 1947.[57] While findings from both her trial and investigation attempted to show that she

was guilty of war crimes, there was doubt over the severity of her guilt. Other members of the court failed to see that she was guilty of any crimes at all, deciding instead that she was innocent.

The trial hearings state, "in spite of the fact that the customary rules of evidence are relaxed in war crimes trials, the evidence for and against the Ilse Koch adduced at the Buchenwald trial was in large measure direct eyewitness testimony." However, there was no direct physical evidence, although examples of shrunken heads and flaps of skin were found in the pathology laboratory,

linking Ilse, "apparently a most bestial woman" to any war crimes.[58] Ilse's complicity was based on direct witness testimony, which was enough to find her guilty of war crimes, even if hearsay evidence was disregarded. According to SS investigators Konrad Morgen and Heinrich Nett, no skins, or products made from skins were found at her home, despite contradictory accounts from survivors.[59]

Due to ongoing controversy surrounding evidence presented at her trial, members of the investigation team continued to question whether her crimes deserved a life sentence.[60] The Judge Advocate of the European Command, Colonel Harbaugh, argued that, based on the evidence presented, life in prison was not a justifiable sentence in Ilse's case; while Harbaugh was convinced that Ilse was guilty of crimes against humanity, he "did not believe she was responsible for the deaths of any of the inmates."[61]

Although Ilse had admitted to beating one, and only one, inmate at Buchenwald, she denied all involvement with the day-to-day operations of the camps. Members of the investigation team also found that the evidence presented at her trial was "legally insufficient to prove Frau Koch's participation in the operation of the concentration camp."[62] Instead, she reminded the court repeatedly that she was just a wife and mother. The investigation decided that her testimony alone justified a review of the case since there was no direct evidence, other than witness testimony, to prove her guilt. Ilse was originally sentenced to life in prison.[63] Arguments came almost immediately that she might not have received a fair trial and that her sentence of life was unjust.

It was also revealed by American investigators that many of the witnesses testifying against Ilse might have been exaggerating their claims that she had lampshades, wallets, and other personal items made from inmates' skins.[64] Reports led by Chief of the War Crimes Board of Review Branch of the Judge Advocate Division questioned the possible reduction in sentence, citing that the original trial had indeed found sufficient enough evidence to justify a life sentence. Moreover, the court found that because of the sensationalism and widespread press about her trial, Ilse might not have received a fair trial. The American court also hesitated before publicly revealing that they were considering, and then had decided to grant, a reduced sentence to time served.[65] Clay ordered Ilse's sentence commuted, arguing "there was no convincing evidence that she selected inmates for extermination in order to secure tattooed skin or that she possessed any articles made of human skin."[66] Ilse did receive a reduced sentence to a four-year term on 16 September 1948, but the furor over her potential release was such that a new trial seemed imminent. The US Senate began talks with West German authorities about her status and possible retrial. Clay tried to block her from being turned over to the West German judicial officials but his protests came to no avail. She was subsequently released by the Americans but was immediately rearrested by West German authorities and charged in May 1950 by the Bavarian Ministry of Justice.[67]

Was Ilse's re-arrest quite possibly a plan by the Americans to have her retried without compromising the double indemnity law found in the American system of justice?[68] It was then decided that "To prevent her being tried twice for the same offence, the German trial had to emphasize her crimes against Germans, since she had already been tried and found guilty of crimes against other nationalities: 'Although it is unfortunate that it may be necessary for the military authorities to adopt this course, it is, at the same time, highly important that Ilse Koch receives the punishment she so justly deserves."[69] Ilse was retried at Augsburg for murder and was sent to a prison in Bavaria known as Aichach. She claimed severe psychiatric illness but doctors found her fit to stand   trial:

> "I am guilty! I am a sinner!" screamed fat-faced Ilse Koch to her jailers. In her frenzy—whether genuine or faked—she smashed the furniture in her cell and babbled about heaven, hell and sin. Later last week the "Bitch of Buchenwald," no longer the doll-eyed ruminant, collapsed in a hysterical heap in an Augsburg courtroom, was carried off to a hospital for mental observation. Several doctors said she was suffering from temporary insanity caused by a guilt complex; others said Ilse was faking in   an attempt to delay justice.[70]

In 1950, Ilse was sent for a period to a psychiatric hospital, and was later sent   back to Aichach.[71]

At this trial (1950/1951), she maintained her same position, that she was innocent and was just a wife and mother. She argued she only became a party member under duress and that she was a victim of a conspiracy against her. Former SS who testified at her trial said she was a "noble wife and mother"   would

be among those who testified in her favor who would be found guilty of perjury.[72]

Ilse's defense strategy failed. She was found guilty and sentenced to life in prison on 15 January 1951. Clemency appeals failed. Ilse Koch, *Die Hexe von*

Buchenwald (witch of Buchenwald), committed suicide by hanging on 1 September 1967, while in prison. She was buried in an unmarked   grave.[73]

In 1971, Ilse's youngest child, son Uwe Köhler, who had been taken away from her when she was in prison, attempted to try to clear his mother's name. He contacted *The New York Times* to raise attention about what he believed were multiple wrongs committed against her by judicial officials. He believed that after his mother's suicide, he was able to gather enough evidence to prove that she "got a raw deal because the three courts [SS, American, and German] that tried her were not able to assemble evidence establishing that she had committed major crimes."[74] Immediately after his birth, Uwe was taken to a Bavarian foster home, where he spent his juvenile years. Uwe revealed to David Binder, the *New York Times* journalist who interviewed him that he had no idea who his parents were until later in life.[75]

When he was eight, he saw his mother's name on his birth certificate, but   it was not until he was nineteen that he made a connection between the name and the Nazi criminal Ilse Koch. He saw a newspaper and then, on a whim, asked his guardian if his mother was indeed, the notorious Ilse. When he was told that she was, he tracked her down. To Binder, Uwe would assert that his father was a German inmate housed near Ilse when she was in American custody. Uwe first   met Ilse in December 1966, and stated that they had "a joyous reunion and he continued to visit her as often as the rules allowed."[76] Uwe told Binder that he did not speak with his mother about the war, but that she "always denied her guilt and said she was the victim of libels, lies, and perjury. I didn't discuss it with her further because it was painful for her. I wanted that my mother would have the hope of getting out, and secondly, after two decades in prison, that she have other thoughts."[77]

Uwe felt that his mother had been unfairly tried, repeatedly, for the same crimes that she was simply not guilty of. He was speaking about the tattoo evidence, which at her two latter trials was a serious charge against her. Uwe argued that the evidence did not prove her guilt about the skinning of men for their tattoos. Although he acknowledged that she had some complicity in crimes   at

the camp, and that she was certainly not entirely innocent of other charges, but that

he felt "that she just slithered into the concentration-camp world like many others

without being able to do anything about it."[78] Further, he wanted his mother to

know that he would try to get her out someday. However, she killed herself on 1

September 1967, a few weeks before she would have turned 61. Uwe went through

his mother's belongings, and tried to come to grips with the legend   of Ilse Koch as

a war criminal, and with the image of the mother he never really had a chance to

know. He reached out to the American press to try to

"posthumously 'rehabilitate' her" by "seeking a kind of rehabilitation through the

press."[79]

Morgen, the SS lawyer who had first investigated Karl Otto Koch and Ilse

under Himmler's directive, was interviewed for Binder's article on Uwe. When asked

to comment on the tattoo evidence and her guilt, Morgen, who in 1971, was a lawyer

in private practice, said that:

> she was no innocent angel ... she was a hussy who rode horseback in sexy
> underwear in front of the prisoners and then noted down for punishment   the
> numbers of those who looked at her. She lay around in the garden in front of
> prisoners. Simply primitive. But she had nothing to do with the lampshade
> business and did not deserve such a draconic punishment. She
> was the victim of horror stories.[80]

---

[1] Testimonies from Ernst Blanck, Kurt Leeser, and Ignatz Wegerer, all survivors of Buchenwald. United States Congress, Senate. *Conduct of Ilse Koch War Crimes Trial: Hearings before the Investigations Subcommittee of the Committee on Expenditures in the Executive Departments, Interim report of the Investigations Subcommittee of the Committee on Expenditures in the Executive Departments pursuant to S. Res. 189, 80th Congress, a Resolution Authorizing the Committee on Expenditures in the Executive Departments to Carry Out Certain Duties.* United States Senate, Eightieth Congress, second session, Sept. 28-Dec. 9, 1948, Submitted, under authority of the order of the Senate, June 19, 1948, by Mr. Ferguson (United States Government Printing Office: Washington, 1948), 10.

[2] Brendan O'Shaughnessy, "Bearing Witness to a Horrific Moment in History," *Chicago Tribune*, 11 November 2001, sec. 2, p. 1.

[3] *The Bitch of Buchenwald: A History of Buchenwald Death Camp and its Notorious Commandante, Ilse Koch.* DVD. Produced by Gerry Malir, 2009. ArtsMagicDVD, 2009.

[4] Smith, pp. 7 and 258.

[5] Ewart, 279.

[6] *The Bitch of Buchenwald.* The film revealed that after her husband was arrested, she had hid her Nazi membership card. The card was later discovered and used against her during her first trial led by the Americans.

---

[7] Smith, pp. 11-12.

[8] For a brief biography of Eicke, see Laqueur, 164.

[9] *The Bitch of Buchenwald.*

[10] Ibid. The documentary also revealed that she was the only SS wife who routinely attended "sport" or any form of punishments. Even when her presence was questioned, Koch made sure that whatever his wife wanted, she received. She purposely sought out attendance at these events and by acting in the same manner in which Eicke prized the men for, she became, in essence "one" of them, even in a temporal, momentary fashion, the vaunted SS.

[11] Ibid. Eicke also trained Rudolf Höss.

[12] Ibid.

[13] See Hackett, 340.

[14] Karl Koch was sent to Lublin (Majdanek) in 1941, the same year the camp was built.   It was clear that by March of 1942, Koch had signed off on final building plans for Majdanek. See Gryn, p. 10, and the foldout map starting on p. 69 for the plans. Refer to p. 19, for a 1943 reference that showed how the camp employment hierarchy was formally instituted, and how the *Oberaufseherinnen* (*Aufseherinnen* are not listed) were only three steps above the kennel wardens. With regard to Majdanek, Elsa Erich, former *Oberaufseherin* at Majdanek, testified at trial that at Majdanek, "the women's camp usually contained 6 to 8 thousand inmates; their number reached even 11,000 during the summer of 1943." See p. 42. See also *The Bitch of Buchenwald.*

[15] *The Bitch of Buchenwald.* The documentary showed numerous Koch family photographs, and once the marriage took place, Manfred disappeared from Ilse's albums.

[16] Ibid. See also Alexandra Przyrembel, "Transfixed by an Image: Ilse Koch, the 'Kommandeuse of Buchenwald'." *German History*, Oct. 2001, Vol. 19 Issue 3, pp. 376-378. Przyrembel revealed what happened to Artwin and Gisela. She studied the correspondence between Artwin and Ilse, and spoke with Gisela in 1996: "While Artwin Koch was apparently destroyed by Ilse Koch's attitude and committed suicide, her daughter Gisela believes to this day that her mother's conviction can be attributed mainly to a press campaign (the author's telephone conversation with Gisela S. in the summer of 1996)." See p. 380, n. 48.

[17] See Laqueur, pp. 97 and 383.

[18] Gedenkstätte Buchenwald, ed. *Buchenwald Concentration Camp 1937-1945 (A Guide to the Permanent Historical Exhibition)* trans. Judith Rosenthal (Wallstein Verlag, 2004), p. 40.   See also pp. 254-255.

[19] *The Bitch of Buchenwald.*

[20] Brown, *The Camp Women*, p. 145. Note the wrong year of her suicide was listed. She died in 1967, not 1957.

[21] Hackett, 336.

[22] United States Congress, Senate, *Conduct of Ilse Koch War Crimes Trial*, see p. 8 for   the testimony of Joseph Lowenstein, inmate, and p. 9, for the testimony of Kurt Titz. In her examination of the German trials, Przyrembel also stated that "the verdict constructed a contrast between the good SS wife, who was mainly restricted 'to her domestic circle of influence' and did 'good' in the camp as far as 'her weak powers permitted', and Ilse Koch, who did not behave according to 'good, womanly sentiments'." See Przyrembel, p. 398.

[23] See Hackett, p. 43, and Smith, *Die Hexe von Buchenwald*, passim.

[24] Hackett, 335.

[25] Smith, p. 94.

[26] Hackett, pp. 43-44, 121-122.

[27] Ibid., 337.

[28] Przyrembel, passim, but especially p. 371, n. 13.

[29] *The Bitch of Buchenwald.*

[30] David Binder, "Ilse Koch's Posthumous Rehabilitation Sought by Son." *The New York Times* (7 May 1971).

[31] United States Congress, Senate. *Conduct of Ilse Koch War Crimes Trial*, Appendix 15: Ilse Koch, p. 25. Several survivors alleged that she would "parade in her briefs, or, according to some versions, stark naked, before the sex-starved males of the concentration camp." See Ewart, 280.

[32] Hackett, pp. 337-339.

[33] Toland, p. 761.

[34] Ibid.

[35] Hackett, pp. 337-339.

[36] Toland, p. 774.

[37] Hackett, 338.

[38] Ibid., 338.

[39] *The Bitch of Buchenwald.*

[40] *The Bitch of Buchenwald* documentary suggested that Himmler had a green marble desk made from Buchenwald labor, although Toland's thesis about Himmler disputes this, as Himmler "never profited from his position." See Toland, p. 764.

[41] Majdanek was an extermination camp.

[42] United States Congress, Senate. *Conduct of Ilse Koch War Crimes Trial*, 5 and Appendix 15: Ilse Koch, item a. Herr Koch was known to have ordered a special lamp made of human bones and skin. See Hackett, p. 64, and Smith, 259. It has also been suggested that Ilse Koch was unable to join her husband at Majdanek for different reasons than a total voluntary one. See Halaw, 247.

[43] Toland, p. 762.

[44] Ibid. Morgen "also did his best to convict Ilse Koch ... but the charges against her   could not be proven." See Ibid., p. 774.

[45] See Hackett, p. 341, the memoir of Stefan Heymann, and Smith, p. 259. A brief biographical description of Karl Koch can be found in Laqueur, 383.   See "Appendix-Ilse Koch" in United States Congress, Senate. *Conduct of Ilse Koch War Crimes Trial*, 23. See also Hackett, pp. 125-127, 336-341.

[46] *The Bitch of Buchenwald.*

[47] Przyrembel, pp. 369-371.

[48] *The Bitch of Buchenwald.*

[49] Smith, 259, and Ewart, 281.

[50] See also photograph of Ilse receiving this sentence: "U.S. Army Trials in Postwar Germany — Photograph" United States Holocaust Memorial Museum at http://www.ushmm.org/wlc/en/media_ph.php?ModuleId=10007145&MediaId=5553.

[51] Smith, 259.   Uwe was given to a Bavarian foster home. Later in life, and interested in his birth parents, he tracked down his mother, and visited her several times in prison. He would last see his mother right before she committed suicide. See Ewart, pp. 249-250. Ewart stated that Ilse Koch's first son Artwin also committed suicide. See p. 250.

[52] See "Appendix-Ilse Koch," United States Congress, Senate. *Conduct of Ilse Koch War Crimes Trial*, 25.

[53] Smith, 16.

[54] United States Congress, Senate. *Conduct of Ilse Koch War Crimes Trial*, 23. Toland revealed an interesting side note to Ilse's first trial. For this, see Toland, p. 774.

[55] Ibid.

[56] Clay was an important figure in the war crimes trials and post-war Germany. Clay would receive volume of mail about his decisions concerning Ilse. During the first war crimes trial, Clay's title was "General, U.S.A., Commander-in-Chief, European Command." See Beals, 272. Appointed Military Governor of Germany by General Dwight D. Eisenhower, Clay played a prominent role in Ilse Koch's trial, and subsequently helped rebuild Western Germany after the war. For more on Clay, see Lucius DuBignon Clay, *The Papers of General Lucius D.   Clay:*

Germany 1945-1949. Volumes I and II (Bloomington: Indiana University, 1974), and Jean Edward Smith, *Lucius D. Clay: An American Life* (Henry Holt & Company, LLC, 1992).

[57] United States Congress, Senate. *Conduct of Ilse Koch War Crimes Trial*, pp. 1-4. Ilse Koch was appointed defense counsel from both the United States Army and a core group of Germany attorneys. See pp. 5. Presiding over her trial were eight officers from the United States Army. See p. 4. Note also Hackett, p. 43.

[58] United States Congress, Senate. *Conduct of Ilse Koch War Crimes Trial*, 5 and Appendix 15: Ilse Koch, item a; see pp. 6-7 for the quote.

[59] Ibid., pp. 10-11.

[60] The crimes ranged from ordering murder, possessing the items made from human skin, and various crimes against humanity. Ewart claimed that the skin items were proven to have been made of goatskin. See Ewart, pp. 252 and 316.

[61] United States Congress, Senate. *Conduct of Ilse Koch War Crimes Trial*, p. 14. See p. 16 for Harbaugh's arguments for leniency for Koch.

[62] Ibid., 12.

[63] For much more on Ilse, see also Joshua Greene, *Justice at Dachau: The Trials of an American Prosecutor* (New York: Broadway Books, 2003), passim.

[64] See Ibid., pp. 11-13, for a review of the Koch prosecutorial witnesses, and note p. 17 for the section that questioned the reliability of these witnesses.

[65] United States Congress, Senate. *Conduct of Ilse Koch War Crimes Trial*, 2.

[66] Jamie McCarthy, "Frau Ilse Koch, General Lucius Clay, and Human-Skin Atrocities," at *The Jewish Virtual Library* http://www.jewishvirtuallibrary.org/jsource/Holocaust/skin.html (15 October 2010).

[67] Przyrembel, p. 373. On p. 376, Przyrembel explained why Ilse was such a crucial focus for constructions of the horrors experienced at Buchenwald: "Two factors were central here, I believe: on the one hand, because of her status as the wife of an SS officer and commandant, Ilse Koch was outside the power apparatus of the SS, which was already unpredictable for inmates. On the other, many survivor testimonies referred to the effect that she as a woman had on the male society of inmates."

[68] Ewart, 250.

[69] Przyrembel, p. 392.

[70] "Germany: Very   Special   Present."   *Time.* http://www.time.com/time/magazine/article/0,9171,859084,00.html#ixzz12ZLQS8hV (1 August 2010).

[71] Smith, 260.

[72] View *The Bitch of Buchenwald*.

[73] See Ewart, 251, and Hackett, 43. Woody Guthrie, American folk artist, wrote a song about Ilse Koch, called "Ilsa [sic] Koch. The first few lines are "I'm here in Buchenwald. My number's on my skin. Old Ilsa Koch is here."
See http://www.woodyguthrie.org/Lyrics/Ilsa_Koch.htm.

[74] Binder.

[75] Ibid.

[76] Ibid.

[77] Ibid.

[78] Ibid.

[79] Ibid.

[80] Ibid.

CHAPTER XV

ILSE LOTHE

Eine Kapo: Block Commander: Not Guilty?

The Jews almost always knew they were about to die and would cry and laugh from shock. Annoyed guards lashed away at them; babies, who hindered attendants while shaving their mother's hair, would be smashed against a wall. If there was any resistance, guards and *Kapos* would use whips to drive the naked victims into trucks bound for the gas chambers.[1]

Ilse Lothe was born 6 November 1914 in Erfurt, Germany. By the time of her trial in 1945, she was unmarried. Minute evidence exists that suggested what kind of social class Lothe came from, and little familial evidence was introduced   at her trial. She worked at a shoe manufacturing plant until 1939. She later claimed she was ordered to work in a munitions factory by the Nazi government.   At her trial, Lothe stated that she had "refused to go there," in reference to the munitions factory. She was sent to Ravensbrück as punishment for her refusal, where she stayed from 1939 until 1942.

Lothe, like many other women caught up in the Nazi régime, was sent to different camps. Lothe stayed at Ravensbrück until March 1942, when she was transferred to Auschwitz Birkenau, where she sometimes supervised pregnant women, who were often immediately sent to the gas chamber upon their arrival at an extermination camp. By April 1942, Lothe was sent to Budin, which was near Auschwitz. By 1943, Lothe was sent back to Birkenau where she was assigned   to work as a *Kapo*, where Lothe was put "in charge of 100 Hungarian Jewesses."[2]   A *Kapo* was a male or female prisoner who was put in charge of a barrack or unit of other prisoners. Lothe's role was different from that of an *Aufseherin*. She was not an employee of the SS, but she was put in a position of relative power over other prisoners as a *Kapo*. Lothe was told that she either work as a *Kapo* or be beaten; she chose the *Kapo* assignment as she would later argue she felt that she had no choice in the matter.[3] She pointed out for any infraction of the rules, punishment would be meted out harshly, no matter who the person was that committed the offense. Lothe stated later at her trial that she was punished by the SS several times while at Auschwitz for smuggling letters out, stealing food and cigarettes, and for burning beds for warmth. Lothe also said that as part of her punishments she would be starved, held in a cell, and beaten, much like the other prisoners would be treated, because, after all, she argued, she was a prisoner herself.[4]

In December 1944, Lothe was sent to a punishment commando known as Vistula. She was sent back to Ravensbrück in January 1945, and then by March of 1945, was sent to Bergen-Belsen. She fell ill for several weeks, recovered, and was then given work details. At Bergen-Belsen, she was told she would again work as a *Kapo*. Elisabeth Volkenrath put her in charge of the vegetable commando. The vegetable commando was a group of prisoners who were assigned to process vegetables. This could include growing, picking, cleaning, and cooking vegetables for other prisoners as well as camp employees.[5] It was while working at the commando that survivors stated Lothe became known for her cruelty, and used her position to convince the *Aufseherinnen* to act against her fellow prisoners that she felt were against her, or in some way violated camp rules.

Survivor Hanka Rozenwayg (who testified for the prosecution against Irma Grese, also testified against Lothe) related her experience with Lothe in Auschwitz when Lothe was unhappy with how Rozenwayg was working:

> In July 1943, whilst at Auschwitz, I was employed digging ditches outside the camp. Whilst so employed I laid down my shovel for a rest, and Lothe, who was in charge of my working party, saw me. I saw her go to the woman SS guard, and I heard her ask the SS woman to set her dog on me. I recognize this SS woman as No. 2 on photograph Z/4/2. I did not know her name, but have since been told that it was Irma Grese. Grese set her dog on to me and as a result I was bitten by the dog on my right

shoulder. I still have a scar on my shoulder where the dog bit me. I was made to continue working and I had to dress the wound myself after I had returned to the block.[6]

Irma Grese would deny that Lothe had come up to her and complained about Rozenwayg, which supported Lothe's assertion that she had never seen Rozenwayg. Lothe argued that she never worked with Grese, and Grese would state the same. Further, when Grese's testimony was reviewed, it was noted concerning Lothe that: "Her answer to Rozenwayg's story was that she had never been with Lothe on an outside working party, and she never had a dog. Ilse Lothe did not work under her as a *Kapo*."[7] Could Grese's testimony be trusted? Was she just trying to defend Lothe given that Grese had nothing to lose at that point? Given the fact that the SS wanted prisoners to act out amongst themselves and resent one another, Grese's statement defending Lothe hardly seemed plausible.

Using prisoners as functionaries was ideal for the SS. If the prisoners could "carry out the administration of the camps, including the maintenance of 'order' through violence, the SS could economize on its own energies and numbers, deflect hate from itself, and turn prisoners against each other" which defined exactly what Lothe was meant, and instructed, to do.[8] Grese did testify that Lothe was never with her in the *Kommando*; Grese also stated in her cross-examination that Lothe did not perform work duty with the *Aufseherinnen*. Therefore, a conclusion could be drawn from Grese herself that Lothe was a prisoner, and was disconnected from the *Aufseherinnen* within the camp structure. This was farthest from the truth. As a *Kapo*, and as a German non-Jewish woman, Lothe's status was certainly above that of other prisoners; her identity may have also allowed her some agency within the camp structure to influence actions against other prisoners. Further, in examining how prisoners themselves could turn against one another, a pattern emerges that was reflective of how the SS wanted the prisoners to act. If they were not marked for immediate extermination, certain prisoners, such as German inmates, or others designated as a *Kapo* (this was not to say that the *Kapo* could not also be killed at a moment's notice) would act in any way possible to save their own lives, even for a short time, since "it is not surprising that some women (as with men) would do anything in order to eat, in order to survive."[9]

When Bergen-Belsen was liberated, Lothe managed to evade arrest for a short period. She remained in the area of Bergen-Belsen until she was arrested in June of 1945 by Allied forces.[10] She stood trial along with other women at the Belsen Trial, on two counts of war crimes at Bergen-Belsen and at Auschwitz alongside with Irma Grese, Elisabeth Volkenrath, Juana Bormann, Herta Bothe, and others with whom she had worked closely with. Her trial began on 17 September 1945, and lasted until 17 November 1945. Lothe maintained throughout her trial that she was not responsible for the same atrocities as the *Aufseherinnen*, as she was just an innocent German prisoner herself and did not want to mistreat prisoners, nor did she do so; consequently, she stated, she was punished because of her unwillingness to go along with the SS and the *Aufseherinnen*:

> Cross examination by Col. Boyd: 'I suggest that to save your own skin you were prepared to fall in with this system of ill-treatment of prisoners and to put yourself at the behest of the S.S.?' Lothe: On the contrary, I did not fall in with that policy and as a matter of fact I was beaten much more frequently because I did not do so.[11]

Lothe maintained at her trial that she was just a prisoner, and had no real power as a *Kapo*. Her argument rested on the fact that she had refused to work for the Nazis and as a prisoner, she had no choice but to obey orders. She denied that she ever acted in any way that was untowardly against any other prisoner such as herself. Further, Lothe related that she was often punished by the SS men for infractions ranging from cigarette smoking to smuggling of food and letters. At her trial, she stated that she was a victim of the "Stalin swing." The "Stalin swing" was when prisoners were hung and beaten.

Lothe described her experience with the "Stalin swing" to the court, and a reporter from *The Argus* revealed that "she [Lothe] was suspended on a triangular frame to which she was lashed, with her hands pinioned. Then she was swung   from one side to the other, and each time received a stroke with a rubber truncheon from two SS men until she had 25 lashes."[12] Lothe also asserted that, like other prisoners, she was beaten and tortured, and denied any involvement in the abuse of her fellow female inmates, despite numerous claims from camp survivors that Lothe was extremely cruel and abusive and had indeed received preferential treatment, especially from *Aufseherinnen*. [13]

Testimony from survivors who interacted with Lothe maintained that Lothe was close friends with Grese. Eyewitnesses also related that Grese often did favors for Lothe. The story of Grese setting her dog on prisoners that Lothe did   not like emerged as a crucial detail for the prosecution in trying to show that   Lothe indeed did have more power than her defense ever alluded to. The prosecution reiterated Rozenwayg's testimony about how Lothe would point out   to Grese the women she did not like and Grese would let her dog attack the inmate.[14]   Moreover, witnesses also related that Lothe whipped and beat

prisoners, usually without provocation. Lothe still never admitted her guilt. Insistent, she repeated that she was just a prisoner forced to serve as a *Kapo*. However, she did testify that she occasionally slapped a prisoner to keep order. However, under continued cross-examination, she admitted that when she had been assigned at Bergen-Belsen, she had been working as a nurse. Interestingly, Lothe used the excuse that she, too, underwent the same form of punishment as   the other women inmates, and could not be held accountable for any   crime:

> Neither at Auschwitz nor at Belsen did she carry a weapon or stick, beat a prisoner with a stick, knock one down or kick one while on the ground. While a selection was taking place all *Kapos* were put in one block and forbidden to leave. *Kapos* were punished more often than other prisoners and received no extra food. Lothe had herself received severe punishment from the SS.[15]

When accused of punishing, beating, and torturing prisoners, Lothe vehemently repeated in her defense that she only acted in the way that she did so that she   could maintain order amongst her charges and not be punished   herself.[16]

Witness testimony contradicted claims by Lothe that she shared the same status as the prisoners. Ewa Gryka, a survivor from Bergen-Belsen, related that   on one instance when she and other inmates were digging mass graves, Lothe refused to let a woman prisoner go to the latrine. When the prisoner could no longer hold her bowels, she walked away from the graves and Lothe attacked her. Lothe beat the woman with a stick so severely that blood poured out her skull.   The woman was sent to the gas chamber, or so Gryka believed, because no one ever saw her again.

Gryka stated that Lothe "has been responsible for sending many people to the gas chamber."[17] Lothe also beat Gryka several times a week, usually with a stick. These abusive and murderous actions destroyed any theory Lothe came up with at her trial as to why she had no choice but to treat the women the way she   did. Although no witnesses testified on behalf of the prosecution to Lothe's attempts at friendly overtures toward the inmates, some Nazi did become friends with the prisoners, sometimes forming strange bonds in the midst of total horror.[18] However, survivors did testify to the fact that Lothe continually beat prisoners   with her fists or other objects. Prosecutorial evidence argued that Lothe would assist in marking for selection those inmates she felt did not work up to the standards sent for prisoners at the camps; however, her defense reiterated that   when selection took place, the *Kapos* were kept away and Lothe never once took part in any selection.[19]

Several survivors testified as to Lothe's cruelty and inhumane treatment of prisoners. However, Zofia Litwinska, survivor of Auschwitz, said that Ilse Lothe was "originally an ordinary prisoner at Auschwitz. I never saw Ilse Lothe beat anybody. She never interfered with the girls who were doing their duty."[20] In summary arguments against Grese, the prosecution had reminded the court of Lothe's involvement with Grese during roll call, and evidence of the same was introduced at Lothe's trial.

These roll calls, when Lothe was the *Kapo*, were prime opportunities for both women to inflict abuse on the prisoners.   During these roll calls, survivors related that Grese would use her dog against prisoners while Lothe beat other prisoners. Therefore, evidence existed that proved Lothe's culpability and connection with crimes against humanity. Moreover, the prosecution stated, several survivors testified that Lothe was horribly cruel and inflicted many beatings of her own accord, often without Grese or other *Aufseherinnen* by her side.[21] Her defense lawyer, Major I.S.W. Cranfield of the British Honourable Artillery Company argued that Lothe was the victim of false eyewitness testimony.

Cranfield cited that when Belsen was liberated, Lothe stayed behind for unknown reasons. One day while Lothe was walking through the camp, three young women who had been at Auschwitz and Bergen-Belsen recognized Lothe as a *Kapo*. These women, who Cranfield said were ill educated, began to shout that Lothe was responsible for crimes in Auschwitz, which resulted in Lothe being taken away by a British soldier. Cranfield argued that the women had manufactured their stories in order to find someone to blame for what they had endured at the camps.

Moreover, he argued, the prosecution had been too willing to take what these women had said as the truth, and any charges of abuse could not be proven against Lothe. He stated that a tremendous amount of evidence introduced at the trial against the *Aufseherinnen* and *Kapos* was "embroidered and exaggerated."[22] Whether or not the eyewitnesses were telling the truth about Lothe's actions, she was found not guilty of war crimes at either Auschwitz or Bergen-Belsen. Her life after the trial and date of death remain unknown at present time.

---

[1] Toland, p. 765.

[2] Taken from "Evidence for the Defendant Ilse Lothe," Fyfe, 267. See p. 272 for more on the fate of pregnant women in the camps.

[3] Ibid., 267.

[4] "Ilse Lothe" from Bergen-Belsen Trial Documents at BergenBelsen.co.uk.

[5] Fyfe, 267.

[6] Ibid., 746. Quote also noted in my chapter on Grese. See also United Nations War Crimes Commission. *Law Reports of Trials of War Criminals: The Belsen Trial*, Vol. II (London: Published for the United Nations War Crimes Commission, by His Majesty's Stationery Office, 1947), p. 16.

[7] United Nations War Crimes Commission, London, 46.

[8] Smith, 324.

[9] Ibid., 325.

[10] Fyfe, pp. 268-270.

[11] "Ilse Lothe" from Bergen-Belsen Trial Documents at BergenBelsen.co.uk.

[12] "Stalin Swing was Belsen Punishment." *The Argus* (Melbourne, Vic: 1848-1954), Friday 19 October 1945, p. 20.

[13] Fyfe, pp. 268-270.

[14] Ibid., 268.

[15] United Nations War Crimes Commission, London, 46.

[16] Fyfe, 268-270, 273. Lothe was found, shockingly, not guilty of crimes in Auschwitz and Bergen/Belsen despite so much survivor testimony against her.

[17] Ibid., 749.

[18] Examples of friendships formed by Nazi women and prisoners are noted throughout, but can be especially found by referring to Heike's scholarship.

[19] Ibid., 747. One survivor referred to Lothe as an SS policewoman and asserted that she was quite close with Irma Grese. See "1,000 More in Reich Sought for War Crimes: Woman Guard Accused Again" *New York Times*, 28 September 1945, 8 (L).

[20] Anthony Mann, "Noted Jurist for Defence: Application Allowed." *The Scotsman.* 28 September 1945. See: http://www.bergenbelsen.co.uk/pages/Staff/StaffPhotographs.asp?CampStaffID=51&PhotographsID=586&index=17 (1 October 2010).

[21] United Nations War Crimes Commission, *The Belsen Trial*, p. 114.

[22] Ibid., pp, 85-88.

CHAPTER XVI

HERTA OBERHEUSER

Schlimme Ärztin: Evil Doctor

Herta Oberheuser was born on 15 May 1911, in Köhn, Germany. Her parents were Anton and Elsbeth Oberheuser, and Herta was raised in a Christian, educated, conservative lower to middle-class household. She went to medical school in Bonn, Germany, and would later graduate as doctor of medicine.[1] Conjecturing on what her career would have been like had Hitler and the Nazis   not come to power, one can imagine that she would have worked in infectious diseases and dermatology since she had specialized in the latter area at the Medical Academy at Düsseldorf.[2] Joining with the SS as a physician contractor,
however, allowed her to go beyond any form of medical research and experimentation she could have possibly imagined while in medical   school.

Once she went to work in SS medical institutions and then the camp structure, her approach to medicine went against any oath to preserve life, and certainly went against any ethical teachings. Oberheuser used live human beings   to experiment on. From children to adults, if selected for experimentation, Oberheuser conducted such barbarities against them that included bone and muscle experiments, using hammers to break apart bones while still in a person's leg or arm, amputations of limbs of the mentally disabled, injecting prisoners (including children) with poisons and other toxic agents, burn   experiments,
freezing and re-warming, and withholding anesthesia, antibiotics, and pain medications.[3] Use of human beings was allowed by the government since animal testing was banned or later, very tightly controlled. The Nazi view   towards protecting the use of animals in medical experimentation originated well before

Oberheuser became a SS physician. On 28 August 1933, Hermann Göring gave a radio speech where he stated

> an absolute and permanent ban on vivisection is not only a necessary law to protect animals and to show sympathy with their pain, but it is a also a law for humanity itself ... I have therefore announced the immediate prohibition of vivisection and have made the practice a punishable offense in Prussia. Until such time as punishment is pronounced the culprit shall be lodged in a concentration camp.[4]

Göring, who had someone sent to a concentration camp for segmenting a frog to bits, was the same man who authorized *Endlösung der Judenfrage*, or the Final Solution to the Jewish Question.[5]

There were strict limits on the use of animals for vivisection. Restriction over the use and treatment of animals as lab experiment subjects was made into law on 24 November 1933, called the *Reichstierschutzgesetz* (Reich Animal Protection Act). Thus, some SS doctors felt that since animal experimentation was so restricted, they had no choice but to use people, especially since humans were made so readily available to them as experimentation subjects with little to no controls imposed as to what could be done against the innocent victims in medical settings.[6] Nazi doctors then used animals sparingly for vivisection. While dogs were not allowed for any surgical experiments whatsoever, humans were unhesitatingly made available for any form of testing. The Nazis willingly supplied the SS doctors with an endless supply of subjects.[7] The contradictory nature of animal rights legislation with the Nazi view of human life was, and is, still astonishing. Hitler and other Nazis, as well as doctors such as Oberheuser, certainly felt themselves as salient, caring beings, but not when it came to treatment of a government designated "enemy" of the state. This excerpt from the Nuremberg Trials summation described the 1933 law, and the SS use of humans for vivisection and other experimentations as that

> We need look no further than the law, which the Nazis themselves passed on the 24th of November 1933 for the protection of animals. This law states explicitly that it is designed to prevent cruelty and indifference of man towards animals and to awaken and develop sympathy and

understanding for animals as one of the highest moral values of a people. The soul of the German people should abhor the principle of mere utility without consideration of the moral aspects. The law states further that all operations or treatments which are associated with pain or injury, especially experiments involving the use of cold, heat, or infection, are prohibited, and can be permitted only under special exceptional circumstances. Special written authorization by the head of the department is necessary in every case, and experimenters are prohibited from performing experiments according to their own free judgment. Experiments for the purpose of teaching must be reduced to a minimum. Medico-legal tests, vaccinations, withdrawal of blood for diagnostic purposes, and trial of vaccines prepared according to well- established scientific principles are permitted, but the animals have to be killed immediately and painlessly after such experiments. Individual physicians are not permitted to use dogs to increase their surgical skill by such practices. National Socialism regards it as a sacred duty of German science to keep down the number of painful animal experiments to   a
minimum.

If the principles announced in this law had been followed for human beings as well, this indictment would never have been filed. It is perhaps the deepest shame of the defendants that it probably never even occurred to them that human beings should be treated with at least equal humanity.[8]

Although the vegetarian Hitler and other top Nazis were thought to have wanted to ban all animal experimentation, because of medical and pharmaceutical opposition to a total ban on animal vivisection, the government did allow some animal experimentation to continue, under very strict guidelines. Animals could not suffer undue pain or harm. With few exceptions, animals were ordered to be anesthetized before experiments took place, and experiments were only permitted   if no other methods were available. The men and women used for experiments   such as those performed by Dr. Oberheuser received no special treatment at all.   The women used by her in medical experiments received very little, if any, in the way of medication, anesthesia, or medical care. These same victims were also executed if they survived experimentation for fiscal reasons as well as to cover up the crimes. If it were not for fellow prisoners, sheer luck, and liberation, the human victims of the Nazi medical experiments would have all died. Humans used by Nazi doctors were already, because of their incarcerated status, considered enemies of the state and therefore   disposable.[9]

The SS allowed Oberheuser and other doctors full, unprecedented access   to human victims for vivisection purposes in the camp structures as well as in SS controlled 'hospital' facilities. In 1935, Oberheuser worked as a *Ringärztin* (female doctor) for the *Bund Deutscher Mädchen*, the German Girls League or   the girl version of the Hitler youth. In 1937, she joined the Nazi party.[10] She volunteered for a position at Ravensbrück, where she performed several medical experiments for the benefit of the German Armed Forces.[11] In June of 1943, she worked at Hohenlychen Hospital, the same hospital where Irma Grese first worked. At Hohenlychen, Oberheuser was appointed assistant physician to Karl Gebhardt, another SS doctor.[12] She worked under SS *Obersturmbahnführer* Dr. Enno Lolling, Chief of Office IIID at Oranienburg who supervised and assigned doctors to medical duties in the camps, including Oberheuser, and with a number of doctors, including SS-*Obersturmbahnführer* Dr. Ludwig Stumpfegger,   who later became Hitler's physician. Dr. Gerhard Schiedlausky, who had worked in four camps, including Ravensbrück, was another key associate of Oberheuser. Lolling assigned "assigned Dr. Schiedlausky and the defendant Oberheuser as co-workers."[13] As a Nazi doctor, Oberheuser was not a member of the SS because of her gender, but was considered an important and highly valued SS employee. The fact that she was assigned to the same duties as male SS doctors demonstrated that her gender played no role in how her core competencies were perceived and in the posts that she was given.

While at Ravensbrück and Hohenlychen, Oberheuser was responsible for some of the cruelest and most appalling medical experiments performed on prisoners. Her superiors assigned her to specific areas and duties, gave her orders, and she followed them: "The defendant Oberheuser's duties at Ravensbrück in connection with the experiments were to select young and healthy inmates for the experiments, to be present at all of the surgical operations, and to give   the experimental subjects post-operative care."[14] However, in following this logic, choice was removed from Oberheuser, and survivors of her experiments stated at Oberheuser's trial that she purposely acted in a cruel manner, withholding medicine at her own personal whim.

Witnesses testified that Oberheuser personally selected prisoners, known as "rabbits" or her "guinea pigs" for experimentation. SS doctors specifically requisitioned the majority of victims, and the requisition was sent directly to the camp commandant. However, Oberheuser asked for and also received victims under her own jurisdiction. The fact that she assisted with selections, and also took part in experiments alongside of the male SS doctors, meant that she acted in the same capacity as the men. Therefore, gender cannot play a role in assessing her culpability since she acted in the same way that her male counterparts did, simply because she could. She was perceived as a skilled, and necessary part of the war effort. Oberheuser, like her male counterparts

> regarded the order given them by the Head of the State as a measure of war which was conditioned by special circumstances, caused by the war itself, and by means of which a question should be answered which was of decisive importance not only for the wounded, but beyond that, should furnish a contribution in the struggle for the foundations of life of the German people and for the existence of the Reich.[15]

Following the logic of the defense argument, the "existence" of the Reich meant that for the greater Nazi vision to be implemented, medical experimentation had to take place. The SS doctors such as Oberheuser knew no boundaries and engaged in whatever experimentation they felt necessary for the war effort and to protect the greater whole of Nazi Germany.

Oberheuser forced the prisoners to take part in increasingly horrifying experiments, and "killed some prisoners, including children, with injections of oil and Evipan."[16] For over a year, Oberheuser performed sulfanilamide experiments at Ravensbrück. Sulfanilamide experiments were conducted in order to help injured German soldiers on the battlefield. In order to perform these experiments, Oberheuser would deliberately inflict wounds of varying sizes and shapes on different areas of a prisoner's body. She then introduced bacteria in the form of a disease such as gangrene, and purposely prevented blood circulation by tying up the limb where the cut was made. She would then intentionally let the wound fester to view the results. In order to promote infection, Oberheuser would force foreign objects such as metal shavings, broken glass, rusty nails, as well as other sharp and dangerous materials into the wounds.[17]

In one experiment on a group of Polish women at Ravensbrück, Oberheuser observed the women's rotting legs by smelling the wounds. Since this experiment took place in the hot summer, flies were rampant and maggots invaded some leg wounds. The legs of the women who were experimented on festered so badly that a slight shift of the leg would allow masses of pus and other liquids to drain. At one point, Oberheuser entered the ward to observe these women. She walked by the beds, sniffed the air, and announced, after seeing the pus-filled legs dripping with ooze, that "it smells revolting in here."[18] After some women survived these experiments, Oberheuser forced the women to walk out of the ward.   When one woman could not walk at all, and protested to Oberheuser,
the doctor replied, "Hop if you cannot walk!" She then attempted to force the woman to walk out of the ward, yelling, "Get up and be off with you.   Quickly,"
but when the woman could not move, Oberheuser dragged her out of the ward herself.[19]

In addition to these experiments, Ravensbrück survivor Marguerite Buber related that it was known among prisoners that Oberheuser might have also performed "experimental transfers of bone and muscle" on young Polish women interred at Ravensbrück. The bone and muscle experiments performed by Nazi doctors such as Oberheuser were especially cruel. These experiments involved the doctors removing sections of bones, muscles, and nerves from prisoners and transplanting them to other prisoner-patients. Oberheuser would be tried for these inhumane bone and muscle experiments at her trial, and based on evidence submitted by the prosecution, would be found guilty of this charge.[20]

Oberheuser also performed sterilization experiments at Ravensbrück. The sterilization experiments were performed in order to find a way to inexpensively and quickly sterilize a large number of people. These experiments were performed against the prisoner's will, and various means to sterilize the women were used. These methods included surgery, drugs, radiation, and other invasive methods.[21] Due to the sterilization and sulfanilamide experiments, thousands of people died or were permanently disfigured because of medical ministrations performed by Nazi doctors like Oberheuser. With seemingly unlimited human subjects for experiments, the barbarities of the SS doctors would not stop until the war was lost and the camps liberated.

Oberheuser was arrested on 8 May 1945. She was one of the few women employed by the SS as an *Ärztin* (woman doctor), and in the Nuremberg Medical Trials, out of twenty-three defendants, was the only woman tried at this trial. She was charged with having committed war crimes (Count II) and crimes against humanity (Count III). The charges, as mentioned, brought against her included   war crimes, but with the added "special responsibility" to having taken part in the following: sulfanilamide experiments from July 1942 to September 1943; sterilization experiments, from March 1941 until January 1945; and bone, muscle, and nerve experiments, from September 1942 to December 1943.[22] Oberheuser was tried in the Military Tribunal No. 1, Case No. 1, brought by the United States of America, notable "because it was the first in the series of proceedings after the IMT Trial."[23] The trial began on 9 December 1946, and continued until 20 August 1947.   The lead prosecutor in the case was American Brigadier General Telford Taylor, the presiding judge was Walter B. Beals, and Oberheuser's defense council was Dr. Alfred Seidl.[24]

Oberheuser pleaded not guilty to all charges. Seidl argued that Oberheuser was forced to perform the experiments, and that she did not personally select anyone for experimentation. However, prosecution witnesses continually belied her claims of ignorance and innocence. One of the witnesses for the prosecution was Jadwiga Dzido, a Ravensbrück survivor, who related her experiences undergoing forced medical experimentation at the hands of Oberheuser. Dzido was forced to undergo horrific medical experiments on her leg. Dzido, a Catholic, was born on 26 January 1918 in Suchowola, Poland, but spent her childhood in Lukow.[25] To support the family after Dzido's father died, her mother worked in a pharmacy. The owner of the pharmacy convinced her to enroll in the pharmacology program at the University of Warsaw. During the summer of 1939, she came home to work for the pharmacy. When the Nazis invaded Poland on 1 September 1939, she became a resister by working with the Polish underground, the ZWZ (youth organization for the Polish army).[26] The Gestapo arrested her in March of 1941, and after subjecting her to horrific abuses at Lublin, she was sent to Ravensbrück. While there, she was then assigned to work detail, and was then turned over to Oberheuser to serve as one of Oberheuser's "rabbits."[27] Dzido was injected with *staphylococcus aureus* a bacteria.[28] Dzido's leg was then sliced open without any anesthesia or medication to treat her wounds; it then took over twenty weeks for the wounds to mend. The pain was horrible, and would last throughout her life.[29]

Dzido also revealed her encounter with Dorothea Binz, who was under order to round up specific prisoners for experimentation:

> In the spring of 1943 the operations were stopped. We thought that we could live like that till the end of the war. On the 15th of August a policewoman came and called ten girls. When she was asked what for, she answered that we were going to be sent to work. We knew very well that all prisoners belonging to our transport were not allowed to work outside the camp. The chief of the block where we were living was forbidden under capital punishment to let us outside the camp. That's why we know that it was not true. We didn't want to let our comrades out of the block. The policewoman came, and the assistants, the overseers, and with them Binz. We were driven out of the block into the street. We stood there in line 10 at a time and Binz herself read off the names of 10 girls. When they refused to go because they were afraid of a new operation and were not willing to undergo a new operation, she herself gave her word of honor that it was not going to be an operation and she told them to follow her.

> We remained standing before the block. Then several minutes later our comrades ran to us and told us that SS men have been called for in order to surround them. The camp police arrived and drove our comrades out of the line. We were locked in the block. The shutters were closed. We were 3 days without any food and without any fresh air. We were not

given parcels that arrived in the camp at that time. The first day the camp commandant and Binz came and made a speech. The camp commandant said that there had never been a revolt in the camp and that this revolt   must be punished. She believed that we would reform and that we would never repeat it. If it were to happen again, she had SS people with weapons. My comrade, who knew German, answered that we were not revolting, that we didn't want to be operated on because five of us died after the operation and because six had been shot down after having suffered so much. Then Binz replied: "Death is victory. You must suffer for it and you will never get out of the camp." Three days later, we learned that our comrades had been operated on in the bunker.[30]

The fact that Dzido survived Binz and then lived through the terrible experimentation done on her was a miracle in itself. Further, Dzido was able to escape death when fellow survivors hid her during the SS round up of all living vivisection victims for extermination as the end of the war loomed closer.[31] Dzido, in her testimony at Oberheuser's trial, like many of the other survivors   who also served as prosecutorial witnesses, served as living eyewitnesses to the horrendous Nazi medical experiments performed on unwilling   victims.

Another Oberheuser victim was Maria Kusmierczuk. Born in 1920, she   was studying science and math at the Stefan Batory University when the Nazis invaded Poland.[32] Like Dzido, she became involved with the resistance   movement the ZWZ. She was arrested in January 1941, and sent to Lublin. After undergoing months of persecution and violence, she was sent to Ravensbrück, where she was forced to work as a laborer. Against her will, on 7 October 1942, like many others of Oberheuser's victims, she was injected with morphine and was experimented   on. Her right leg was slit open and was purposely injected with tetanus, as well as "bacteria, dirt and slivers of glass, in order to simulate the combat wounds of German soldiers fighting in the war. The inflamed area was then treated with sulphonamide drugs."[33] Her leg did not heal properly and her leg bone "remained exposed and she unable to walk."[34] Kusmierczuk said that pain medicines were withheld on purpose by Oberheuser's direct order. She would be the only woman of her group who lived that underwent this experiment. After surviving   the experiments, vivisection victims would be killed but Kusmierczuk survived execution because she assumed the identity of another woman. She also testified   at Oberheuser's trial, and her experiences further affirmed the doctor's   guilt.[35]

Several other women were also brought to the stand, and repeated examples of Oberheuser's cruel and inhumane treatment of prisoners reverberated throughout the courtroom. Oberheuser took part in "experiments in high altitude, freezing, typhus and malaria … mass sterilization, mass murder of 'useless eaters'" and other horrific abuses, all within complete violation of any medical ethics.[36] Further, Oberheuser admitted that she was assigned to select healthy women for experiments by SS doctors, with her statements somehow seeking to assign culpability because of her inferred lack of choice in the matter.[37]

Survivor Vladislava Karolewska stated at Oberheuser's trial that the doctor knew fully well what she was doing concerning selection. To infer otherwise was ludicrous, especially when Oberheuser herself seemed to relish in referring to prisoners from whom she selected her victims, as "those girls are new guinea pigs."[38] Female prisoners who were victims of vivisection revealed how Oberheuser ignored them when they were in horrific pain and needed further medical treatment. Survivor and prosecutorial witness Dr. Zofia Maczka, who witnessed firsthand the experiments led by Gebhardt and Oberheuser, that Oberheuser "utterly neglected basic nursing requirements and her treatment of subjects was cruel and abusive."[39]

It was further revealed that Oberheuser physically abused prisoners by hitting or kicking them with her bare hands or instruments. In addition, and by   her own admission, Oberheuser stated that not only had she performed experiments but admitted that she had taken part in human euthanasia, using such chemicals as gasoline, oil, and other substances to cause death. She argued that   all people who were put to death at her hands were near death anyway, and were not worthy of life to begin with, due to their diminished physical state. However, Oberheuser would maintain, as the core of her defense, that she again had no choice but to take part in the medical experiments as she was only a subordinate to SS doctor Karl Gebhardt, and was only following orders.[40] Before he was charged,

Gebhardt had written to *Wehrmacht* physicians earlier that he accepted "the full

human, surgical, and political responsibility for these experiments."[41] But as

Gebhardt's assistant at Hohenlychen, certainly she bore culpability as well, since she

stood, literally and figuratively alongside of him during selection and

experimentation. Her testimony at her trial validated her guilt:

> The responsibility of the defendant Gebhardt for these experiments is also
> proved by the affidavit of Oberheuser. She stated: "The experiments with
> bone transplantations were carried out, as far as I can remember, at the end of
> 1942 and beginning of 1943 by Dr. Stumpfegger of Hohenlychen. I helped
> Dr. Stumpfegger in the same way as I helped Dr. Fischer with the
> sulfanilamide experiments, and as I have described already in paragraph 4 of
> this affidavit. Before the operation I had to examine, as in the other case,
> the condition of health of the selected persons. The operations consisted of
> the removal and transplantation of a piece of the bone from the tibia. Fifteen
> to twenty persons were used for these experiments. The persons necessary for
> these experiments were requisitioned by Dr. Schiedlausky from the camp
> commander. Dr. Karl Gebhardt was in charge of the sulfanilamide
> experiments and bone transplantations. I do not know whether he himself
> performed operations of this type. But I know that all these experiments were
> performed under his direction and supervision and upon his instructions. He
> was assisted by the doctors already mentioned, Dr. Fischer and Dr.
> Stumpfegger, and also by Drs. Schiedlausky and Rosenthal. Also only healthy
> Polish prisoners were used for these experiments. I cannot remember that a
> single one of the experimental subjects used was pardoned after the
> completion of the experiments."
> (NO-4.87, Pros. Ex. 208.)[42]

Oberheuser was found guilty of both war crimes (Count II) and crimes against

humanity (Count III). Dr. Seidl petitioned the court that Oberheuser's sentence reflect

time served. On 20 August 1947, Oberheuser was sentenced to twenty years in prison,

and Judge Beals granted Dr. Seidl's request that allowances be made for time she

had already served.[43] Seidl further petitioned the court that the sentence be modified

even further, but the court denied his request:

> as it found that evidence relating to this defendant shows that she is a cruel,
> merciless woman. She became a concentration camp doctor of her own free
> will (Record, p. 5485). She assisted the defendant Gebhardt in performing the
> experiments and was in charge of the postoperative care.

> The evidence is convincing that she badly neglected the experimental subjects and was many times needlessly cruel (Record, pp. 1436, 1443-4). It appears that she frequently kicked, beat up and threw out women who came to her for treatment (Prosecution Document NO-871). She admitted killing a number of sick inmates by injections (Prosecution Document NO-487). The argument that the defendant could not have prevented the experiments is not significant. The basis of her guilt is her voluntary and active participation on the atrocities."[44]

The court found further that Oberheuser's sentence, because of the crimes committed by her, was "exceedingly mild."[45] Did gender play a role in the sentencing? Oberheuser referred to her gender in this excerpt from her final defense statement: "In administering therapeutical care, following established medical principles, as a woman in a difficult position, I did the best I could."[46]   The Nazis and her superiors certainly did not consider gender a factor when assigning Oberheuser to her duties as a SS contracted doctor, but her sentence suggested that perhaps gender did indeed play a role in her sentence. When comparing her sentence to that of her male co-defendants, a case could be made

for this supposition. Oberheuser's sentence was exceptionally light given the barbarity of her work in the camps, as well as for her role in the deaths of many prisoners, who were all innocent victims in the name of Nazi medicine.

Per her attorney's request, Oberheuser was sent to War Crimes Prison No. 1, in Landsberg, Bavaria.[47] Since allowances were made for time served, after appeals her sentence was reduced to ten years imprisonment, but   American General of Germany John McCloy released her in 1952.[48] After she was   released from prison, Herta Oberheuser went back to work as a doctor. She tried to start her life over again, and began performing pediatric and family medicine in private practice in Stocksee, near Kiel, in Schleswig-Holstein, West Germany. She practiced for almost six years with financial assistance made interest free to her   by the West German government.[49] Oberheuser received prisoner of war status   from the government, and granted insurance as well.[50] On 4 March 1958, the *Daily Express* newspaper broke the story of Oberheuser's practicing medicine again. A firestorm of controversy emerged, notably in the correspondence section of *The British Medical Journal.*

In the 10 May 1958 issue of *The British Medical Journal,* Dr. Armstrong Davison expressed great anger that Oberheuser was practicing medicine again while also condemning the fact that little restitution had been made to   her victims.[51] This was followed by the 24 May 1958 edition where Dr. Eric Townsend wrote that "it is in no spirit of revenge or Shylockian desire to extract the last pound of flesh that one is horrified to know that the Federal German government sees fit to reinstate a practitioner such as Herta Oberheuser."[52] Dr. Wilhelmina C. Maguire, who was a former senior medical officer with the International Refugee Organization, also wrote about her outrage that Oberheuser was practicing again. Maguire had "personal contact with the disfigured and mutilated victims of the Nazi concentration camps." She further revealed that when applying to entry to another country, the medical state of the survivors brought upon them by the Nazis made it impossible to them to leave, because the

countries to which they applied for refugee status refused them. She stated further that "Is Herta Oberheuser to be allowed the opportunity to practise medicine again, she who has already so vilely dishonoured the Hippocratic   oath?"[53]

Other protest letters in the Correspondence section followed. In the 5 July 1958 edition, Dr. A. P. Tait discussed the Maguire letter, but added "I wonder if it would not be more adult for Dr. Maguire to present us with the facts as they are now. We might find that this person is now a dedicated practitioner, doing good

work. It is possible."[54] Numerous letters followed Tait's comments to the Correspondence section. Dr. S. Bennett's comments in the 12 July 1958 issue revealed just how shocking Tait's letter was seen by the medical community: "Dr. A. P. Tait's suggestion that Dr. Herta Oberheuser might now be a 'dedicated practitioner, doing good work,' is staggering in its naïveté. Does he not realize   that the very idea is an insult to her countless victims?"[55] Bennett, who   witnessed, firsthand, the victims of the Nazis at Bergen-Belsen, expressed his outrage further in referring to Oberheuser as "this war criminal, found guilty of crimes against humanity so dreadful that the mind boggles at the thought, has forfeited all right   to be accepted by civilized people."[56]

In the supplement to *The British Medical Journal* for the annual representative meeting, the meeting notes were recorded. Dr. Townsend's protests against the Federal German Government allowing Oberheuser to practice medicine were outlined. Other doctors at the meeting also registered their protests and raised concerns that the West German government allowed her to practice.   The letters in the Correspondence section raised enough attention to the Oberheuser case that Dr. I. D. Grant discussed how the International Relations Committee wrote a letter to the West German Medical Association outlining not only their concerns, but pointedly asked how Oberheuser could be allowed to practice medicine when she had been convicted of war crimes and crimes against humanity. He wrote to the West German Medical Association that it was felt by some British doctors that the "British Medical Association should make some official protest against the return of Herta Oberheuser to medical practice" and

that "It may be necessary for our International Committee to consider this matter."[57] The West German Medical Association replied that they "had no power to take away from Dr. Oberheuser the right to practise her profession" but that they had registered their protests to the Ministry of the Interior of Schleswig- Holstein that her license to practice be revoked. They wrote that they were also incensed that she had been practicing medicine and sought to distance themselves from the Nazi doctors.[58] An official protest was made and letters in the Correspondence section continued to catalogue what the medical community was doing to get Oberheuser's license revoked.

In the 26 July 1958 Correspondence section of *The British Medical Journal*, it was revealed that the Western German Medical Association and the Ministry of the Interior of Schleswig-Holstein began proceedings to   revoke Oberheuser's medical license.[59] A letter from Dr. Felix S. Besser quoted the Hippocratic oath, and outlined some specifics of Oberheuser's crimes concerning gasoline injections. He further questioned the logic of Tait's letter. Dr. A. Meyer further argued against Tait, and said "It is bad enough that this monster is at   liberty

at all, but the thought that she is once more one's 'colleague' is downright revolting,

and it is revealing, though not unexpected, that the German authorities have given her

their blessing."[60] Maguire wrote again, and this time she brought   up a supposition

of how patients of these former Nazi doctors could experience great anguish if they

found out what their doctors did under the Nazi régime after entering into a trusting

doctor/patient relationship.[61]

Letters continued to express anger at Oberheuser and other former SS doctors

being allowed to practice medicine. The victims of these doctors suffered with

constant physical reminders of what they endured. They also faced constant struggles

medically and financially after the war. Frances Blackett, Honorary Secretary for the

British League for European Freedom outlined how former Nazi doctors such as

Oberheuser received monies from the West German government   as former prisoners

of war, whereas their surviving victims now with refugee status, received nothing,

despite post-war discussions to do so, and also because   of a promise by the West

German government to recompense the survivors for   their suffering. Blackett also

called attention of the failure of the U.N. Secretary

General to follow up on reparations.[62] European media ran stories about

Oberheuser, and the attention grew globally about how former SS doctors were

practicing medicine. By 9 August 1958, Tait wrote to Correspondence seeking to

clarify his earlier position.

Tait wrote that he by no means sought to endorse Oberheuser in any way.

Instead, he sought to bring attention to the fact that she was indeed practicing

medicine, and that he "did not state that she was a 'dedicated practitioner,' only that

she might be, which is a very different thing." Further, he felt "it important to

know something about her now. I felt that justice demanded such knowledge and that

our verdict should have been tempered by it."[63] A few days after Tait's rebuttal

was published, both the *Daily Telegraph* and the Medical News section   of

The British Medical Journal revealed that Helmut Lemke, the Minister of the Interior

of Schleswig-Holstein revoked Oberheuser's medical license. The British

Medical Association certainly helped influence this decision, as the Medical News column stated.[64] Oberheuser filed the first of many appeals and media attention did not abate.

An investigation published in the *Sunday Times* issue of 7 June 1959, found that over two dozen former SS doctors were practicing medicine in West Germany. Dr. Michael E. M. Cook wrote to Correspondence and asked that all doctors in Great Britain "should make the strongest protest to the German Medical Association." He argued that unless something was done by the German Medical Association to revoke more licenses, "further action could be taken to express our feelings. This is not a case of just a few bad people stigmatizing the majority; so long as these doctors remain in practice the majority are conniving at

their crimes and therefore are morally approving them."[65] Despite the continued outcry against her and other SS medical personnel, Oberheuser did not simply just accept the revoking of her license. She kept appealing the Minister's order, and did not seem to want to give up in her battle to have her license reinstated.

In 9 November 1960, *Der Spiegel* published a report that Oberheuser was still fighting to get her license returned. She again petitioned the High Court to overturn Lemke's decision. The 10 December 1960 Medical News section of *The British Medical Journal* revealed that her appeal was rejected.[66] The Medical News section of *The British Medical Journal* later reported in its 15 July 1961 issue that Oberheuser had stopped all appeals, ceased practicing medicine, and relinquished the designation of doctor.[67] It was believed that by 1967, a pharmaceutical laboratory employed her. Oberheuser died on 24 January 1978, in a nursing home in Linz am Rhein.[68]

---

[1] Tillion, 76. See also Ulrike Steenbuck, "Herta Oberheuser – Ärztin in Ravensbrück. Biographie einer Täterin," in Jutta Dalhoff and Sabine Kock, *Ich habe mir Deutschland vom Leibe zu halten versucht: Frauen in Nationalsozialismus und der Umgang 'nachgeborener' Frauen mit dem Gedenken: Dokumentation einer Veranstaltungsreihe vom Mai 1995*. Keil: Universität Kiel, 1996. Note that Oberheuser's name has been spelled one of two ways: Oberhauser, and Oberheuser, which was the correct form. I have used the correct German Oberheuser throughout this text.

[2] Wolfgang Weyers, *The Abuse of Man: An Illustrated History of Dubious Medical Experimentation* (London and New York: Ardor Scribendi, 2003), pp. 285, 286, and 359 for more on Oberheuser.

[3] See *Trials of War Criminals before the Nuremberg Military Tribunals under Control Council Law No. 10 Nuremberg, October 1946-April 1949* (Washington, D.C.: U.S. G.P.O, 1949-1953), passim, for Oberheuser.

[4] Kathleen Marquardt, Herbert M. Levine, and Mark LaRochelle, *Animal Scam: The Beastly Abuse of Human Rights* (Washington, DC: Regnery Books, 1993), p. 124.

[5] Ibid.

[6] Spitz, p. 62.

[7] Ibid.

[8] See p. 71 in *Trials of War Criminals before the Nuremberg Military Tribunals under Control Council Law No. 10 Nuremberg, October 1946-April 1949* (Washington, D.C.: U.S. G.P.O, 1949-1953).

[9] I draw the comparison between animal and human experimentation to show how little regard the Nazis had for human life. However, a distinction has to be further made between so- called "Aryan" as well as "Jewish" pets to demonstrate how far the Nazis were willing to take their murderous ideology, even down to animals and pets. If Jews owned animals, then their animals would not receive the same preferential status as pets owned by non-Jews or Aryans.   When their owners were arrested, Jewish pets were hung, shot, tortured, or terribly and often publicly, abused. Jews were banned from owning pets in 1942. Jewish owned pets found to be hidden after this law was passed were horrifically abused and killed, actions which were designed to psychologically terrorize the pet's owners. See Boria Sax, *Animals in the Third Reich: Pets, Scapegoats, and the Holocaust* (New York and London: Continuum, 2000), pp. 112-113, 119, and 176-177. Also, Newman and Kirtley related a story where a prisoner came across one of the SS men's dogs. The prisoner was able to approach the dog, and petted it, talking softly to the animal. The SS man caught this interaction, and shot the dog. Because the dog showed kindness to the prisoner, it had to die. See Newman, p. 237.

[10] Tillion, 30.

[11] Beals, 254.

[12] Ibid., 254.

[13] *Trials of War Criminals before the Nuremberg Military Tribunals under Control Council Law No. 10 Nuremberg, October 1946-April 1949* (Washington, D.C.: U.S. G.P.O, 1949- 1953), p. 356.

[14] Ibid., p. 45. See also the testimony of Fritz Fischer, p. 377, where he related how Oberheuser and Schiedlausky, camp doctor at Ravensbrück from December 1941 until August 1943, assisted him in experiments where people died. Specific charges against Oberheuser included sulfanilamide experiments; bone, muscle, and nerve regeneration and bone transplantation experiments, and sterilization experiments. See Ibid., p. 695.

[15] Ibid., p. 963.

[16] Tillion, 76.

[17] See section E in *Trials of War Criminals before the Nuremberg Military Tribunals under Control Council Law No. 10 Nuremberg, October 1946-April 1949* (Washington, D.C.: U.S. G.P.O, 1949-1953). These same experiments were carried out at Hohenlychen, the hospital where Irma Grese worked, using female prisoners from Ravensbrück. See Brown, *The Beautiful Beast,* pp. 22-25.

[18] Póltawska, pp. 84-85. Gertrude Tillion, survivor of Ravensbrück, related one instance where Dorothea (Theodora) Binz, was having problems controlling women, one of whom was Wanda Póltawska, who refused to allow them to be subjected to experiments such as the ones Oberheuser performed. See Tillion, pp. 82-83, Póltawska, pp. 113-125, and my chapter on Binz.

[19] Póltawska, 90. Note that Dorothea (Theodora) Binz would often by responsible for rounding up prisoners for medical experiments performed by Oberheuser.

[20] Buber 253.

[21] Póltawska, section I.

[22] Beals, pp. 184, 193-195, and Dalhoff, pp. 31-34.

[23] Robert M.W. Kempner, "The Nuremberg Trials as Sources of Recent German Political and Historical Materials." *The American Political Science Review*, vol. 44, no. 2 (Jun., 1950): 454.

[24] Beals, 11.

[25] United States Holocaust Memorial Museum, courtesy of Anna Hassa Jarosky and Peter Hassa. "Friday February 26, 1943: Ravensbrück [Brandenburg] Germany; War Crimes Investigation Photo of Jadwiga Dzido." Washington: USHMM. Note: Jarosky is the daughter of Dzido (later Hassa).

[26] Ibid.

[27] Ibid.

[28] According to the U.S. Department of Health and Human Services, Food and Drug administration, *staphylococcus aureus* is: "S. aureus is a spherical bacterium (coccus) which on microscopic examination appears in pairs, short chains, or bunched, grape-like clusters. These organisms are Gram-positive. Some strains are capable of producing a highly heat-stable protein toxin that causes illness in humans." See Bad Bug Book: Foodborne Pathogenic Microorganisms and Natural Toxins Handbook *Staphylococcus aureus* at http://www.fda.gov/Food/FoodSafety/FoodborneIllness/FoodborneIllnessFoodbornePathogensNaturalToxins/BadBugBook/ucm070015.htm (21 October 2010).

[29] United States Holocaust Memorial Museum, courtesy of Anna Hassa Jarosky and Peter Hassa.

[30] *Trials of War Criminals before the Nuremberg Military Tribunals under Control Council Law No. 10 Nuremberg, October 1946-April 1949* (Washington, D.C.: U.S. G.P.O, 1949-1953), pp. 384-385.

[31] United States Holocaust Memorial Museum, courtesy of Anna Hassa Jarosky and Peter Hassa.. The biography of Dzido revealed that she escaped the first round of executions (the SS would kill any living experimentation victim to conceal any proof of the medical barbarities) but was then sent on a death march. After liberation, she returned to her home town to find out her mother had been killed and the pharmacist, Teodozjuz Nowinski, who had convinced Dzido to enroll in school, was sent to and was known to have died in Auschwitz.

[32] United States Holocaust Memorial Museum, courtesy of Anna Hassa Jarosky and Peter Hassa. "Saturday, June 01, 1946-Thursday, August 01, 1946: Poland; War Crimes Investigation Photo of Maria Kusmierczuk." Washington: USHMM.

[33] Ibid.

[34] Ibid.

[35] Ibid. Her biography at this source revealed that Kusmierczuk became a doctor after the war. See also Spitz, pp. 140-141.

[36] Kempner, p. 454.

[37] Spitz, p. 116.

[38] Ibid., p. 129. Karolewska revealed an encounter with Binz. She said that when selected for experimentation again, the women formed a line similar to what they must have witnessed when prisoners were about to be killed. Binz asked, "why do you stand in line as if you were to be executed?" Karolewska said the women told her they would rather die than endure more vivisection. The women were punished for saying this to Binz. See Ibid., p. 129.

[39] Ibid., 116.

[40] Beals, 255.

[41] Spitz, pp. 143-144.

[42] *Trials of War Criminals before the Nuremberg Military Tribunals under Control Council Law No. 10 Nuremberg, October 1946-April 1949* (Washington, D.C.: U.S. G.P.O, 1949- 1953), p. 393.

[43] *Benjamin B. Ferencz Collection: Correspondence and Related Records Regarding Restitution for Victims of Medical Experiments. 1957-1981*, at United States Holocaust Memorial Museum. Washington, D.C. http://www.ushmm.org (31 December 2001). See also Beals, p. 211.

[44] Beals, 255. Gebhardt, the same doctor who referred Irma Grese to Ravensbrück, was tried along with Oberheuser, and was sentenced to death.   See Ibid., 227, and Robert Jay Lifton, *The Nazi Doctors: Medical Killing and the Psychology of Genocide* (New York: Basic Books,   Inc., 1986), p. 290.

[45] Ibid., 255.

[46] Spitz, p. 263.

[47] Beals, 272.

[48] Leigh Fraser, interview by Marian Salkin, Transcript of Audio-taped Interview, 18 and 27 October; 9 November 1993 (Holocaust History Archive, Melrose Park, PA), pp. 67-68. Fraser was a British subject who worked as a Wren. She spent a considerable period in Bergen-Belsen after liberation, and among other duties, assisted with processing prisoners, and interacted with the Nazi women.

[49] Eric Townsend, "Reinstatement by Federal German Medical Authorities of Practitioner Guilty of Medical War Crimes." *The British Medical Journal*: Annual Representative Meeting.   (19 July 1958): p. 56.

[50] Ibid.

[51] See letter by M. H. Armstrong Davison, "Medical War Crimes." *The British Medical Journal* vol. 1, no. 5079 (10 May 1958): 1121.

[52] See the letter by Eric Townsend, "Medical War Crimes." *The British Medical   Journal* vol. 1, no. 5081 (24 May 1958): 1237. Shylock has been interpreted many ways by scholars, including as demonstrative of anti-Semitism. I refer the reader to Harold Bloom. Bloom said that Shakespeare's own anti-Semitism cannot be proved, but that "*The Merchant of Venice* is nevertheless a profoundly anti-Semitic work." See p. 171 in Harold Bloom, *Shakespeare: The Invention of the Human* (New York: Riverhead Books, 1998).

[53] Wilhelmina Maguire, "Medical Correspondence." *The British Medical Journal* vol. 1, no. 5084 (14 June 1958): 1420.

[54] For Tait's astonishing letter, see E.T. Wright, and A.P. Tait. "Medical War Crimes." *The British Medical Journal* vol. 2, no. 5087 (5 July 1958): 51.

[55] H. Livingstone Peake, and S. Bennett. "Medical War Crimes." *The British Medical Journal* vol. 2 no. 5088 (12 July 1958): 108.

[56] Ibid.

[57] Townsend, p. 57.

[58] Ibid.

[59] Arnold Sorsby, Felix S. Besser, A. Meyer, Wilhelmina Maguire, Frances Blackett. "Medical War Crimes." *The British Medical Journal* vol. 2, no. 5090 (26 July 1958): 246-247. Dr. Arnold Sorsby discussed how Dr. Hans Eisele, who worked at Buchenwald, and who was originally sentenced to die at his post-war trial, had his sentence reduced to seven years and began practicing medicine again. See Ibid., p. 247.

[60] See the letter of Felix S. Besser, in Ibid.

[61] See the Maguire letter, in Ibid.

[62] See the letter of Frances Blackett, in Ibid., pp. 247-248.

[63] See A.P. Tait, "Medical War Crimes." *The British Medical Journal* vol. 2, no. 5092 (9 August 1958): 390.

[64] See the entry marked "Medical War Crimes" in "Medical News." *The British Medical Journal* vol. 2, no. 5093 (16 August 1958): 460.

[65] Michael E. M. Cook, "Medical War Crimes." *The British Medical Journal* vol. 1, no. 5137 (20 June 1959): 1588.

[66] "Medical News." *The British Medical Journal* vol. 2, no. 5214 (10 December 1960): 1748.

[67] "Medical News." *The British Medical Journal* vol. 2, no. 5245 (15 July 1961): 187.

[68] Dalhoff, pp. 34-38, and Fraser, 68.

PART IV: *AUFSEHERINNEN UND ANDERE FRAUEN*: WHY?

CHAPTER XVII

CONCLUSION

Society is afraid of both the feminist and the murderer, for each of them,
in her own way, tests society's boundaries.[1]

The Nazi régime lasted from 30 January 1933 until 7 May 1945. Throughout
this period, thousands of women worked for and with the Nazi party. Other women
were involved with Nazism because of their spouses or because they were forced
to do so, though either conscription or as prisoners. Nazism, which held such
contempt for women, taught these women that the goal of the enemy of the state
(which was personified for the Nazis in the Jew) was to destroy the Aryan master
race. Consequently, women were led to believe that their lives were in danger unless
the enemy was suppressed. Women who were then put in a position of authority over
an enemy, and with almost all social mores removed, often treated prisoners in their
charge any way that they wished since they were allowed to and simply because they
chose to do so. Even if restrictions had been placed on them, women like Grese found
ways to circumvent authority so that they could fulfill their duty, which some felt
was to destroy the enemy of the state.

Having been imbued with propaganda to believe that the enemy, defined as
the Jew and prisoners in their custody, wanted to cause them harm, myriad guards did
not see the inmates as human. Any violent or sadistic means necessary to ensure that
the prisoner-enemy did not usurp their authority or disturb the camp structure was
acceptable. Even if prisoners did not do anything to upset an *Aufseherin*, it was not a
guarantee that they would be immune from punishment or

even murder. Several of the women who worked in the camps attacked prisoners without provocation and without explanation. Prisoners could suffer any kind of abuse or torture at the hands of the women involved with the camps because it was acceptable. Violence was often used as a means of control. Thousands of women involved with the Nazi party were indoctrinated and instructed to "take a hard attitude toward prisoners, and for some of them this attitude and the arrogance that came from wielding such power led almost effortlessly into a kind of mindless, almost juvenile, type of brutality.[2]

For the women who truly believed in the racist ideology of the Nazis, and if they felt a form of collectivism by agreeing with Nazi tenets, fighting against the enemy vis-à-vis work was a way that women served their state. They could also take part in the war this way; albeit at home or in occupied areas. Women could have babies for Hitler, or could work as an *Aufseherin*. Many women chose instead to fight for the Nazi-constructed racial war against the Jews and others by working in the camp structure. Although Hitler and the Nazis identified the Jew as the primary enemy, not all other enemies were as clearly defined. Anyone who was imprisoned in the camp structure was fair game. Prisoners could be subjected to arbitrary torture or could be killed for no apparent reason, and equally without provocation.[3] Working against the perceived enemy became a way for some women to do their part for the Nazi state. Most did so willingly, and were not programmed by the Nazis to abuse or murder.

Although the Nazi indoctrination theory may seem plausible to some, it still does not explain why so many women acted so violently towards others in their charge. SS superiors recognized women who were especially evil and vicious as having done a good job. Quite often, these same cruel and sadistic women received promotions for their brutality.[4] Since women who worked for the SS in the camps lived with "a self-important consciousness of their superior achievements, rank, and authority, their membership in some prestigious group," any violent means necessary to achieve SS recognition was acceptable and encouraged.[5] Involvement with the SS in the camp structure gave women an opportunity to define an authoritative role for themselves. They were also able to use their authority against prisoners in a way that they could personally control. Although Nazi regulatory guidelines for guards to follow for inflicting proper punishment on prisoners existed, many women such as Grese with her alleged custom-made cellophane whip came up with individualized ways to abuse their enemies.

Having authority gave many of the women, such as Bormann, a purpose, and a way to achieve not only recognition, but to make more money (this was rarely true). Was more money and a sense of purpose really reasons for Braunsteiner to murder infants? Was there any rationale for Lächert to abuse prisoners, Volkenrath to stomp on women, or for Binz to hack someone to death? How can the women, such as Oberheuser, who were not *Aufseherinnen* be explained?

Oberheuser willingly used human surplus for her experiments, in the name of science. Lothe, on the other hand, decried her role in the Nazi party, saying that she had been forced to do the things she did because she was a prisoner herself. Ilse Koch, whose position of authority was based on her status as a camp commandant's wife, was allegedly responsible for some of the most horrific crimes of the Holocaust. Regardless of any attempts to understand the economic, emotional, physical, or psychological motives of these women, one must understand that for the most part these women were normal, educated, intelligent women who had no other reason to abuse and kill Jews as well as other prisoners except for the fact that their own government allowed them to do so and because they wanted to, for whatever personal reasons that they may have   had.

There may never be an acceptable answer for why so many women took part in sadistic, horrific acts of violence against prisoners. Regardless of any predetermined concepts that existed about women and the ideal feminine sphere, these women defied all preconceived notions of the gentler sex. Women were responsible for many of the most heinous atrocities committed within the camps.

Their gender does not make allowances for their participation in genocide and   other

crimes of the Holocaust.

Nazism gave many of these women a sense of identity and a collective

purpose. Once ensconced in the Nazi structure, or once employed by the SS, women

turned their fears and anxieties against a common enemy into a way to abuse, torture,

and murder innocent victims simply because the women were in a position of power

over their charges. Sadistic violence was a way to assert authority and control, and,

quite possibly, release emotions, constrained anger,

and act out revenge fantasies.[6] These women could feel superior in their positions

of power, and dominate as well as humiliate those who they were told were inferior

or were their enemies. However, despite any attempts to understand the psychological

motives of these women, one must understand that they had no reason to mistreat

and murder other than they were granted a license to do so. Moreover, all of the

women examined herein denied or minimized their culpability for the Holocaust,

despite direct evidence that indicated   otherwise.

Why did Nazism as an ideology help to bring out such horrific and sadistic

behavioral traits in women who were involved with the Nazis or who worked as

Aufseherinnen and in other positions, forced or not? Was it because Nazism offered

women a "sweet sense of belonging to an intimate in-group made up of

comrades of the same blood and the same belief"?[7] However, if this were true,

then all women who worked as *Aufseherinnen* or for the Nazi party would have to

have been anti-Semitic, or at least have believed, perhaps absolutely, in the idea   of

the Aryan master race, and that everyone else deemed as enemies of the state deserved

to die. But not all *Aufseherinnen* were entirely evil as Weissmann Klein noted.

Herbermann discussed her interactions with Johanna Langefeld, an

Oberaufseherin at Ravensbrück. While working at Ravensbrück, Herbermann said

that Langefeld saved several people, including many Jehovah's Witnesses,

whereas others said that Langefeld might have also taken part in selections.[8]

Herbermann further stated that Langefeld, an "unemployed single mother who asked for work as a prison warden so that she could do good among the poorest of the poor," also saved some political prisoners. Because of her sympathy towards prisoners, Langefeld was brought before an SS court, and she was subsequently fired from Ravensbrück.[9]

These women could be categorized as violent sadists, incapable of understanding the horror of their actions in the name of biological and ideological camaraderie, but some were more violent than others, often using extreme means to control or even murder prisoners. Fists, dogs, guns, and whips were used to control. Binz used both a pickaxe and her own boots to kill female prisoners. What remains true of some of the women who worked for or who were involved with the Nazi party was that they took an active part in crimes against humanity   or war crimes at different levels. Nazism encouraged ordinary women to help destroy the enemy of the German state. Therefore, Nazism advocated and encouraged abuse, humiliation, and murder of those deemed not worthy of life: "The mind of the German, especially the mind of a national Socialist and member

of the SS, was drilled into one particular channel and the broad view of humanity was lost sight of."[10] Despite their culpability, the majority of women on trial for war crimes committed under the Nazi régime denied their responsibility for the crimes committed in the concentration and extermination camps. They did what they did because they could. Did these women experience "pleasure at the prospect of punishing someone who wronged" them, with the "someone"

constructed by the Nazis as the Jew and others deemed unworthy of   life?[11] Perhaps. How many women escaped punishment because their gender allowed them to assimilate back into post-war society? Are any remaining perpetrators still alive? If so, their accountability diminishes with   time.[12]

By disregarding female perpetrators in the study of genocide and war, the suffering of the victims is discounted, and culpability is removed from the *Aufseherinnen, Kapos,* and *die Ärztin* merely because of their gender. The crimes of the Nazi female perpetrators, however small or large their role was, cannot be overlooked. The women who were involved with or who worked for the Nazis may have been aberrations or even pawns for Hitler and his ideology, but many of the women, even those who had been conscripted, chose their own path: good or evil. The female perpetrators did not have to molest, torture, or kill prisoners. Women such as Ilse Koch, Bormann, and Volkenrath abused prisoners on their own, without direct orders to do so. Oberheuser was a doctor, someone who was supposed to uphold human life. She strayed from adherence to the Hippocratic oath to do no harm. These women all made a choice to consciously act in the way that they did, which was, and still is, a frightening concept.

[1] Jones, 13.

[2] Morrison, 26.

[3] Such examples were found with Geneviève de Gaulle, a Christian French resister (and niece of General Charles de Gaulle), and Nanda Herbermann, a Christian German whose brother was a member of the SS. Both women were imprisoned at Ravensbrück.

[4] Morrison, 26. The Nazi indoctrination theory was used at Herta Bothe's trial in her defense. See chapter on Bothe in my book.

[5] Shapiro, 105.

[6] Term "revenge fantasies" from Marilyn Elias, "Revenge." *Sunday. Chicago Tribune* (14 November 2010): 22-23.

[7] Kirkpatrick, 294.

[8] See Heike, "Female Concentration Camp Guards as Perpetrators," pp. 131-132.

[9] See Herbermann, pp. 125-126, n. 3, and Brown, *The Camp Women*, p. 18.

[10] United Nations War Crimes Commission, *The Belsen Trial*, p. 132.

[11] See Elias, "Revenge." This article discussed how "revenge fantasies" lead people to believe that getting revenge against a perceived enemy (or someone a person believes did them wrong) "would feel tremendously satisfying." The article pointed out that while acting out on such a fantasy might indeed not prove to be rewarding in the end, the brain is stimulated by just the thought of engaging in revenge. It cited numerous studies done recently on test groups and the idea of revenge. One such group was comprised of 14 people. When given the chance to retaliate against the person designated as the "enemy," 12 opted to do so. The article did mention that gender can play a role in how revenge fantasies are acted out, suggesting women take a more passive role than men; however, this is not always true, as studies of female perpetrators and serial killers have shown. Refer also to Vronsky, passim. Miami psychologist Michael McCullough was cited in the "Revenge" article, taken from his research in his book *Beyond Revenge: The Evolution of the Forgiveness Instinct*. McCullough and Elias illustrated how "Although it can be a misguided, costly craving in the modern world, evolutionary psychologists believe the thirst for revenge ensured our ancestor's survival—retaliation was the only way for the victims to deter aggressors from harming them or their tribes in the future." Nazi propaganda conceptualized the Jews (and others) as aggressors who would harm German women (and the human race) unless something was done to stop them. Many women who worked for the Nazis believed this was truth and acted against their (falsely constructed) aggressors in the concentration and extermination camps.

[12] Remember Hermine Braunsteiner was the first Nazi war criminal to be extradited from the United States. She was a woman.

APPENDIX I

Excerpt from the Application for *Aufseherinnen*

You only have to watch over prisoners; consequently, applicants, who should be between the ages of 21 and 45, don't need professional training. The salary of hired *Aufseherinnen*, who become employees of the Reich, is determined by [Schedule] TOA IX and a step raise will be given after a three-month probationary period. Community food allotment as well as a "well-furnished official residence" and service clothes (fabric and fatigue uniforms) are assured.[1]

---

[1] From *"Das Frauenkonzentrationlager Ravensbrück,"* in Brown, *The Beautiful Beast*, 26.

Women Working For The Nazis: Further Analysis

Women could not join the SS, but they could work for them as contractors. The SS did not permit women to become members because of their gender. The SS was designed to control and protect the interests of the state. Hitler's second in command, Hermann Göring, in his only official authorized biography, described the SS, and outlined the duties of the SS men. Their duties, according to Göring, varied, and included secret surveillance, supervision of political activities, as well as providing protection for Hitler against insubordination by people opposed to him. As an umbrella organization, the SS had many subsidiaries that carried out duties as designated by the state, including running the camps. The duties of the SS were not limited to what Göring envisioned; terror, violence, murder, and other vile acts were also part of SS

duties.[1] Women as SS contractors were not addressed. SS functionaries helped   the Nazis carry out their crimes such as what was seen with the T4 program, which Juana Bormann might have been involved with. However, when trying to determine initial female involvement outside of the camp structure, it was important to view the war crime sector samples obtained by historian Michael Mann, in which he indicated, "95% of my samples were men. Women were more than 5% only in T4 [Centre in the Tiergarten Strasse N. 4] (as nurses and secretaries)."[2] T4 was the abbreviation for the medical euthanasia program ordered by Hitler.

In September of 1939, Hitler personally signed an order for the establishment of this program, designed to grant a mercy death to children, men, and women classified as not worthy of life. The Reich Chancellory developed   the

T4 program as an official euthanasia program to rid Germany of criminals, the disabled, injured, mentally ill, people of mixed racial origin, and the chronically sick. Both children and adults were murdered and killing centers were established solely for this purpose. Secretly named T4 because its main office was located in Berlin on Tiergarten Strasse Nr. 4, the T4 program was the predecessor to the extermination camps that had already employed many women.

With regard to women employed by the Nazis: "Women formed about 10% of concentration camp staff, as they did among all camp staff."[3] Women were less likely to be promoted to higher ranks and were consigned to either administrative or medical type of jobs, unless they were hired or conscripted for a position as an *Aufseherin*. In the job description it did not state, nor did it hint at what would be required as guards of prisoners, but some SS women reconstructed their position, and created a gendered agency of power for themselves that defied even Nazi hierarchies of cruelty; these women did so willingly simply because they had the opportunity to do so. Can the phenomenon of women such   as Lächert, Mandl, or Grese, who "rose to the top of the women's SS" be explained?[4]

These women were certainly not secretaries, nor were these women nurses; they were instruments of abuse and death. Women were not considered on equal standing with men in the SS, but they did receive promotions and were recognized for their work. No definitive figures can be given as to the actual numbers of female Nazi perpetrators. Whether they were volunteers, or were conscripted, some of these women were drawn to Nazism or had "male family members who were active Nazis" and that while "some must have had strong Nazi views, though few had previously acted upon them and few seemed caged within Nazism or prewar violence."[5]

Can the actual figures of female perpetrator participation in genocide and other crimes of the Holocaust be actually determined based on the few findings that remain post-war and were not destroyed by the Nazis? Can available data be truly reflective of women who actually participated in war crimes and crimes against humanity at the camps?[6] With emerging scholarship, decades of silence towards analysis of female perpetrators can be   re-dressed.

---

[1] See Erich Gritzbach, *Hermann Göring: The Man and His Work* (London: Hurst and Blackett, Ltd., 1939), pp. 33, 41, 79, and 136.

[2] See Michael Mann, "Were the Perpetrators of Genocide 'Ordinary Men' or 'Real Nazis'? Results from Fifteen Hundred Biographies" *Holocaust and Genocide Studies* 14, no. 3 (winter 2000): 331-366.

[3] Ibid., pp. 340-341.

[4] Smith, p. 323.

[5] Mann, pp. 340-341.

[6] For more on T4, see Lifton, pp. 95-97.

APPENDIX III

Popular Constructions of Nazi Women: She-Wolf to Wonder   Woman

Hypersexualized images of Nazis emerged after World War Two with men's magazines of the 1950s and 1960s, but notably in film in the 1970s.[1] The hypersexualization of German woman was nothing new in erotic literature or images. Though in film, combining German women with Nazi women in violent, pornographic ways became, and, apparently, still continues, as a popular underground theme for some. Erotic, sexually explicit depictions of the *Aufseherin* in film were seen in *Ilsa, She-Wolf of the SS* (1975). In this film, Ilsa, an *Oberaufseherin*, raped, performed medical experiments, and committed other barbaric acts. Following *Ilsa, She-Wolf of the SS*, other films continued these
graphic, sadistic themes, and while "one can debate endlessly the meaning of the mostly male sexual fascination with beautiful blond Nazi killer bitches" it does   not justify their existence.[2]

There were so many other films in this genre it became problematic to list them all, not to mention to attempt to deconstruct, view, and somehow make sense of appalling, as well as incredibly grotesque, materials that were made during the 1970s (and beyond), but a few are discussed here. I can offer no rationale or explanation for the need for these films that include constructions of *Aufseherinnen* and SS men in an extreme pornographic and horror filmic fashion. In these films, victims of the Nazis are continually debased in sexually
derogatory, and in very intense, brutal ways. Many of these films have been banned, notably in the United Kingdom.[3] *Deported Women of the SS Special Section* (1976) featured women prisoners sent to camps run by lesbian guards and
perverted men who rape and torture the women. The *Gestapo's Last Orgy* (1977)

was a film so appalling that researching this particular entry was incredibly upsetting. The film features rape, Nazi cannibalism of Jewish prisoners, the boiling of a Jewish baby for dinner, and other scenes that defy logical description. Other exploitation films included *SS Camp 5: Women's Hell* (1977), which apparently was part of a series of SS "camp" films. The Internet Movie Database describes this film as: "During the last days of WW2, several female prisoners arrive at Camp 5 to work as sex slaves for officers and guinea pigs for horrific experiments by Nazi doctors who are trying to find a cure for burns."[4] SS female doctors also appear in some of these films. Another 1977 entry was *Women's Camp 119*. In this film, SS doctors experimented with freezing prisoners and then rewarmed them with nude women, which was depicted in a very graphic and pornographic manner. These filmic depictions, although pornographic, and constructed in an extraordinarily grotesque sexual manner, were partially based   on freezing and rewarming experiments performed at Dachau and other camps. Oberheuser took part in such experiments. Holocaust survivors, scholars,   and

others have denounced these films.[5] However, Nazi pornographic/exploitation films have continued and the subject materials remain the same. Not all constructions of female Nazis were pornographic, yet they were still heavily sexualized. An example of these images was found in the television show *Wonder Woman*. Wonder Woman as a comic was created in December 1941, and she battled Axis powers. This theme carried into the 1970s television show where actress Lynda Carter played Wonder Woman. In one episode, Nazis officials and   a blond, curvy SS woman named "Fausta" wanted to steal Wonder Woman's

special powers. They kidnapped Wonder Woman and torture was suggested.[6] Campy, sexy, but shown in a heroic fashion, Wonder Woman defeated Fausta and emerged as an American hero, unlike many other 1970s media presentations. Along with recurrent hyper-sexualized images of German women, filmic constructions of SS women in pornographic settings continued into the twenty-   first century. Occasionally, the two constructions   intermingled.

A film released in 2008 was *Blitzkrieg: Escape from Stalag 69* whose theme was not too dissimilar from other such films that emerged in the 1970s   about SS women. German women were shown in a dominant fashion, and the   Nazi element played a key role in the plot line. Sexualized constructions of German women continue in television commercials, and promotion of these   images as well as continuous explicit presentations of SS women have grown with the advent of the Internet and social networking sites. At the time of this writing, there were numerous web pages devoted to the idealization of sexy German female constructs, *Aufseherin* (both real and imagined), and   also   fallacious   Nazi/SS woman models; these depictions were found in close to dozen different languages by searching online for the subject material. Not all were found   online.

German women as sexualized constructs were seen during the 2009 Superbowl, with a GoDaddy.com commercial that featured a "Miss Schmidt," a blond German woman who was featured in a shower scene with Danica Patrick, the racecar driver.[7] In 2010, a Dos Equis beer commercial was shown   on broadcast television where the "world's most interesting man" emerged, obviously post-coitus, from a train car with two women in traditional German costume still inside.[8] These commercials demonstrate an ongoing fascination   with German women as objects of sexual desire. Obviously, these constructs differ greatly than the use of Nazi or SS women in pornographic   settings.

The use of SS women as sexual objects intersects with what one would think would be norms of decency. In 2010, Irma Grese had a social networking page created for her that linked to more Nazi sexual exploitation type web pages, including a semi-nude woman wearing a SS cap while holding a weapon. Grese was, and is, an especially popular topic on the Internet and has many web sites devoted to her, perhaps more than any other *Aufseherin*.[9] Numerous other SS female constructs are featured in amateur pornographic films that abound on the web and appear not to abate any time soon. After a conversation with a colleague about how top Nazi leaders such as Hitler have been made into action-type toys, a search for Nazi figurines on Google turned up a site that sells SS women dolls,

with bright blond hair, china-blue eyes, and very tight SS *Aufseherin* uniforms.

And so the desecration of the memories of the Nazi victims continues.

---

[1] Vronsky, pp. 370-371. Filmic representations in a historical construct were seen in the 1947 film *The Last Stop* and also in *The Passenger* (1963).

[2] Ibid., 371.

[3] See http://www.parliament.uk/.

[4] *SS Camp 5: Women's Hell* (1977). http://www.imdb.com/title/tt0147310/ (3 November 2010).

[5] See Geoffrey Cocks, *The Wolf at the Door: Stanley Kubrick, History, and the Holocaust* (New York: Peter Lang Publishing, 2004), p. 165.

[6] See *Wonder Woman: Fausta, The Nazi Wonder Woman*. VHS. Directed by Directed by Barry Crane, 28 April 1976. Terra Haute, IN: Columbia House Video for DC Comics, 1999 and also *Wonder Woman Meets Baroness von Gunther*. VHS. Directed by Barry Crane, 21 April 1976. Terra Haute, IN: Columbia House Video for DC Comics, 1999.

[7] See www.godaddy.com.

[8] The commercials can be viewed at http://dosequis.com/.

[9] Links to these pages are purposely omitted from citation.

GLOSSARY

Anschluss. Annexation of Austria to Nazi Germany in March 1938.

Ärztin. Female doctor.

Aufseherin. Female overseer, or ward guard. Irma Grese, Juana Bormann.

Anweiserin. Female concentration-camp supervisor, manager.

Appell. Roll call, usually led, at least in the women's camps, by an *Aufseherin*.

Arbeitsdienst. Labor service.

Arbeitsdienstführer, *Arbeitsdienstführerin*. SS Labor Control Officer, male and female. Position Irma Grese was promoted to while at Bergen-Belsen.

Arbeitskommando. Working squad.

BDM. *Bund Deutscher Mädchen*, the League of German Girls or the girl version of the Hitler Youth.

Blockältester. Block leader.

Blockältesten. Female block leaders.

Einsatzgruppen. Mobile battalions of special action soldiers, which often employed women who served as aides in a variety of capacities.

Einsatzkommando. A unit of the *Einsatzgruppen*.

Erstaufseherinnen. Head guard.

Flakhelferin. Female anti-aircraft auxiliary.

Frau. Woman, or wife.

Frauenfront. German women's movement.

Frauenlager. Women's compound.

Frauenwerk. Women's Bureau.

Gefolgschaft. Factory staff.

Gestapo. Geheime Staatspolizei, secret police, or a terrorist unit of police officers that was later absorbed, under Heinrich Himmler, into the SS. The Gestapo, under the SS umbrella, became both the state security police and the regular state police.

Goebbels, Joseph. Reich Minister for National Propaganda.

Göring, Hermann. *Reichsmarshall,* Reich Air Force Marshall and head of the Luftwaffe, he signed off on the Final Solution.

Häftling. Prisoner.

Helferinnen. Women who worked as aides, assistants, guards, or helpers.

Heydrich, Reinhard. *SS Obergruppenführer.* Coordinator of the Final Solution.

Himmler, Heinrich. *Reichsführer* (Head of the SS).

Hitler, Adolf. Leader (*Führer*) of Germany.

Hundeführerinnen. Women dog handlers or leaders.

Kapos. Block commanders; male or female prisoners worked in these positions.

Kommandant. Commander, or chief officer of a concentration camp.

Kommando. A commando or squad. Could also refer to a person assigned to work as head of a squad under SS control, such as Herta Bothe.

Kommandoführerin. Chief female commander, post Irma Grese was promoted to.

Lager. A camp, concentration, extermination, holding or transit.

Lagerführer. A camp leader.

Lagerkommandant. Camp commander.

Mengele, Josef. Notorious Auschwitz doctor and mass murderer.

Nazism. Fascist system of power led by Hitler, 1933-1945.

Nazi Women's League (NS-*Frauenschaft*) NSDAP organization for women.

NSDAP. Nationalsozialistische Deutsche Arbeiterpartei, the National Socialist German Workers Party.

Oberaufseherin. Female head overseer, e.g. Dorothea (Theodora) Binz.

Reichsführer. Head of the SS and minister of the interior, Heinrich Himmler.

Reichsfrauenführerin. Leader of the Reich's German Women's movement, such as Gertrude Scholtz-Klink.

Ringärztin. Female BDM doctor.

Schutzstaffel (SS). Protective Squadron. Established in 1925, the SS remained a division of the Nazi party until 1933, when it became an important part of the bureaucracy of the Third Reich. Heinrich Himmler, who took over the SS from Hermann Göring, was Hitler's *Reichsführer*, and was the architect of the complex SS hierarchy. Himmler was also known as *Chef der Deutschen Polizei*, the chief of the Reich police. It was under his direction that the SS grew into several different police units, including the unit that would be in charge of the concentration and extermination camps, the SS *Totenkopfverbände* (SS Death Head Special Units).

Schutzhaftlagerführer. Camp Leader.

Sicherheitsdienst (Security Service). Women worked for this unit typically in administrative positions.

Sonderkommando. A special unit.

Speer, Albert. Architect, and Architectural Inspector of the Reich.

SS-Helferinnenkorps. The Corp of SS assistants. Status for women who applied for positions as *Aufseherin*, unlike women who were drafted.

SS-Kriegshelferinnen. (War auxiliaries). Women who were conscripted for work after 1939 in Nazi Germany and later occupied areas.

SS-Retinue. Designation for groups of female guards who guarded female prisoners.

SS-Schwestern. Nurses of the SS, pertains to the nurses who worked in the camps. The German word "*Schwester*" has three meanings: sister, nurse, and nun.

SS-Wächterin. Term for guard.

Stellvertreter. Replacement (position some women held in the camps).

Sturmabteilungen (SA, Storm Troopers).

Tiermenchen. Subhuman designation given to Nazi victims.

Totenkommando. A death squad, a group responsible for executions.

Totenkopfdivision. SS Death Head Division.

Totenkopfverbände. SS Death Head Special Units. Theodor Eicke was the Commander of these units.

Volksgemeinschaft. "People's community," term defined the Nazi construction of community.

Waffen-SS. Elite unit of the SS.

Wehrmacht. The German armed forces.

Wehrmachtshelferinnen. Women who worked for the armed forces of Germany.

Weltanschauung. Ideological world outlook. Especially used to describe Hitler's ideology. In order to find acceptance for their anti-Semitic policies, Hitler and his top Nazis needed a way to influence and convince the public, in a twisted form of social Darwinism, that unless the world was rid of Jews, the entire human race would suffer. Hence, Hitler appointed Goebbels as the man responsible for creating, administering, and supervising propaganda to spread Nazi *Weltanschauung.* The Nazi propaganda message centered not only on anti-Semitism, but also stressed racial purity.

BIBLIOGRAPHY

Primary Sources

Biographical Accounts

Gritzbach, Erich. *Hermann Göring: The Man and His Work.* London: Hurst and Blackett, Ltd., 1939.

Hitler, Adolf. *Hitler's Secret Conversations: 1941-1944.* New York: Signet, 1953.

__________. *Mein Kampf.* München, F. Eher Nachf., 1939.

Höss, Rudolph. *Death Dealer: The Memoirs of the SS Kommandant at Auschwitz.* New York: Da Capo Press, 1996.

Eyewitness Accounts

Bar-On, Dan. *Legacy of Silence: Encounters with Children of the Third Reich.* Cambridge, MA and London: Harvard University Press, 1989.

Bonhoeffer, Emmi. *Auschwitz Trials: Letters from an Eyewitness,* trans. Ursula Stechow. Richmond: John Knox Press, 1967.

Fénelon, Fania and Marcelle Routier. *Playing for Time.* Syracuse: Syracuse University Press, 1997.

Fraser, Leigh, interview by Marian Salkin, Transcript of Audio-taped Interview, 18 and 27 October; 9 November 1993, Holocaust History Archive, Melrose Park, PA.

Lewis Jon E., Ed. *The Mammoth Book of Eyewitness History: Firsthand Accounts of History in the Making from the Ancient to the Modern World.* New York: Carroll & Graf Publishers, Inc., 1998.

Owings, Alison. *Frauen: German Women Recall the Third Reich.* New Brunswick, NJ: Rutgers University Press, 1994.

Scholtz-Klink, Gertrud. *Die Frau im Dritten Reich.* Tübingen: Grabert, 1978.

Schoppmann, Claudia. *Days of Masquerade: Life Stories of Lesbians During the Third Reich*. New York: Columbia University Press, 1996.

Steinhoff, Johannes, Peter Pechel and Dennis Showalter. *Voices from the Third Reich: An Oral History*. Washington, D.C.: Regnery Gateway, 1989.

Survivor Accounts

Anthonioz, Geneviève De Gaulle. *The Dawn of Hope: A Memoir of Ravensbrück*, 2 ed. New York: Arcade Publishing, 1999.

Buber, Margarete. *Under Two Dictators*, trans. Edward Fitzgerald. New York: Dodd, Mead and Company, 1946.

Dufournier, Denise. *Ravensbrück: The Women's Camp of Death.* London: George Allen and Unwin, Ltd., 1948.

Gedenkstätte Buchenwald, ed. *Buchenwald Concentration Camp 1937-1945 (A Guide to the Permanent Historical Exhibition)* trans. Judith Rosenthal. Wallstein Verlag, 2004.

Hackett, David A., Ed. *The Buchenwald Report.* Boulder: Westview Press, 1995.

Herbermann, Nanda.   *The Blessed Abyss: Inmate #6582 in Ravensbrück Concentration Camp for Women.* Detroit: Wayne University Press, 2000.

La Guardia Gluck, Gemma. *Fiorello's Sister: Gemma La Guardia Gluck's Story (Religion, Theology, and the Holocaust)*. Syracuse, NY: Syracuse University Press, 2007.

Levi, Primo. *Survival in Auschwitz: The Nazi Assault on Humanity*. New York: Simon and Schuster, 1996.

Levy, Isaac. *Witness to Evil: Bergen-Belsen, 1945*. London: Peter Halban in association with the European Jewish Publication Society, 1995.

Milla, Liana. *Smoke over Birkenau*. New York: Jewish Publication Society, 1991.

Miller, Joy Erlichmann. *Love Carried Me Home: Women Surviving Auschwitz*. Deerfield Beach, FL: Simcha Press, 2000.

Póltawska, Wanda. *And I Am Afraid of My Dreams.* London: Hodder & Stoughton, 1987.

Tillion, Germaine. *Ravensbrück: An Eyewitness Account of a Women's Concentration Camp.* Garden City, NY: Anchor Books, 1975.

Trial Transcripts and Military Tribunal Accounts

Davidson, Eugene. *The Trial of the Germans: An Account of the Twenty-two Defendants before the International Military Tribunal at Nuremberg.* New York: The MacMillan Company, 1966.

Fyfe, Sir David Maxwell. *War Crimes Trials: Volume II, The Belsen Trial.* London: William Hodge and Company, Ltd., 1949.

Neal, Judge Walter B. and United States Government, *The First German War Crimes Trial: Chief Judge Walter B. Neal's Desk Notebook of the Doctor's Trial, Held in Nuremberg, Germany, December, 1945 to August, 1947,* ed. W. Paul Burman, 2 vols. Chapel Hill, NC: Documentary Publications, 1985.
Office of United States, *Chief Counsel for Prosecution of Axis Criminality,* vols. 1-8.Washington: United States Government Printing Office, 1946.

Phillips, Raymond. *Trial of Josef Kramer and Forty-Four Others (The Belsen Trial).* London: William Hodge and Company, Ltd, 1949.

Trials of War Criminals before the Nuremberg Military Tribunals under Control Council Law No. 10. Nuremberg, October 1946-April 1949. Washington, D.C.: U.S. G.P.O., 1949-1953.

United Nations War Crimes Commission. *Law Reports of Trials of War Criminals: The Belsen Trial,* Vol. II. London: Published for the United Nations War Crimes Commission, by His Majesty's Stationery Office, 1947.

United Nations War Crimes Commission. *Law Reports of Trials of War Criminals: The Belsen Trial,* 2d ed. New York: Howard Fertig, 1983.

United States Congress, Senate. *Conduct of Ilse Koch War Crimes Trial: Hearings before the Investigations Subcommittee of the Committee on Expenditures in the Executive Departments, Interim report of the Investigations Subcommittee of the Committee on Expenditures in the Executive Departments pursuant to S. Res. 189, 80th Congress, a Resolution Authorizing the Committee on Expenditures in the Executive Departments to Carry Out Certain Duties.* United States Senate, Eightieth Congress, second session, Sept. 28-Dec. 9, 1948, Dec. 27, 1948, Submitted, under authority of the order of the Senate, June 19, 1948, by Mr. Ferguson. United States Government Printing Office: Washington, 1948.

United States, Office of Chief of Counsel for the Prosecution of Axis Criminality. *Nazi Conspiracy and Aggression*, 1946, 1971.

Secondary Sources

Articles

Armstrong Davison, M. H. "Medical War Crimes." *The British Medical Journal* vol. 1, no. 5079 (10 May 1958): 1121.

"Belsen and Dachau," *The New York Times* (15 December 1945): 16 (L).

"Belsen Girl Guard Blames all of SS," *Newsweek*, 7, no. 2 (6 October 1945).

Binder, David. "Ilse Koch's Posthumous Rehabilitation Sought by Son." *The New York Times* (7 May 1971).

Burleigh, Michael. "Euthanasia and the Third Reich," *History Today* 40 (February 1990): 11-16.

Campbell, D'Ann. "Women in Combat: The World War II Experience in the United States, Great Britain, Germany, and the Soviet Union," *Journal of Military History* 57, no. 2 (1993): 301-323.

"Case Opened Against Belsen Guards: Prosecution's Tale of Horror, Application for Separate Trial Refused," *London Times* (18 September 1945): 4   (F).

Cook, Michael E. M. "Medical War Crimes." *The British Medical Journal* vol. 1, no. 5137 (20 June 1959): 1588.

Elias, Marilyn. "Revenge." *Sunday. Chicago Tribune* (14 November 2010): 22-23.

"Female Nazi War Criminals."
http://www.capitalpunishmentuk.org/nazigirls.html (3 November 2010).

"Germany: Very Special Present." *Time.*
http://www.time.com/time/magazine/article/0,9171,859084,00.html#ixzz12ZLQS 8hV (1 August 2010).

Harvey, Oliver. "A 'kind, sweet' granny hiding an evil secret" in *The Sun* http://www.thesun.co.uk/sol/homepage/showbiz/film/2259283/Kate-Winslet-plays-an-evil-Nazi-guard-in-her-Oscar-nominated-film-The-Sun-reveals-the-real-life-story-behind-the-character-she-plays.html?print=yes (21 February 2009)

"Helene Grese." Bergen-Belsen Trial Documents at BergenBelsen.co.uk. http://www.bergenbelsen.co.uk/pages/Trial/Trial/TrialDefenceCase/Trial_036_Grese.html (1 August 2010).

Heike, Irmtraud und Langefeld, Johanna. "Täterinnen im Konzentrationslager: Die Biographie einer KZ-Oberaufseherin" *Werkstatt Geschichte* 4, no. 12 (Nov 1995).

"Irma and the Whip," *Newsweek*, (11 October 1945): 3e.

Johnson, Richard L. "Nazi Feminists: A Contradiction in Terms," *Frontiers*, vol. 1, no. 3 (1975): 55-62.

Kempner, Robert M. W. "The Nuremberg Trials as Sources of Recent German Political and Historical Materials." *The American Political Science Review*, vol. 44, no. 2 (Jun., 1950): 447-459.

Knapp, Gabriele. "Music as a Means of Survival: The Women's Orchestra in Auschwitz." *Feministische Studien* trans. Katherine Deeg, Anette Bauer, and Liana Curtis. vol. 1 (1996).

Lower, Wendy. "Male and Female Perpetrators and the East German Approach to Justice," 1948-1963. *Holocaust and Genocide Studies* 24, no. 1 (spring 2010):   56-84.

Maguire, Wilhelmina. "Medical Correspondence." *The British Medical Journal* vol. 1, no. 5084 (14 June 1958): 1420.

Malone, Andrew. "Stolen by the Nazis: The tragic tale of 12,000 blue-eyed blond children taken by the SS to create an Aryan super-race." *The Daily Mail Online.* www.dailymail.co.uk/news/article-1111170/Stolen-Nazis-The-tragic-tale-12-000-blue-eyed-blond-children-taken-SS-create-Aryan-super-race.html (23 April 2010).

Mann, Anthony. "Noted Jurist for Defence: Application Allowed." *The Scotsman.* 28 September 1945. See: http://www.bergenbelsen.co.uk/pages/Staff/StaffPhotographs.asp?CampStaffID=51&PhotographsID=586&index=17 (1 October 2010).

Martin, Douglas. "A Nazi Past, a Queens Home Life, an Overlooked Death" *The New York Times*.

http://www.nytimes.com/2005/12/02/international/europe/02ryan.html (19
September 2010).

Mason, Timothy. "Women in Germany, 1925-1940: Family, Welfare, and Work.
Part II," *History Workshop* (January 1976): 5-32.

________. "Zur Lage der Frauen in Deutschland: Wohlfahrt, Arbeit, und   Familie,"
        Gesellschaft: Beitreage zur Marxschen Theorie (June 1976):   118-193.

McCarthy, Jamie "Frau Ilse Koch, General Lucius Clay, and Human-Skin
Atrocities," at *The Jewish Virtual Library*
http://www.jewishvirtuallibrary.org/jsource/Holocaust/skin.html (15 October
2010).

"Medical News." *The British Medical Journal* vol. 2, no. 5093 (16 August 1958):
460.

"Medical News." *The British Medical Journal* vol. 2, no. 5212 (26 November
1960): 1612.

"Medical News." *The British Medical Journal* vol. 2, no. 5214 (10 December
1960): 1748.

"Medical News." *The British Medical Journal* vol. 2, no. 5245 (15 July 1961):
187.

Moss, Stephen. "Memories of Auschwitz." *The Guardian*. (13 January   2005).

Peake, H. Livingstone and S. Bennett. "Medical War Crimes." *The British
Medical Journal* vol. 2 no. 5088 (12 July 1958):   108.

Prusin, Alexander V. "Poland's Nuremberg: The Seven Court Cases of the Supreme
National Tribunal, 1946-1948." *Holocaust and Genocide Studies* 24, no.   1 (spring
2010): 1-25.

Przyrembel, Alexandra. "Transfixed by an Image: Ilse Koch, the 'Kommandeuse
of Buchenwald'." *German History* 19 no. 3, (October 2001):   369-399.

Rollyson, Carl. "Reporting Nuremberg: Women Journalists at the Nuremberg
Trials" *New Criterion* 17 (September 1998): 74 (I).

Rupp, Leila J. "Mother of the Volk: The Image of Women in Nazi Ideology,"
Journal of Military History 3, no. 3 (winter 1977):   362-379.

________. "Women, Class, and Mobilization in Nazi Germany," *Science and Society* 43 (1979): 51-69.

Schwarz, Gudrun. "SS Aufseherinnen in N-S Konzentrationslagern   (1933-1945)" *Dachauer Hefte* 10 (1994): 32-49.

Smith, Roger W. "Women and Genocide: Notes on an Unwritten   History" *Holocaust and Genocide Studies* 8 no. 3, (winter 1994):   315-334.

Sorsby, Arnold, Felix S. Besser, A. Meyer, Wilhelmina Maguire, Frances Blackett. "Medical War Crimes." *The British Medical Journal* vol. 2, no. 5090   (26 July 1958): 246-248.

Sprenger, Isabell. "Täterinnen im Konzentrationslager: Aufseherinnen in den Frauenaussenlagern des Konzentrationslagers Gross-Rosen" *Werkstatt Geschichte* 4, no. 12 (Nov 1995).

"The SS Garrison in Auschwitz-Birkenau." Auschwitz-Birkenau Memorial and Museum. http://en.auschwitz.org.pl/h/index.php?option=com_content&task=view&id=20& Itemid=17 (9 October 2010).

"SS Female Overseers in Auschwitz." DEGOB: National Committee for Attending Deportees. http://degob.org/index.php?showarticle=2018 (20 October 2010).

"Stalin Swing was Belsen Punishment." *The Argus* (Melbourne, Vic: 1848-1954), Friday 19 October 1945, p. 20.

Strebel, Bernhard. "Täterinnen im Konzentrationslager: Verlängerter Arm der SS oder Schützende Hand? Der Fallbeispeile von weiblichen Funktionshäftlingen im KZ Ravensbrück" *Werkstatt Geschichte* 4, no. 12 (Nov 1995).

Tait, A.P. "Medical War Crimes." *The British Medical Journal* vol. 2, no. 5092 (9 August 1958): 390.

"1,000 More in Reich Sought for War Crimes: Women Guard Accused Again" *New York Times*, 28 September 1945, 8 (L).

Townsend, Eric. "Medical War Crimes." *The British Medical Journal* vol. 1, no. 5081 (24 May 1958): 1237.

__________. "Reinstatement by Federal German Medical Authorities   of Practitioner Guilty of Medical War Crimes." *The British Medical Journal*: Annual Representative Meeting. (19 July 1958): pp.   56-57.

United States Holocaust Memorial Museum, courtesy of Anna Hassa Jarosky and Peter Hassa. "Friday February 26, 1943: Ravensbrück [Brandenburg] Germany; War Crimes Investigation Photo of Jadwiga Dzido." Washington: USHMM.

United States Holocaust Memorial Museum, courtesy of Anna Hassa Jarosky and Peter Hassa. "Saturday, June 01, 1946-Thursday, August 01, 1946: Poland; War Crimes Investigation Photo of Maria Kusmierczuk." Washington: USHMM.

Weindling, Paul. "From International to Zonal Trials: The Origins of the Nuremberg Medical Trials" *Holocaust and Genocide Studies* 14 no. 3, (winter 2000): 367-389.

Wiggerhaus, Renate. "Women in the Third Reich" *Connexions*, 36 (1991): 10-11.

Williams, G. E. Grenville. "Medical War Crimes." *The British Medical Journal* vol. 1 no. 5086 (28 June 1958): 1546.

Wright, E.T. and A.P. Tait. "Medical War Crimes." *The British Medical Journal* vol. 2, no. 5087 (5 July 1958): 51.

Books

Adele-Marie, Wendy. "History of the Holocaust." *Encyclopedia of the Modern World*, edited by Peter N. Stearns. Oxford: Oxford University Press, 2009.

__________. Wendy. "Adolf Hitler." *Encyclopedia of World War II*, edited by Spencer C. Tucker. Santa Barbara, CA: ABC-CLIO,   2005.

__________. "Hermann Göring." *Encyclopedia of World War II*, edited by Spencer C. Tucker. Santa Barbara, CA: ABC-CLIO, 2005.

__________. "Hitler   and   the   National   Socialist   Party."   in   Encyclopedia   of Documentary Film, edited by Ian Aitken. New York: Routledge,   2006.

__________. "The Nuremberg Trials." in *Germany and the Americas*,   edited by Thomas Adam. Santa Barbara, CA: ABC-CLIO,   2005.

________. *Women and Work* (Chicago: Roosevelt University,   2004).

Allen, Ann Taylor. "The Holocaust and the Modernization of Gender: A Historiographical Essay." *Zygmunt Bauman: Volume II, Part Three, The Holocaust,* edited by Peter Beilharz. London: Sage Publications, Ltd.,   2002.

Baer, Elizabeth and Myrna Goldenberg. *Experience and Expression: Women, the Nazis, and the Holocaust.* Detroit: Wayne State University Press,   2003.

Bauer, Yehuda. *Rethinking the Holocaust.*   Yale University Press: New Haven   and London: 2001.

Bell, Carl C. Ed., *Psychiatric Aspects of Violence: Issues in Prevention and Treatment.* San Francisco: Jossey-Bass, 2000.

Blandford, Edmund L. *SS Intelligence: The Nazi Secret Service.* Edison, NJ: Castle Books, 2001.

Bleuel, Hans Peter. *Sex and Society in Nazi Germany.* Philadelphia and New York: J.B. Lippincott Company,   1973.

Boyd, Kelly, Ed. *Encyclopedia of Historians & Historical Writing, Volume One* London: Fitzroy Dearborn Publishers, 1999.

Bracher, Karl Dietrich. *The German Dictatorship: The Origins, Structure, and Effects of National Socialism.* New York and Washington, D.C.: Praeger Publishers, 1970.

Bramsted, Ernest K. *Goebbels and National Socialist Propaganda*, 1925-1945. Michigan: Michigan State University Press, 1965.

Bridenthal, Renate, Atina Grossman, and Marion Kaplan, Eds. *When Biology Became Destiny: Women in Weimar and Nazi Germany.* New York: Monthly Review Press, 1984.

Brown, Daniel Patrick. *The Beautiful Beast: The Life and Crimes of SS- Aufseherin Irma Grese.* Ventura, CA: Golden West Historical Publications,   1996.

________. *The Camp Women: The Female Auxiliaries Who Assisted the SS in Running the Nazi Concentration Camp System.* Atglen, PA: Schiffer Military History, 2002.

Bruce, George. *The Nazis.* London: The Hamlyn Publishing Group, 1974.

Buchmann, Erika. *Die Frauen von Ravensbrück.* Berlin: Kongress Verlag, 1959.

Chartock, Roselle and Jack Spencer, Eds. *Can it Happen Again?: Chronicles of the Holocaust.* Black Dog & Leventhal: New York, 1995.

Cosner, Shaaron. *Women under the Third Reich.* Westport: Greenwood Press, 1998.

DeGrazia, Victoria. *How Fascism Ruled Women: Italy, 1922-1945.* Berkeley: University of California Press, 1992.

Dicks, Henry V. *Licensed Mass Murder: A Socio-Psychological Study of Some SS Killers.* London, Chatto; Heinemmann Educational Society for Sussex University Press, 1972.

Dijkstra, Bram. *Evil Sisters: The Threat of Female Sexuality and the Cult of Manhood.* New York: Alfred A. Knopf, 1996.

__________. *Idols of Perversity: Fantasies of Feminine Evil in Fin-De-Siècle Culture.* Oxford: Oxford University Press, 1986.

Dornemann, Louise. *German Women Under Hitler Fascism: A Brief Survey of the Position of the German Women up to the Present Day.* London: Allies Inside Germany, 1943.

Ebbinghaus, Angelika. *Opfer und Täterinnen: Frauenbiographien des Nationalsozialismus.* Nördlingen, Germany: Delphi Politik, 1987.

Edelheit Abraham J. and Hershel Edelheit. *History of the Holocaust: A Handbook and Dictionary.* Boulder, CO: Westview Press, Inc., 1994.

Erpel, Simone, Ed. *Im Gefolge der SS: Aufseherinnen des Frauen-KZ Ravensbrück: Begleitband zur Ausstellung.* Berlin: Metropol Verlag, 2007.

Eschebach, Insa. *Die Geschichte einer NS-Täterin: Versuch einer Rekonstrukion nach den Akten.* 1994.

__________, with Jens Ebert. *Erna Dorn: Zwischen Nationalsozialismus und Kaltem Krieg.* Berlin: Dietz Verlag, 1994.

Edvardson, Cordelia. *Burned Child Seeks the Fire: A Memoir.* Boston: Beacon Press, 1997.

Ewart, Andrew. *World's Wickedest Women: Intriguing Studies of Eve and Evil Through the Ages*. New York: Taplinger Pub. Co. 1964.

Feig, Konnilyn G. *Hitler's Death Camps: The Sanity of Madness*. New York and London: Holmes and Meier Publications, 1979.

Feinman, Ilene Rose. *Citizenship Rites: Feminist Soldiers and Feminist Antimilitarists*. New York and London: New York University Press, 2000.

Flowers, Ronald Barri. *Women and Criminality: The Woman as Victim, Offender, and Practitioner*. New York: Greenwood Press, 1987.

Fritzsche, Peter. *Germans into Nazis*. Cambridge, MA: Harvard University Press, 1998.

Frommann, Eberhard. *Die Leader der NS-Zeit: Untersuchungen zur Nationalsozialistischen Liedpropaganda von den Anfängen bis zum Zweiten Weltkrieg*. Köln: Pappy Rossa, 1999.

Füllberg-Stolberg, Claus, Martina Jung, Renate Reibe, and Martina Scheitenberger. *Frauen in Konzentrationlagern: Bergen-Belsen, Ravensbrück*. Bremen: Ed. Temmen, 1994.

Gilbert, Martin. *Atlas of the Holocaust*. Oxford: New York: Pergamon Press, 1988.

Gilligan, Carol. *In a Different Voice: Psychological Theory and Women's Development*. Cambridge: Harvard University Press, 1982.

Glass, James M. *Life Unworthy of Life: Racial Phobia and Mass Murder in Hitler's Germany*. New York: Basic Books, 1997.

Goodman, Katherine R. *Amazons and Apprentices: Women and the German Parnassus in the Early Enlightenment*. Rochester, NY: Camden House, 1999.

Gordon, Sarah. *Hitler, Germans, and the 'Jewish Question'*. Princeton, NJ: Princeton University Press, 1984.

Graber, G.S. *History of the SS*. New York: D. McKay, 1978.

Greene, Joshua. *Justice at Dachau: The Trials of an American Prosecutor*. New York: Broadway Books, 2003.

Gryn, Edwin and Zofia Murawska. *Majdanek Concentration Camp*. Lublin: Wydawnictwo Lubelskie, 1966.

Guenther, Irene. *Nazi Chic? Fashioning Women in the Third Reich*. New York: Berg, 2004.

Gutman, Yisrael and Michael Berenbaum, Eds. *Anatomy of the Auschwitz Death Camp*. Bloomington: Indiana University Press, 1994.

Haste, Cate. *Nazi Women: Hitler's Seduction of a Nation*. London: Channel 4 Books, 2001.

Herbert, Ulrich, Karin Orth, and Christoph Dieckmann. *Die Nationalsozialistischen Konzentrationslager: Entwicklung und Struktur* (German Edition). Göttingen: Wallstein, 1998.

Heike, Irmtraud. "Female Concentration Camp Guards as Perpetrators: Three Case Studies" in *Ordinary People as Mass Murderers: Perpetrators in Comparative Perspectives*, edited by Olaf Jensen and Claus-Christian W. Szejnmann. New York: Palgrave Macmillan, 2008.

Jones, Ann. *Women Who Kill*. New York: Holt, Rinehart and Winston, 1980.

Kenney, Theresa. *Women Are Not Human: An Anonymous Treatise and Responses*. New York: The Crossroads Publishing Company, 1998.

Kershaw, Ian. *Hitler: 1936-1945, Nemesis*. New York: W.W. Norton and Company, 2000.

Kirkpatrick, Clifford. *Nazi Germany: Its Women and Family Life*. New York: Bobbs-Merrill, 1938.

Knapp, Gabriele. *Das Frauenorchester in Auschwitz: Musikalische Zwangsarbeit und Bewaltigung*. Hamburg: von Bockel Urlag, 1996.

Koonz, Claudia. *Mothers in the Fatherland: Women, the Family, and Nazi Politics*. New York: St. Martin's Press, 1987.

__________. "A Tributary and a Mainstream: Gender, Public Memory, and Historiography of Nazi Germany" in *Gendering Modern Germany History: Rewriting Historiography,* edited by Karen Hagemann and Jean H. Quataert. New York: Bergbahn Books, 2007.

Laqueur, Walter, Ed. *The Holocaust Encyclopedia*. New Haven and London: Yale University Press, 2001.

Lifton, Robert Jay. *The Nazi Doctors: Medical Killing and the Psychology of Genocide*. New York: Basic Books, Inc., 1986.

Lustgarten, Edgar. *The Business of Murder*. New York: Charles Scribner, 1968.

Mann, Michael. *The Dark Side of Democracy: Explaining Ethnic Cleansing*. Cambridge: Cambridge University Press, 2005.

Marcuse, Harold. *Legacies of Dachau: The Uses and Abuses of a Concentration Camp, 1933-2001*. Cambridge, MA: Cambridge University Press, 2001.

Merlo, Alida V., and Joycelyn M. Pollock. *Women, Law, and Social Control*. Needham Heights, MA: Allyn & Bacon, 1995.

Mielke, Siegfried, Ed. *Gewerkschafterinnen im NS-Staat: Verfolgung, Widerstand, Emigration.* Essen: Klartext Verlag, 2008.

Morrison, Jack G. *Ravensbrück: Everyday Life in a Women's Concentration Camp, 1939-1945.* Princeton: Markus Wiener Publishers, 2000.

Newman, Richard and Karen Kirtley. *Alma Rosé: Vienna to Auschwitz*. Portland: Amadeus Press, 2000.

Ofer, Dalia and Weitzman, Lenore J. *Women in the Holocaust*. New Haven and London: Yale University Press, 1998.

Paechter, Heinz. *Nazi Deutsch: A Glossary of Contemporary German Usage*. New York: Frederick Ungar Publishing, Co., 1944.

Pine, Lisa. *Nazi Family Policy: 1939-1945*. Oxford: Berg, 1997.

Potter, Jane. "Women in War and Peace." *The Routledge History of Women in Europe since 1700*, edited by Deborah Simonton. London and New York: Routledge, 2007.

Rittner, Carol and John Roth. *Different Voices: Women and the Holocaust*. St. Paul, MN: Paragon House, 1998.

Rupp, Leila J. *Mobilizing Women for War: German and American Propaganda, 1939-1945.* Princeton: Princeton University Press, 1978.

Sax, Boria. *Animals in the Third Reich: Pets, Scapegoats, and the Holocaust*. New York and London: Continuum, 2000.

Sayer, Ian and Douglas Botting, *The Women Who Knew Hitler: The Private Life   of Adolf Hitler*. New York: Carroll and Graft, 2004.

Sayers, Michael and Albert E. Kahn. *The Plot Against the Peace: A Warning to the Nation!* New York: Book Find Club, 1945.

Schmittroth, Linda and Mary Kay Rosteck. *People of the Holocaust*. Detroit: UXL, 1998.

Schwarz, Gudrun. *Eine Frau an seiner Seite: Ehefrauen in der SS-Sippengemeinschaft* (A Woman at His Side: Women in the SS Community). Mittelweg: Hamburger Edition HIS Verladsges, mbH, 1997.

Segev, Tom. *Soldiers of Evil: The Commandants of the Nazi Concentration Camps*. New York: McGraw-Hill, 1988.

Shapiro, David. *Autonomy and Rigid Character*. New York: Basic Book, Inc., 1981.

Sigmund, Anna Maria. *Women of the Third Reich*. Richmond Hill, Ontario: NDE Pub., 2000.

Smith, Arthur L. Jr. *Die Hexe von Buchenwald: der Fall Ilse Koch*. Köln: Böhlau, 1983.

Sofsky, Wolfgang. *The Order of Terror: The Concentration Camp*, trans. William Templer.   Princeton: Princeton University Press, 1997.

Spielvogel, Jackson and David Redles. *Hitler and Nazi Germany*: A History, 6th ed. Boston: Prentice Hall, 2010.

Spitz, Vivien. *Doctors from Hell: The Horrific Accounts of Nazi Experiments on Humans*. Boulder, CO: Sentient Publications, 2005.

Stephenson, Jill. *Women in Nazi Society*. New York: Barnes & Noble Books, 1975.

Sydnor, Charles W. *Soldiers of Destruction: The SS Death Head's Division, 1933-1945*. Princeton, NJ: Princeton University Press, 1977.

Taake, Claudia. *Angeklagt: SS-Frauen vor Gericht*. Oldenburg: BIS, Bibliotheks- und Informationssystem der Universität Oldenburg, 1998.

Toland, John. *Adolf Hitler*. New York: Doubleday & Co., Inc.,   1976.

United States Holocaust Memorial Museum. Washington, D.C. *Benjamin B. Ferencz Collection: Correspondence and Related Records Regarding Restitution for Victims of Medical Experiments.*   1957-1981.

Vermehren, Isa. *Reise durch den letzen Akt: Ravensbrück, Buchenwald, Dachau: Eine Frau berichtet.* Hamburg: Christian Wegner Verlag, 1946.

Vronsky, Peter. *Female Serial Killers: How and Why Women Become Monsters.* New York: Berkley Books, 2007.

Wall, Donald D. *Nazi Germany and World War II*, 2nd ed. Belmont, CA: Wadsworth, 2003.

Weckel Ulrike and Edgar Wolfrum. *"Bestien" und "Befehlsempfänger": Frauen und Männer in NS-Prozessen nach 1945.* Göttingen: Vandenhoeck & Ruprecht, 2003.

Weiner, Irving B. *Personality and Clinical Psychology Series: The Quest for the Nazi Personality: A Psychological Investigation of Nazi War Criminals.* Hillsdale, NJ: LEA Publishers, 1995.

Weyers, Wolfgang. *The Abuse of Man: An Illustrated History of Dubious Medical Experimentation.* London and New York: Ardor Scribendi, 2003.

Wittmann, Rebecca. *Beyond Justice: The Auschwitz Trial.* Cambridge, MA: Harvard University Press, 2005.

Wistrich, Robert S. *Who's Who in Nazi Germany.* New York: Routledge, 1995.

Book Reviews

Weindling, Paul. *The Nuremberg Medical Trial: The Holocaust and the Origin of the Nuremberg Medical Code* by Horst Freyhofer. *The English Historical Review* Vol. 121, No. 490 (Feb., 2006), pp. 349-350.

Conference Proceedings

Dalhoff, Jutta, and Sabine Kock, *Ich habe mir Deutschland vom Leibe zu halten versucht: Frauen im Nationalsozialismus und der Umgang 'nachgeborener' Frauen mit dem Gedenken: Dokumentation einer Veranstaltungsreihe vom 8. Mai 1995.* Kiel: Universität Kiel, 1996.

Katz, Esther and Joan Ringelheim, eds. *Proceedings of the Conference on "Women Surviving the Holocaust."* New York: Institute for Research in History, 1983.

Schwarz, Gudrun "Forgotten Perpetrators: Women in the SS." Presentation. United States Holocaust Memorial Museum. 9 January 2001.

Film

The Bitch of Buchenwald: A History of Buchenwald Death Camp and its Notorious Commandante, Ilse Koch. DVD. Produced by Gerry Malir, 2009. ArtsMagicDVD, 2009.

Holocaust: Ravensbrück and Buchenwald. ArtsMagicDVD, 2008.

The Last Stage (Ostatni Etap). VHS. Directed by Wanda Jakubiowska, 1948. Sarasota, FL: Polart Distribution (USA), Inc. 1997.

March of Time (outtakes) Krakow scenes; War Crimes Trial: "Butchers of Auschwitz." Story RG-60.0983, Tape 917. Steven Spielberg Film and Video Archive at USHMM. http://resources.ushmm.org/film/display/main.php?search=simple&dquery=Ausch witz&cache_file=uia_qcezwC&total_recs=123&page_len=25&page=1&rec=5&fi le_num=1467 (1 November 2010).

One Survivor Remembers. DVD. Directed by Kary Antholis, 1995. The United States Holocaust Memorial Museum and Home Box Office, 1995.

Wonder Woman: Fausta, The Nazi Wonder Woman. VHS. Directed by Directed by Barry Crane, 28 April 1976. Terra Haute, IN: Columbia House Video for DC Comics, 1999.

Wonder Woman Meets Baroness von Gunther. VHS. Directed by Barry Crane, 21 April 1976. Terra Haute, IN: Columbia House Video for DC Comics, 1999.

INDEX